1

Biblical-Catechetical Homilies
for Sundays and
Holy Days

BIBLICAL-CATECHETICAL HOMILIES
for Sundays and Holy Days (ABC)

Based on the Lectionary
and Reflecting the Syllabus of
the Pastoral Homiletic Plan

By Rev. David Q. Liptak

ALBA · HOUSE   NEW · YORK

SOCIETY OF ST. PAUL, 2187 VICTORY BLVD., STATEN ISLAND, NEW YORK 10314

Library of Congress Cataloging in Publication Data

Liptak, David Q
  Biblical-catechetical homilies for Sundays and
holydays (ABC)

  1. Church year sermons. 2. Catholic Church—
Sermons. 3. Sermons, American. I. Title.
BX1756.L56B52   252'.02   79-27895
ISBN 0-8189-0400-3

Nihil Obstat:
Gene E. Gianelli
Censor Librorum

Imprimatur:
†John F. Hackett
Auxiliary Bishop of Hartford
June 6, 1979

Designed, printed and bound in the United States of
America by the Fathers and Brothers of the
Society of St. Paul, 2187 Victory Boulevard,
Staten Island, New York, 10314, as part of their
communications apostolate.

2 3 4 5 6 7 8 9 (Current Printing: first digit).

This Collection of Homilies
Is Dedicated to
Mary, *Sedes Sapientiae*
and *Regina Clerum*
with a special prayer to
St. Bernard, Priest
and Doctor of the Church
and a Word of thanksgiving for
Pope John Paul II, Bishop of Rome
and Supreme Pastor, 1978—

TABLE OF CONTENTS

Author's Preface

The Background Of This Book

When in the Fall of 1978 Alba House discussed my writing a collection of homilies on the Bible readings for the Sundays and Holy Days in the three-year cycle of the new Lectionary, I proposed that the sermons reflect the contributions of the Programmed Homilies Committee, an interdiocesan panel then several months into its task; specifically, to draft a practical, doctrinal-catechetical syllabus compatible with the themes suggested by the A, B, and C sets of Scriptural texts in the Lectionary for every Sunday and Day of Precept.

During the 1977 Synod of Bishops in Rome, Archbishop John F. Whealon of Hartford addressed himself to the importance, in preaching, of aligning the treasures of Catholic Tradition with the Lectionary Readings. The Archbishop also suggested that a syllabus be drawn up to help homilists implement this. His remarks were reported in the March 1978 issue of *Notitiae* (140: pp. 143-145).

In my conversations with Alba House during the Fall of 1978, it was decided that the homilies in this book would largely reflect the Programmed Homilies Committee's final blueprint, known as the Pastoral Homiletic Plan. Among the specific reasons for this Plan was the desire to help priests and deacons preach about all the Church's key teachings and practices against the thematic background provided by the Lectionary, through the individual sets of Bible texts assigned to each Sunday and Holy Day within the three-year cycle. The possibility that some aspects of the Church's message can be overlooked, especially in Sunday sermons, was raised by Church historian and liturgist, Father Robert F. McNamara, of

St. Bernard's Seminary, Rochester, in his manual, *Catholic Sunday Preaching: The American Guidelines 1791-1975*, published in 1975 by the Word of God Institute.

Although the final version of the Pastoral Homiletic Plan was not ready until early 1979, I found it necessary to begin writing these homilies in late 1978, in order to meet a projected deadline. However, the Committee's notes were made available to me as its work progressed. I also consulted by telephone and mail with one of the Committee's members, Father William Graf of Rochester, New York.

This book for the most part represents the Committee's published document, which appeared in the August/September 1979 issue of *The Homiletic and Pastoral Review*. However, several variant topics or aims have been introduced. Most are minor changes. One reason for modification is that, as I indicated above, the completed syllabus was not available until early 1979, after I had completed about a third of this book to meet its deadline date. Another reason is simply one of personal preference: options of approach which the syllabus takes into account and respects. Some of the variations result from combining two or more topics or aims. Others arise from differing degrees of emphasis from the Committee's final document. All major topics and goals have been incorporated in one way or another.

How To Use This Book

Preaching during the Eucharist is not reading, or even reading from, a printed sermon. Preaching is an *event* involving a graced word, a word effective of faith for those who open their hearts through listening. The role of the homilist—the bishop, priest, deacon—is to explain and relate the Biblical theme or themes of a particular Mass in the concrete Now situation of a congregation. To do this, the preacher must first review and exegete the assigned Scriptural readings, together with the intervenient verses; discover a pastorally applicable unifying theme (or themes); and both nourish and shepherd the assembled faithful with God's word. This book is a brief and admittedly simple illustration as to how this can be accomplished according to a familiar catechetical idiom. Each homily includes an instruction based on the syllabus.

The homilies in this volume are intended as models for amplification and application. The basic material for the homilist is present; what is required is further reflective study on the texts of the Lectionary and on the doctrines or observances cited, some thought as to how the topics and goals can best be presented to a particular congregation, and a specific elaboration of the conclusion. There is of course a fundamental prerequisite: prayer, which in the final analysis, is the essential ground from which the ministry of the word is exercised.

Appreciation

I am especially grateful to Archbishop Whealon for his encouragement and advice in the preparation of these homilies. A word of thanks is also due to Father McNamara and Father Graf for their glimpses into the working of the Programmed Homilies Committee. Among others, I should like to cite in appreciation are Mrs. Joyce Boudreau and Denise Stankovics, for their help, respectively, in typing and editing the manuscript; Fr. Francis J. Lescoe, who encouraged me to undertake this work; and Father Anthony Chenevey, Editor of Alba House, for his advice and help.

Scriptural quotations in this book were all taken from the New American Bible. The exegesis for the homilies was drawn chiefly from *The Jerome Biblical Commentary* (Englewood Cliffs, N.J.: Prentice-Hall, 1968), and Archbishop Whealon's brief explanatory notes for the Bible readings in *The Vatican II Sunday Missal* (Boston: St. Paul Editions, 1974). Other Biblical volumes I used to a large degree were the *Dictionary of Biblical Theology* by Xavier Leon-Dufour (New York: Desclee, 1967) and *Sacramentum Verbi*, 3 vols., ed. J.B. Bauer (New York: Herder and Herder, 1970). Quotations from Vatican II are taken from *The Documents of Vatican II*, ed. Walter M. Abbott (New York: America Press, 1966).

The theology mirrored throughout is Magisterial. Besides consulting classical volumes such as *Enchiridion Symbolorum Definitionum et Declarationum de rebus fidei et morum, editio XXXV*, ed. H. Denzinger, rev. ed. Alphonsus Schönmetzer (Rome: Herder, 1973), and solid current works like *Sacramentum Mundi*, ed. Karl Rahner et al., 6 vols., (New York: Herder and Herder 1968-1970) and *Theological Dictionary*, ed. K. Rahner and H. Vorgrimler; ed. C. Ernst (New York: Herder and Herder, 1965), I also utilized catechetical manuals such as *Sharing the Light of Faith, National Catechetical Directory for Catholics of the United States* (Washington D.C., National Conference of Catholic Bishops, 1979) and *The Teaching of Christ, A Catholic Catechism for Adults*, ed. Ronald Lawler, Donald Wuerl and Thomas Comerford Lawler (Huntington, Ind.: Our Sunday Visitor, 1976).

If one modern theologian's insights seem to be especially evident, that theologian is Karl Rahner. Yves Congar's theologizing is also represented, especially in the area of Christology; likewise, Cardinal Joseph Ratzinger's. There are also traces of Bernard Lonergan, and citations from Pope John Paul II.

For homiletic style, I owe a notable debt to Monsignor Ronald Knox and Bishop Ottokar Prohaszka.

D.Q.L.
Feast of the Visitation, 1979

Foreword

The Second Vatican Council brought to the Catholic community a welcome insistence on the preaching of homilies. The homily, as contrasted with the sermon, was to be based on the day's Scripture readings. It was to be an application of the proclaimed Scripture to the lives of the listeners.

Since Vatican II there have been two major problems with homilies as preached from Catholic pulpits.

The first problem has been a general lack of doctrinal content. There have been more exhortations than instructions, more generalizations than specific doctrines, more appeals to the emotions than to the understanding as well as emotions. As a result many laity have complained about the lack of solid doctrinal content in homilies.

The second problem has been the general absence of homilies based on post-Scriptural doctrines, devotions and Christian living. Many are the Catholic beliefs and practices that have not been mentioned from our pulpits since the mid-1960's. Yet we are a Church that finds God's Revelation in Tradition as well as Scripture. And we know that the homily is the main stay for directing Catholic living.

In general, homilies since Vatican II have not presented very well the breadth and depth of Catholic belief and practice. In this one area the teaching Church has not taught well her children—for part of preaching is teaching.

Father David Liptak is eminently qualified to supply solid doctrinal content—as well as scholarly illustrations—for homilies. His theological background, experience as a writer and his service as editor of a question-and-answer column in our diocesan newspaper have kept him in close touch with the problems of people as well as with Catholic doctrine and the development of doctrine.

In this set of homilies he has had the advantage of a new homily plan developed precisely for the twin purposes of covering in balance all major teachings of Catholic faith while remaining anchored in the assigned Scripture.

Therefore I see this approach of Father Liptak as overcoming simultaneously the two major weaknesses in Catholic homilies since Vatican II.

This is a needed work which should help many Catholic homilists—deacons, priests, bishops—to preach God's Word more effectively. To all of them I warmly commend this helpful book.

†Most Reverend John F. Whealon
Archbishop of Hartford
June 2, 1979

CYCLE A

FIRST SUNDAY
OF ADVENT (A)

The Meaning of Advent

Isaiah 2:1-5; Romans 13:11-14; Matthew 24:37-44

Aim: (1) to explain Advent as referring to the three comings of Christ (at Bethlehem, at the end of the world and into our hearts by grace this Christmas); (2) to encourage the faithful to make up their minds to lead a good Catholic life.

The Old Testament prophet Isaiah in today's First Reading projects the gathering of all people into the Lord's house forever—that well known passage about beating swords into plowshares is part of this lesson. (There is a statue reflecting this theme in front of the United Nations Buiding in New York City.)

In the Second Reading, St. Paul, in his greatest writing, the monumental Letter to the Romans, reminds us that judgment approaches; hence temptations to sins such as carousing, drunkenness, sexual excess, lust, quarreling, jealousy—all the rest—should be scrupulously avoided.

And in the Gospel, from St. Matthew's account, we are advised to remain awake: for judgment will surely come "like a thief in the night"—a figure of speech we would not dare use unless Christ had so taught us.

Jesus' coming with salvation and judgment, both at Bethlehem and now, is one theme sounded clearly in today's liturgy, therefore.

Another is the divine promise of an eternal homecoming for all who accept Christ as Lord, both at Bethlehem and now. For this same Lord born at Bethlehem will surely come again to this world as Lord of Lords and King of Kings.

Advent provides a unique occasion each year not only to reflect on these truths, but also to determine how we can best respond to Jesus' drawing us to himself, to that final meeting place and perfect fulfillment.

Do we want to respond? If so—the choice is ours—the key to Advent activity is the Church. The Church, Father Yves Congar has nobly put it, is "the sacrament of the return of the world to God in Christ." He adds: "what Christ saves and must one day reunite in his Kingdom is mysteriously projected and assumed by this sacrament of salvation. . . What Christ must one day reunite in his Kingdom is projected by the sacrament and by the spiritual reality of his body on earth: the Eucharist and the Church" (*Jesus Christ*. New York: Herder and Herder, 1966).

Advent faith, therefore, is primarily a homecoming to the Church. Advent faith implies freshly renewed participation at Sunday Mass, a well-prepared and especially contrite confession, a return to the Eucharist with the consciously-recalled fervor of a first Communion. Advent faith means that Christ is close to us precisely in his Church, that he is coming nearer and nearer to us in his Church.

A specific word about confession. The concept implies sin; personal sin; guilt, therefore. Sin means an offense against God; there are still Ten Commandments. Moreover, Sacred Scripture is replete with references to "death" resulting from sin. Our faith is that every free and fundamental decision that seriously contravenes God's will for man, is a sin. A free and fundamental decision means a human election deliberately made with full knowledge and liberty.

In what state will we be when Jesus, who was born at Bethlehem, comes again to this world in judgment? If we recognize him now in his principal sacrament, the Church, and if we live by virtue of this recognition, our preparation will be solid. Our homecoming to the Church will gloriously end in our homecoming to the Kingdom of Christ forever.

Advent is the time to ponder these thoughts. Christmas, the beginning, should remind us of the end, our destiny, our eternal goal.

The celebration of Jesus' first coming as Savior should keep our hearts focused on his return as Judge.

SECOND SUNDAY
OF ADVENT (A)

Repent Your Sins; the Kingdom is Coming.

Isaiah 11:1-10; Romans 15:4-9; Matthew 3:1-12

Aim: (1) to show repentance of sins as a required preparation for the Lord's coming; (2) to encourage timely use of the Sacrament of Reconciliation and of Advent Penitential Services.

Reading today's beautiful prophecy from Isaiah (the first reading), that great religious genius of Israel, one is reminded of Vergil's mysterious *Fourth Eclogue*, written about three decades before Christ's birth.

Vergil was the supreme Roman poet. More than anyone else, it seems, he broadcast the Latin tongue throughout the world; in England the ruins of ancient military barracks still bear graffiti—inscriptions from Vergil's poems, made by Roman legionnaires. Vergil was so revered by the medievals that Dante, in Christianity's greatest poem, *The Divine Comedy*, chose him as his guide through the first two books (the *Inferno* and the *Purgatorio*); for Dante, Vergil was the model of *the* best of human wisdom: that of the Greek philosophers, for example, or the pyramid-builders of Egypt.

Vergil's famed *Fourth Eclogue, Bucolic IV*, written in a pastoral tradition invented in Sicily, is known as the *Messianic Eclogue*. In it Vergil foretells the imminent advent of a golden age, inaugurated by a boy endowed with divine honors, an age in which poisonous serpents will disappear, when the herds of cattle will not fear the lion; when peace with justice and freedom from want will be realized all over the world.

The *Eclogue* is obviously one of the most mysterious writings of antiquity. Could Vergil have known about Christ's coming? Whereas the medievals perhaps tended to accept Vergil's prophetic powers too readily, we of today seem too quick to reject them. Meanwhile the questions remain unsolved.

Besides, as philosopher Karl Jaspers has observed, there was a world-wide interest in a messianic age from about 800 B.C. down to at least 200 B.C. During this period, Isaiah was not only prophesying the advent of a Messiah, but in various parts of the world highly intelligent men—philosophers, poets and dramatists—were anxiously looking forward to a day when—as Isaiah says in today's first lesson—the wolf shall be a guest of the lamb and there will be peace and justice everywhere.

All of this was realized, of course—Isaiah's prophecies, Vergil's mysterious predictions, the yearnings of wise men throughout the ancient world—when Jesus, God made man, was born at Bethlehem. Jesus is the longed-for Messiah of God; knowing him means knowing the keys to justice and peace, wisdom and goodness, security and hope. He is the way, the truth and the life, whom Isaiah foretold, and whom God-fearing men like Vergil sought.

Knowing Jesus begins with knowing the Scriptures, as today's Second Reading, from Paul's Epistle to the Romans, reminds us. To meet God's final and perfect word, his Word made flesh, one must search for him in the Bible as we read within his Church.

John the Baptizer, called to announce Christ's public mission, could not have recognized Christ on the banks of the Jordan that historic day—the story of today's Gospel, from Matthew—unless he had previously met the Savior in the pages of the Old Testament, profoundly contemplated. In fact, when John first met Jesus, he used Biblical language to point him out; John called Jesus the Lamb of God, an obvious reference to the Old Testament Exodus.

To know Christ we too should get to know the Scriptures, all the Scriptures. From them we come to believe that through repenting our sins—as St. John the Baptizer bids us do—we can achieve possession of Christ's eternal Kingdom, unveiled by him in the Gospels.

There is no more apposite way of joining the Baptizer in this Advent season anticipatory to Christmas than, very simply, to read some of the Bible every day. The Bible has a way of convincing us of our sinfulness, and, consequently, of our need to join the Baptizer in repentance in order to enter Jesus' Kingdom—which, our Lord reminds us, has a very narrow door (Luke 14:22 ff.).

THIRD SUNDAY
OF ADVENT (A)

John the Baptist As Our Advent Guide

Isaiah 35:1-6, 10; James 5:7-10; Matthew 11:2-11

Aim: (1) to describe the fearless honesty, humility and discipline of John the Baptist; (2) to encourage those virtues in our lives, and during this Advent.

Today's Gospel—that beautiful story of how John's Disciples were sent to Jesus to ascertain his messianic credentials, and of Christ's moving answer for the sake of John's disciples and for *us*—focuses on the person and example of the Baptizer, the last major prophet of the Old Covenant, and the precursor of the New Testament inaugurated by Christ.

John's entire reason for being—his *raison d'etre*—is epitomized in both the question he sent to Jesus, and in the answer given by the Lord. John represents the summit of prophecy, even the prophecies of Isaiah, that religious genius who spoke for Yahweh centuries before the Christmas event, and from whom today's poetic first Mass lesson is taken.

St. John's mysterious emergence on the biblical scene has become considerably less enigmatic as a result of recent archaeological discoveries, especially the Dead Sea Scrolls. Prior to these discoveries, John seemed to have taken stage center from a point beyond our capacity to see. He is of course introduced to us through the narratives of his father Zechariah's encounter with the angel Gabriel in the Temple, and through the event of Mary's Visitation—

both of which are recorded in St. Luke's Gospel. But how do we explain John's sudden appearance on the religious scene in the fifteenth year of the reign of Tiberius Caesar—a highly dramatic appearance, at that?

Today it seems likely that as a youth St. John had some contact with the monks of Qumran, the Essenes, in whose caves, in the vicinity of the Dead Sea, remnants of these precious scrolls were first chanced upon by a shepherd boy in 1949. John must have trained for his ascetic life from his early days; the principle of spiritual preparation through discipline and penance was emphasized in the Qumran documents. And penance and discipline were at the core of the Baptizer's message.

But St. John's vocation was clearly distinct from, and higher than, that of the Essenes. Actually, it was unique. To John alone was given the role of announcing the need for penance in preparation for the imminent advent of the Messiah, whom he alone, again, was chosen to identify in the moving words we repeat just before Communion at every Mass: "This is the Lamb of God who takes away the sins of the world."

Scores of his own countrymen went out to the desert to hear St. John and to renew—or for the first time openly to witness to—commitment to penance in expectation of the Messiah—a fact which, incidentally, rebuts the often voiced notion that the Israelitic nation in large part had repudiated such biblical values before the Savior's public life commenced.

Unlike many preachers of his age (the times were marked by the emergence and decline of several pseudo-prophets who achieved popularity by misusing current messianic yearnings), John the Baptizer repeatedly stated his nothingness before the Son of God—merely precursor.

When the Eternal Lamb of God, Jesus, finally appeared, moreover, the Baptizer retreated to the shadows, eventually dying a martyr, the victim of the insane hatred of Herodias, whose adulterous union with King Herod John did not hesitate to label as sinful.

Every Christian mirrors St. John in that every Christian is in some sense a precursor of the Incarnate God. In the darkness of this world, we carry the light of Christ. Or, more precisely, we are called to diffuse this light; whether we do it or not is left to our own choosing. Shall we be content, for another Advent and Christmas, to let this light burn fitfully, hesitatingly, as we continue to stumble for lack of better illumination? Or shall we intensify this light for ourselves and others?

Turning up the flame of faith in our hearts can be accomplished by renewed penitential love. Isaian-like optimism (today's First Reading) and loving patience (the theme of St. James' exhortation in today's Second Reading) are also important, of course. John exemplified both. But since all virtue comes from God, it is first necessary to acknowledge our nothingness, indeed our unworthiness, before his loving mercy. Though John was unworthy, Christ called him. In our sinfulness—when we affirm it—Christ calls us too, to diffuse his light.

An initial step in this direction could be made this morning at Mass, especially at Communion time, when we look up at the Sacred Host and hear the priest say—"This is the Lamb of God who takes away the sins of the world."

The response—"Lord, I am not worthy. . .Only say the word. . ."—is as soul-fixing a commitment as can be expressed in our weak human language.

FOURTH SUNDAY
OF ADVENT (A)

Mary and Joseph Prepare for Christmas

Isaiah 7:10-14; Romans 1:1-7; Matthew 1:18-24

*Aim: (1) to show Mary and Joseph as faithful to God's
will; (2) to encourage similar faithfulness—to God's
Commandments, to the Church, to one's commitments.*

Well, here it is, the fourth and last week in Advent. Christmas is
only a few days away.

We lament, "Where has the time gone?" The time *has* gone—
whatever *time* is. (No one knows precisely; those clocks we must
watch are only mechanical reminders of a mystery we don't fully
understand. Philosophers offer one kind of answer; physical
scientists, another.) Advent means of course "getting ready," "getting
ready" for Christmas. And the time left us to do so is now very brief.

Getting ready for anything important usually means work. The
training an athlete endures to prepare for an event is a classic
example; likewise, the process a woman goes through to ready her
table for guests during the holidays. Or take the case of a young lady
getting ready for her first date; she seeks to make herself as attractive
as possible.

Advent has the same purpose: getting ready by making oneself as
healthy, ready and attractive as possible for experiencing anew the
great mystery recalled each year on December 25: God's entering this,
our world, by being born in Bethlehem.

So today we ask—it's the last great opportunity to do so before Christmas suddenly falls upon us—how we might get ready. What are the spiritual means available—the best training process—the most effective spiritual etiquette?

One means, surely, is a conscious recommitment to God's will, a freshly affirmed word of fidelity to God's law, and to the Church. Mary, the Mother of the Lord, is, of all creatures, the perfect model; her explicit desire to do God's will is implied in today's Gospel passage, which takes up the story of our salvation where the Angel Gabriel's visit had left off; namely, after her dramatic *Yes of Consent* to be the mother of Jesus.

But Joseph, too, especially as he is presented to us in today's Gospel, is a powerful model of fidelity and commitment to divine invitation. Simply because he was asked by the Lord to take Mary as wife, Joseph assented, immediately and unreservedly. There was no hesitating, no doubting.

Mary and Joseph's fidelity occasioned a new beginning for mankind. Today's First Reading, that mysterious prophecy about a virgin's being with child whose name would be Emmanuel, is employed by the liturgy as pointing down the centuries, albeit indirectly, to the Virgin Birth of Jesus—that ancient doctrine we recall each Sunday in the Creed at Mass when we profess our faith in Christ "born of the Virgin Mary."

God, who created the first human being out of nothing in order to share his life with him, was born of a virgin to show us that his coming is totally gratuitous. (St. Paul emphasizes this in today's Second Reading.) It means a totally new start.

A totally new start: this is what Christmas still means to anyone who appreciates its true meaning. A new start in affirming and implementing fidelity to God, in his law and in his Church.

To this end, we ask Mary and Joseph, our primary Advent guides, to help us. Specifically, we could ask for the grace of a most sincere confession, this final week of Advent, and a keener capacity to see "Christ with-us"—Emmanuel—in our Church and its sacraments.

CHRISTMAS (Vigil Mass)

Christ is Savior

Isaiah 62:1-5; Acts 13:16-17; Matthew 1:1-25

Aim: To emphasize that Christmas reminds us of our need for a Savior.

We are met for the Vigil Mass of Christmas. Vigil implies waiting with expectation. In a few hours, at midnight, we shall mark the holy night of "our dear Savior's birth"—to borrow a phrase from one of our most beloved carols. With the arrival of this holy night, all the messianic prophecies—today's First and Second Readings, for example—will be assured of fulfillment. Paul says this explicitly in today's Second Reading. For on the first Christmas, almost 2,000 years ago, was born to us a Savior, Jesus Christ, who suffered and died for us so that he might redeem us and, having risen from the tomb, might *live* with us forever.

December 25 is the traditional liturgical date for Jesus' birth, which we in English call Christmas, meaning "Christ's Mass."

The precise, historical date of Jesus' birth is unknown. December 25 seems to have been chosen because it marks the beginning of the lengthening of daylight following the winter solstice. The shortest day of the year appears just before December 25. For many of the ancient pagans, it was a time of great anxiety, since they believed in a cosmic struggle of darkness with light. In late December they used to keep vigil, hoping that the sun would begin to grow stronger again. Inevitably, the sun would begin to show fresh power, and the days begin to lengthen; they celebrated the solstice as the Feast of the Invincible Sun.

What better time can Christians assign to Christmas? Christ, the Light of the World, dispels the darkness of sin and ignorance.

For one thing, Christmas tells us that humanity is good. The Second Person of the Blessed Trinity became a human being; he did not simply take on the appearances of a human being. He was born of a woman. He has a genealogy (today's Gospel), which only a true human being can have. Everything about humanity therefore, is good. This is all related in a matter-of-fact way in today's Gospel.

God was not only born among us; by his birth he came close to us. At Christmas, God literally embraced us in our humanity; *all* of us. No one who is human is excluded from this embrace.

Moreover, Christ's embrace is a saving embrace; Jesus, true to his name, revealed that God has willed to save us. Christ is our Savior.

This truth cannot be fully understood theoretically. To grasp it, one must first be conscious of his or her own need *to be saved*; be aware, in other words, of his or her unworthiness, indeed, sinfulness. What need is there of a *Savior* unless there is a need for us to be *saved?*

Christmas therefore presumes that we know our place; our sinfulness, in other words, together with our desperate need for divine help. This means that the first step toward understanding Christmas is contrition. And without understanding, there can be no true appreciation of the Feast.

This means, doesn't it, that Christmas is an adult celebration. Only we who have sinned and desperately need forgiveness can profoundly comprehend and value it.

Without a sincere confession, without repentance, without contrition, Christmas has no real meaning. The night of our dear Savior's birth can only be appreciated against the backdrop of the dark night of our longing for God's loving forgiveness and Redemption.

"Fall on your knees"—as the carol bids us—is necessary for a true Christmas celebration.

CHRISTMAS (Mass at Midnight)

God Dwells Among Us

Isaiah 9:1-6; Titus 2:11-14; Luke 2:1-14

Aim: to explain the gifts of Christmas: (1) God's greatest gift to us, his Son; (2) our gifts in return: faith, dedication to others; imitation of his Christ-life.

St. Luke's account of the birth of Jesus at Bethlehem, from which we just read, is one of the world's most loved Gospels. It is thought that our blessed Lady related the story of the first Christmas to St. John, into whose care Jesus commended her during his agony on the cross of Calvary. John in turn narrated the story to the early Christian community, from which Luke, a second-generation Christian, received it.

The key message of course is that God has manifested himself in the flesh, as the First Epistle to Timothy later concretized it (3:16). The Word of God—the eternal Father's self-expression—became man, as we say in our Creed. St. John's Gospel says, literally, that the Word of God became man and "pitched his tent" in our very midst. Today at Mass we genuflect, when during the Creed, we profess that the Son of God became man.

Christmas teaches us first of all that God is not merely a God transcendent—a God *out there*, a God who dwells only in the heavens—but also a *God bestowed*, a God who wills to communicate himself to us so that he might draw us to him in faith, hope and love.

Christmas also teaches us the reason why God *bestows* himself: a reason only God could reveal, of course, since it is his own mind. This reason is defined in the Epistle to Titus from which today's Second Reading is taken: God became one of us because he *loves* us (3:4-7). The divine motive underlying the Incarnation—the Enfleshment of the Word of God—is love. The Father gives his supreme Gift to us, the Gift of his own Son, because he is in love with us.

All this was prophesied by Isaiah of old who, in today's First Reading, foretells the incomparable joy that the Incarnation should ensure for those who despite the darkness of this world nonetheless search for him and his light.

Jesus is the image of the invisible God; Jesus mirrors God. The infant lying in the manger of Bethlehem is God manifested to us in human form, for love of us. God, while remaining God, became a true man because he loves us.

How shall we accept God's supreme love-Gift? First, surely with a profession of faith. This Christmas we are invited to renew our affirmation of Christ as true God and true man: the way, the truth and the life.

Secondly, we are reminded today that as God comes to us in a manifestation of love, so we can approach God only through love. We must love God as Jesus loved. But since in Jesus God has joined himself to mankind, love of God cannot be separated from love of our fellow men. In Christ God has made men—all men—his brothers and sisters.

Finally, Christmas tells us that to be truly human, we must be Christ-like. Jesus is the perfect model of humanity; hence to fulfill ourselves as persons, we must imitate his way, follow his truth, live his life.

This alone is the gate to a *merry* (the word really means "blessed") Christmas.

CHRISTMAS (Mass at Dawn)

Christ the Light of the World

Isaiah 62:11-12; Titus 3:4-7; Luke 2:15-20

Aim: (1) to describe the lights of the first Christmas: in the cave, of the angels, of the star; (2) to describe this Child as the Light of the World, our guide through life.

In Ancient Greece, the great and etherial philosopher Plato once envisioned men as chained in an underground cave where they see only the shadows of objects cast upon the cave walls. In this situation, he said men would readily conclude that the shadows of things constituted reality. What if these chained men could escape, he asked, and see things as they are? Plato's famous vision is called his "view from the cave."

Christmas provides us with another view from a cave, the cave of Bethlehem, in which men and the world are seen for the first time in an entirely new light, the light which our Tradition calls the "Sun of Justice," Jesus, the Light of the World.

It is true, the Christ-event tells us, that our vision as human beings is clouded by the cave-like confines of this earthly existence. Through intense self-searching (like that of Plato) man can free himself from the chains that bind him (ignorance, superstition, prejudice) and acquire a sound glimpse of reality and its meaning. But only when man can see being as a reflection of the "Son of Justice," of God the Infinite Creator and Sustainer of all that exists, can he perceive creation as it actually is.

Christmas means the descent of the Eternal Light upon this world. It represents God's gratuitous Yes to man's ageless prayer as expressed in the traditional "O" Antiphon for December 21:

"O Dawn of the East, Brightness of the Light Eternal, and Son of Justice: Come and enlighten them that sit in darkness and in the shadow of death."

The shepherds were in darkness that first Christmas night. The shepherds symbolize most of us: ordinary people; responsible, hard-working, seriously-minded people looking for answers, searching for light in the grey corridors of our existence, recognizing our lack of righteousness—as today's Second Reading reminds us. Like the shepherds we too are invited to the cave of Bethlehem, where the key illumination for our lives can be found. We are reminded today through angels, as the shepherds were in today's Gospel.

For the great intellects of this world—our contemporary Platos—there was the Star, which the Magi followed. The light of Christmas, as Isaiah foretold in today's First Reading, is meant for all peoples, "to the ends of the earth."

It is Christ, God-made-man, Emmanuel, who enters the cave of man's imprisonment and gives meaning to his life, and enables him to see all reality as mirroring the divine Light. The "view from the cave" that Bethlehem gives us is a view of heaven on earth, of God's living among men, of insuperable light in the midst of darkness, of freedom despite chains.

CHRISTMAS
(Mass During the Day)

The Word Was Made Flesh

Isaiah 52:7-10; Hebrews 1:1-6; John 1:1-18

Aim: (1) to explain "the Word" as the Second Person of the Trinity; (2) to explain the theological meaning of Christmas and the benefits for our life of the Incarnation.

"In the beginning was the Word," today's Gospel begins.

The Word means God the Son, the Second Person of the Blessed Trinity, the Father's eternal self-image. When the Word—the Son of God—became a real human being, the invisible God manifested himself so concretely that we can literally hear him, touch him, embrace him.

Before the first Christmas, today's Second Reading from Hebrews tells us, the invisible God revealed himself by his actions and his words; primarily through the prophets. At Christmas, he revealed himself by the *Word*; namely by the Son of God himself made man, "the reflection of the Father's glory and the exact representation of his being."

This is what the word "Incarnation" means; a Latin derivative, it recalls that God literally took on flesh, a humanity. Christmas doesn't mean simply that God took for himself the disguise of a man, to live as a masquerade. This has been suggested several times in Church history by thinkers who tend to minimize man, or to dismiss him as something less than sublime. The Incarnation, the Enfleshment of the Word—the truth we recall at Christmas—means that God, while remaining God, really became a human being.

Doesn't this tell us that being a human being is good—that there is nothing ignoble about being human—that everything human, if viewed in God's light, is good?

Doesn't this also mean that God became close to us—very close in fact—that God is *for me*? (The liturgy says, "Unto *us* a child is born.")

Finally, doesn't this mean that God's coming is for all persons, everywhere, "to the ends of the earth," as today's First Reading, from Isaiah, exclaims? For if Christ became a human being, surely he united himself with all who participate in human nature: with people who were as ordinary as the shepherds and as lofty (and distant) as the Magi.

The greatest tragedy that can befall us in the context of Christmas is our failing to recognize God's Son incarnate, lying in the manger of Bethlehem. For, as today's Gospel proclaims, to all who do recognize him, he will empower to become children of God.

Christmas, at its deepest level, means that in Jesus, God-made-man, all men are called to be God's adopted children and heirs to his Kingdom.

SOLEMNITY OF MARY, MOTHER OF GOD (ABC)

Mary the Example of Mature Christian Living

Numbers 6:22-27; Galatians 4:4-7; Luke 2:16-21

Aim: (1) to look well at the Lord's mother as we start another year of life; (2) to imitate her prayerfulness, fidelity, energy, sinlessness.

The proximate reason why the Church celebrates today, the Octave day of Christmas, as the Solemnity of Mary the Mother of God, is that Christmas was made possible through her. It was by her *Yes of Consent* that we received Jesus the Savior, while we were still in our sins, as today's Second Reading reminds us. And Jesus' birth is the perfection of the benediction prophesied in today's First Reading.

The name "Jesus" means "God saves"—in other words, "Savior." Christ, the Bible tells us, *had* to be named Jesus. The name was assigned by eternal decree; likewise the reason: "For it is he who will save his people from their sins" (Matthew 1:21). Today's Gospel carefully records Jesus' being given his name.

We honor Mary today, then, first because she brought into our world the only person who *must* be named Jesus, since he alone was the perfect realization of the name's intrinsic meaning: "God saves," or "Savior."

Secondly, we honor Mary on this Octave Day of Christmas because Bethlehem marked a new beginning for the world and men, and Mary made this possible. Jesus, Scripture explains, is the New Adam whose Precious Blood re-created the world. Since newness of life—forgetting the past and starting anew—is so comfortable a thought for January 1, the beginning of a new year, the Church invites us to begin anew in the company of Mary the Mother of the Lord.

A third message can be distilled from today's Solemnity at the start of a new year. A resolution is in order; namely, that our personal pilgrimage to Jesus throughout the coming year might be inspired by the example of Mary—an example summarized by her words to the waiters at Cana of Galilee: "Do whatever he (Jesus) tells you."

Mary is a model of faith; indeed, she is *the* person of faith, always believing, though not always fully understanding. Mary is the exemplar of prayerfulness, of energy in an effort to bring Christ to others, and, of course, of sinlessness: of avoiding anything that might distract from her divine Son, to whom she points with confidence, hope and love.

Sound devotion to the Mother of God can only mean a good and happy year, a year closer to Jesus in our brief pilgrimage of years here on earth. Mary points to Jesus always, as she did at the wedding feast of Cana, when she told the waiters to do Christ's bidding. In like manner she directs us to the Lord, as a sign of faith.

There is a final point to be made at this Christmas time. Just as Jesus chose to come into this world through Mary, so he continues to grace us through her. As the poet Dante Alighieri said in his immortal *Divine Comedy*, anyone who desires grace but ignores our Lady seeks grace in vain (Canto XXXIII).

FEAST OF
THE HOLY FAMILY (ABC)

The Fourth Commandment:
Respect for Parents; Care for Children

Sirach 3:2-6, 12-14; Colossians 3:12-21; (A) Matthew 2:13-15, 19-23; (B)
Luke 2:22-40; (C) Luke 2:41-52

Aim: (1) to show the poverty, simplicity and holiness of
the Holy Family; (2) to contrast this with our affluent,
wasteful society, and (3) to encourage Christian
simplicity in our lifestyle; to stress the need for strong,
united families with devout fathers, mothers, children.

To anyone unfamiliar with the course of the liturgy, today's Feast of the Holy Family seems an abrupt intrusion into the Christmas season. As usual, though, there is a sound reason. The Church, anxious lest we mistakenly identify Christ's presence exclusively by the signs of adoring shepherds and angelsong, quickly changes the scene, as it were, to remind us that the God who became man meets us in the rather ordinary circumstances of everyday home life, characterized by a wood lathe and carpenter's bench in the cellar. Joseph, Scripture informs us, was a carpenter.

Today, the sociologists tell us, the family unit has changed. It has "evolved," they say, from a "consanguine" unit (one that included aunts and uncles and grandparents and cousins) to a "nuclear" or "conjugal" unit, with no room for dependents other than children— "just what you can pack in a station wagon," as one commentator put it. We are also told that the American family unit has not only changed as to its socio-economic base, but that it has partially or wholly surrendered traditional roles, including once sacrosanct educational and religious functions, to non-family institutions.

Any changes in the family—indeed, anything relating to family life—merits study, especially because it is generally acknowledged that the family, whatever its characteristics in changing eras, is nonetheless our primary "socializing institution."

Too, the composition of a nation depends on the moral fiber of the persons who constitute that nation. Thus, if respect as a moral concept is not learned in the home, it will not be learned with reference to any authority: the courts, the school, the Church, society itself. The same as regards honesty, justice, tolerance, and so on.

For a Christian, of course, the family occupies an especially noble status; for a Christian, the family is not only a socializing unit, not simply a prepolitical civilizing institution; it is in fact (though mysteriously) a pastoral unit. Today's Second Reading touches upon this point, and the Gospel concretizes it.

For a Christian, a family is a sanctuary, in which marrieds truly exercise almost "priestly" commitments.

Priestly? How else do we explain that parents are the principal messengers of the Gospel insofar as their children are concerned, by means of the unforgettable example of genuine fatherly and motherly care they exercise; together with their actual work of instructing? Who teaches a child first to read the Bible? That God confirms these priest-like parental duties is clear from today's First Reading.

One way parents can implement the total Gospel message of today's Feast of the Holy Family is literally by giving themselves to their children, as Mary and Joseph did (Today's Gospel). Our faith tells us that parenting means not primarily giving *things* to children, but rather the giving of *oneself*.

EPIPHANY (ABC)

Evangelization: Proclaiming the Gospel to All Nations

Isaiah 60:1-6; Ephesians 3:2-3, 5-6; Matthew 2:1-12

Aim: (1) to explain Epiphany as the Gospel reaching out to all nations; (2) to encourage personal attitudes and programs that are evangelistic.

Today is Epiphany, an ancient feast. "Epiphany" derives from a Greek work for an official state visit: the formal appearance of a king in an outlying district, for example.

Today's Gospel focuses on the mysterious journey of the Magi, an event dimly foretold by Isaiah in the First Reading, and interpreted by Paul, in the Second Reading.

Who were these Magi? (This word also comes from the Greek.) For one thing, they were not really kings (despite the popular carol, "We three kings of Orient are"). They seem to have been astrologers, intelligent men who scanned the heavens. Nor do we know their names. Gaspar, Baltasar, and Melchior are names simply assigned them in the legends. And note that the Bible does not say how many there were. Nor does it cite their precise nationality.

The important point is that these Magi, these wise men, lived outside the Holy Land and went looking for Jesus because they knew he was to be born at Bethlehem at that time.

How did they know? St. Matthew in today's Gospel tells us they saw Jesus' star at its rising. Somehow—we don't know how—they recognized this star and, having seen it, left home and hearth to follow it. (The Dead Sea Scrolls, incidentally, contain a star-chart predicting the Savior's birth. It might prove a key clue to the mystery of the Magi.)

If we want to find a practical lesson today, then, the message of the star is foremost. Jesus himself said: "Seek and you shall find." God sees to it that people who really care, who are really looking for right answers, will find him. For the person who really wants to know where Jesus is, where he—she—*can* find Jesus, a "time of the star" will surely emerge, as it did for the Magi.

A second lesson is that like the star in the heavens, God makes himself available from every corner of the earth, from the darkest recesses even of every human soul. Which is to say that his Gospel of love, forgiveness and redemption reaches out to all people, everywhere.

A third lesson is that we who have experienced the time of the star in our lives can help others—by our witness, kindness, service—to see the star of Christ. Our very stance as Catholics can shout out (as today's First Reading does):

"The glory of God is rising on *you* (too) . . . Lift up your eyes and look around. . . "

In a sense this third lesson is most relevant of all today. All around us, in our neighborhoods, in the offices, factories, stores, schools, or hospitals in which we work or move, there are scores of people who, for various reasons, have never taken the time to look up to see if there is a star in the heavens for them. Our joy in Gospel living, our service to others, even the very way we speak or act, can help these people look up. We call this evangelization: drawing others to search for, and to experience, the light and warmth of the Star of Bethlehem. This Epiphany we ask God especially to aid us in this endeavor.

FEAST OF THE BAPTISM OF THE LORD (ABC)

Jesus is Baptized and Commissioned to Serve

Isaiah 42:1-4, 6-7; Acts 10:34-38; Matthew 3:13-17 (A), Mark 1:7-11 (B), Luke 3:15-16, 21-22 (C)

Aim: (1) to explain Jesus' baptism in the light of the Suffering Servant of Yahweh; (2) to encourage a similar sense of mission in our Christian lives.

Today's First Reading, from Deutero-Isaiah (the Second Isaiah), is one of the most celebrated Old Testament passages. Written during the sixth century B.C., it is substantially the first of the four Servant Songs, all of which point to Jesus and help us understand his mission. The fourth Servant Song is always read before St. John's Passion narrative in the Good Friday liturgy. The third is read on Palm Sunday; the first and second, on Monday and Tuesday of Holy Week. (Today's First Reading, then, is also assigned to Monday of Holy Week.)

Isaiah's four Servant Songs look to a day when an incomparable Servant of God (the Hebrew is *Ebed Yahweh; Ebed* really means a "slave") will grace our world and serve mankind through suffering to the death. Moreover, this servant will alter the course of the world by doing good, and God's Spirit will be uniquely upon him, according to the songs.

Centuries later, when John the Baptizer, who had been baptizing his disciples in the Jordan River, saw Jesus coming toward him, he used a phrase from one of Isaiah's Servant Songs when he referred to our Lord who takes away the sins of the world. And the words spoken by the Father—in the mysterious voice from heaven in today's Gospel—are taken almost word for word from Isaiah's first Servant Hymn.

Jesus had no need of baptism; because he is the Son of God incarnate and the Jordan rivers were blessed *by him.* He voluntarily chose to step into the Jordan, however, as a sign that he willed to assume the burden of our sins—as Isaiah's prophesied Servant was to do.

This symbolic action by Jesus inaugurated his mission, which he himself told us was to serve, not to be served. Christ came to give his life as a ransom for all men (Mark 10:45).

One lesson we learn from today's liturgy, then, is that since Jesus came to be God's Suffering Servant, a key to discipleship is suffering service for others. As St. Peter told the early Christians in the homily recorded in today's Second Reading: "(Jesus) went about doing good works and healing all who were in the grip of the devil. . . "

There are many models of suffering service in the footsteps of Jesus. Parenting is one; motherhood, especially. Another is embracing a life vocation such as priestly ministry, or teaching, or nursing, or health care in any form. Commitment to kindness in one's neighborhood is another mode; or, to justice. The ways are many and are concretized by saints and heroes of faith. Simply witnessing to everyday honesty and godly conversation in a factory or office can be a most effective means: it requires strength of character to sustain the ridicule and dismissal of one's peers for refusing to compromise one's higher values.

To make this world a little better place frequently proves agonizing. Yet we are all called to be Servants of God in our own spheres of living. Today we reflect on this especially.

FIRST SUNDAY OF LENT (A)

Being Dead to Sin

Genesis 2:7-9, 3:1-7; Romans 5:12-19; Matthew 4:1-11

Aim: (1) to explain original sin, and to describe baptism and the Christian life as a burial to sin and rising to new life; (2) to explain the Lenten ashes as illustrating our death to sin.

Today's Bible readings focus on the existence of sin in our world. The First Reading, from Genesis, the opening book of the Bible, is the familiar story of man's fall from grace. The serpent in the story is a symbol of the power of evil; the same symbol is used in the Book of Wisdom (11:24) and the Apocalypse (12:9). The reason why this symbol was chosen is related to the usages and myths of the ancient mideastern world; undoubtedly it was an understood poetic sign of evil in the culture of the age when Genesis was written.

The kind of sin committed by our protoparents was generically one of disobedience. Somehow they had declined God's invitation or mandate.

The *specific* nature of this transgression is not known precisely. What matters here is that through it, sin came into the world, together with all the consequences of sin, basically three: illness, ignorance and death. What also matters is that because of this sin all human beings (save one, Mary) are conceived in a situation of inward alienation from God. This is what we call original sin.

How can we be so certain of this doctrine? There are two clear

Biblical affirmations: First Corinthians 15:21, and Romans 5:12-21. The latter, Romans 5, was today's second Mass reading.

This same reading also reveals that just as sin came into the world and affects all persons as a result of Adam's transgression, so forgiveness from sin came into the world, for all who sincerely desire it, through one man—the new Adam—Jesus of Nazareth.

This same Jesus we see, in today's Gospel passage, preparing to inaugurate his preaching mission. The scene is the mysterious incident of the Temptation in the Desert. In a sense, it is a new Garden of Eden scene—now, the *Son of Man* confronted by Satan. Only the original garden is no longer a garden; it is a desert; sin has symbolically reduced the world to a wasteland.

It was Jesus who, by rising from the tomb, overcame sin and its consequences, including death. We are privileged to share in this awesome mystery by—as Jesus bids us at the beginning of Lent— repenting our sins and believing his Good News.

We make contact with the saving mystery of Jesus' death and Resurrection through faith and the sacraments, beginning with baptism. Our death and burial in Christ are effected through baptism, where we are symbolically plunged into the cleansing and quickening waters, then raised from the font to new life.

Our being marked with blessed ashes every Lent reminds us of this; specifically, death to sin, through repentance and faith, so that we might participate again in another Easter, an infallible sign of new and eternal life in Christ.

In permitting himself to experience Satan's temptations in the parched regions of the new Eden, Jesus meant to teach us, surely, the reality of sin in our world, and our vulnerability to evil as a result of our generation from Adam. But he also wanted to remind us that our hope of avoiding slavery to sin is secure through and in him. He, in other words, will personally help lead us out of the desert of temptation; he will be our guide and protector.

The condition is that we repent—really die to sin—as we began to do in baptism.

SECOND SUNDAY OF LENT (A)

Our Goal of Sanctity

Genesis 12:1-4; Second Timothy 1:8-10; Matthew 17:1-9

Aim: (1) to picture the Transfiguration Mount as our climb up to sanctity; (2) to explain sanctity and how to reach it.

The Mount of the Transfiguration, as glimpsed in today's Gospel, is a symbol of our goal in life: to be *there*, with Christ, forever.

Peter, James, and John wanted to remain there, with the Lord, at the summit. Peter wanted to build a set of permanent dwellings up there. But Jesus allowed his Apostles but a glimpse of heaven, for a blinding instant. Then he *led* them down the mountain, back into this world of crowds and problems. If they were to be authentic Christians, the Apostles would have to follow Jesus as he walked through *this world* (which is frequently no heaven), to his own Passion and death.

The Gospels teach us that Christians can only be true followers of Jesus by following him (or wanting to follow him) *in this life*: by trying to make this life a little better place for others; by searching for Jesus in the pained and hurt faces that confront us in this life.

Not that we do not aspire to be atop the mountain too, where there are no difficulties or ills. In fact, our homeland is in heaven, as St. Paul tells us (Phillipians 3:20). And God has promised us a future even more glorious than that promised Abram in today's First Reading.

As in the case of Abram—whose name was changed by God to Abraham—we too are on pilgrimage to a better land. We, too, must bear the burden of the heat and the dust of the road; and in all our bearing, we must help others make the summit of the mountain too—one day, that is.

Refreshing moments atop the mountain in this life are usually relatively few. For the most part, the business of life goes on relentlessly down here, far below the summit of the mountain, where the roads aren't always well paved, where elbowroom is sometimes lacking, where noise and clatter distract, and where storm clouds frequently gather. St. Paul grants this in today's Second Reading.

But the Gospels show us that it's here that we find Jesus walking in front of us. Didn't our Lord say that we can find him in others? And isn't finding Christ true holiness?

We find Christ in the sad faces of those who are rejected by other people as allegedly inferior in intelligence, or national origin, or circumstances of birth. We find Jesus in the insecure, those who are constantly in need of reassurance, the fearful and the anxious. We find Jesus in the sick: the elderly in convalescent homes whom no one visits, or in the drab walk-up apartments of the inner-city. We find Jesus in youths with problems unprecedented in the history of the world: problems of communication not only with adults, but with their peers. Christ is found out there in the streets and ghettoes and unhappy suburban homes and—well, anywhere in the world where a Christian can help make life better.

The trick, as one writer has put it, is to keep one eye fixed on the top of the mountain, and the other on the wretched situation of men and women and children in need here below.

Lent is the right time to think about all this, and, of course, to determine to do something about it.

THIRD SUNDAY OF LENT (A)

Grace through the Cross of Christ .

Exodus 17:3-7; Romans 5:1-2, 5-8; John 4:5-42

Aim: to explain (1) the meaning of God's sanctifying grace given to us through the death and resurrection of Jesus.

The exciting promise of living water is presented in today's First Reading, (the Exodus story of Moses' striking the rock in response to God's command in the desert) and in today's Gospel (the beautiful story of Jesus at the Samaritan well) is explained in terms of the infusion of God's life and love by St. Paul, (today's Second Reading, taken from his Letter to the Romans). Thus we are invited by the liturgy to identify the living water as the waters of grace: the life of God being poured into our hearts through the Holy Spirit, who has been given to us.

"Grace" is the word used often in the New Testament to describe the generosity by which God bestows upon us his own life. It is also used to describe the gifts themselves that flow from his free and awesome mercy. Every gift God bestows on us is linked with his life; with supernatural and endless life in him.

God freely and lovingly calls us to his life—a new life that transcends our human capabilities—while we are in a state of sinfulness. St. Paul's words in today's Second Reading should be read while on our knees: "It is precisely in this that God proves his love for us: that *while we were still sinners*, Christ *died for us*." We call this divine action "justification." God justifies us because he freely wants to, out of love for us.

Our being justified effects a profound change within our very being. The Council of Trent described this transformation as a "sanctification and renewal of the inner man." As a result of it we become children of God and heirs of heaven. This profound change is called "sanctifying grace," and since it is intended to be an enduring gift, it is also called "habitual grace." Once a person has received it, beginning with baptism, he retains it as long as he does not separate himself from God by deliberate serious sin.

This great gift comes to us through the Passion, death and Resurrection of Jesus, who now as living Lord sends the Holy Spirit into our midst to draw us into the very life of the Blessed Trinity. In today's Gospel, Jesus said to the Samaritan woman at the well, "Give me to drink." This very expression—"I thirst"—was later used by Jesus on the Cross of Golgotha.

Jesus thirsts for us: to lavish us with God's very life, the life he enjoys from all eternity with the Father in union with the Holy Spirit. He thirsts for us so much that (as today's Second Reading reminds us) he went for us to the Cross, where, just before he died, he expressed it again.

Grace—God-life—is the wellspring of living water from which our thirst is satisfied. In Jesus' words to the woman at the well, "If only (we) recognized God's gift. . . "

The wellsprings of this living water are the sacraments. Each time for example, that we receive the Eucharist or experience sacramental absolution—the Sacrament of Reconciliation—we draw from the saving waters by which Christ's own life—the same God-life which he shares with the Father in union with the Holy Spirit—is communicated to us, toward the day when the need for all symbols will disappear in the reality of God's never ending light.

FOURTH SUNDAY
OF LENT (A)

Our Blindness to God and to the Will of God

First Samuel 16:1, 6-7, 10-13; Ephesians 5:8-14; John 9:1, 6-9, 13-17, 34-38

Aim: to show how we too are blind in that we do not:
(1) see our true need for God; (2) to see God's will in the
trials, disappointments and crosses of life.

Today's beautiful Gospel, from John, recalls Jesus leading a man *born* blind from darkness into light, by granting him the capacity to see. The effect of Christ's action is reminiscent of the rush of God-life bestowed upon David, when anointed by Samuel, in today's First Reading. The meaning of the miracle wrought by Jesus is elaborated upon in today's Second Reading, from St. Paul's Letter to the Ephesians; in a word, the light which the blind man received gave him a new capacity of vision for God's honor and glory, and to be diffused in Jesus' name for others to share.

Commenting on today's Gospel, Bishop Ottokar Prohaszka, the brilliant Hungarian preacher who died in 1927, wrote:

"Jesus called forth light with clay, whereas we suppress the divine light in us with clay, with our earthly, lowly way of thinking. What darkness there is everywhere. . . "*

Baptism gives us a new capacity for vision. The clay of which we are fashioned is so graced by God that we have the ability, in principle, at least, to see beyond what the senses record.

Unfortunately this sounds like empty poetry to one who has lost his sense of mystery. To secularist-minded contemporary man, seeing means visual sighting, nothing more; hearing means the ear's registering sounds, nothing more. Yet this is a crude assessment of reality. Real vision, real hearing, surpass by far the merely physical and intellectual outlines of phenomena.

Think, for example, of the composer Beethoven. Beethoven composed his famed *Missa Solemnis*, regarded by many as the greatest Mass ever written, when he was deaf. (This was the Mass performed in St. Peter's Basilica before Pope Paul VI, and televised around the world.) When Beethoven attended the first performance of this Mass, which he could not hear in the conventional way, he broke down with joy. He heard every note in a manner of transcending the standard assumptions regarding hearing.

A parallel can be expressed about sight, as anyone who has experienced blind people on tours or pilgrimages can testify. In seeing, too, it is what the soul encounters that matters most.

In the pilgrimage of life, we place ourselves at a distinct disadvantage if we proceed merely by means of what our senses detect. A new kind of vision, a new kind of hearing is given to us by Jesus, through baptism. As Christ's disciples we are gifted with a capacity to detect the reality of the mystery in which we are immersed, a mystery that says to us, before all else: God exists, Jesus who is God *lives*; Jesus intervenes in my life, even in the trials and crosses I experience; and Jesus *is needed by me.*

Real blindness is not seeing any of this.

As Christians we can see that the obstacles that seem to fall before our paths in life are only like the frozen branches of trees that crash to the ground on wooded paths in wintertime. They do not really impede our progress, but simply compel us to get down on our knees in a foot of snow to clear our passage, all the while inviting us—as the poet Robert Frost once suggested—to ask ourselves who we really are and what our goals should be.

---

* *Meditations on the Gospel*, trans. M. de Pal Westminster, Md.; The Newman Press, 1952.

FIFTH SUNDAY OF LENT (A)

The Evil of Mortal Sin

Ezekiel 37:12-14; Romans 8:8-11; John 11:1-45

Aim: to explain (1) the three conditions necessary for a mortal sin; (2) the horror of mortal sin; (3) the need to avoid mortal sin and to get rid of it immediately.

The raising of Lazarus from the grave (today's Gospel) points toward the raising of the sinner through Jesus' merciful love in the Church, primarily through the Sacraments of Baptism and Penance. Our exaltation, essentially more marvelous than the infusion of fresh life seen by the prophet Ezekiel in the familiar vision of the dry bones (First Reading), constitutes a rushing upon us of Christ's very life, so much so that St. Paul could say, "God dwells in us" (Second Reading).

In Jesus, we, like Lazarus, are freed from the constraints of death—but from *eternal* death, which is the only death that really matters, the only death that endures.

We mean the death of sin, of course: mortal sin. Mortal sin constitutes a conscious, free decision of the whole personality, in serious matter, against God's will as known through nature, reason or Revelation. In our catechism days we used to say that mortal sin involved a serious offense against God, done with full advertence and consent of the will.

That there are actions which are seriously wrong if performed knowingly and freely, is a Biblical datum. Read, for some examples,

First Corinthians 6:9-10; or Galatians 5:19-21; or First Timothy 1:9-11.

This means that there are objective norms of human conduct. Certain acts (e.g., blasphemy, perjury, adultery, abortion) are sinful in themselves if done with sufficient reflection and voluntary assent. The Church, aided by the Spirit, helps us assess such serious aberrations.

Mortal sins are so called because they deprive us of Christ's life in us, and consequently, lead away from Christ, where only death awaits. The word "mortal" comes from the Latin for "death." Separation from Christ means the zenith of meaninglessness, the summit of nonfulfillment.

For a follower of Christ, therefore, mortal sin is a horrendous prospect, to be avoided always. As a contradiction of all we believe, it is essentially ugly and repugnant. There is nothing good or beautiful about it; it is never justified, never tolerable, never neutral. If one could draw a picture of mortal sin, one would draw Jesus, the Son of God, crucified, his Precious Blood pouring forth, his voice crying, "My God, My God, why have you forsaken me?" This is what sin looks like.

Jesus prayed from the Cross, "Father, forgive them. . ." In him we have forgiveness of our mortal sins. Through a contrite sacramental confession, we can literally place ourselves under the cross of Golgotha and hear our Savior's words of pardon addressed to us—to you and to me. Through the Sacrament of Reconciliation we can hear Jesus' words summoning the dead Lazarus to come out, referred to us.

What happened to Lazarus pales before what happens to the sinner who, having made a contrite sacramental confession, receives the Church's absolution. The mortal sinner passes from *real* and *lasting* death into the life of Jesus' resurrection.

PASSION (PALM) SUNDAY (A)

The Events of the Holy Week

Isaiah 50:4-7; Philippians 2:6-11; Matthew 26:14-27:66

Aim: (1) to reconstruct the final week in Jesus' public ministry as the Lord's great sacrifice for us, a synopsis of his entire life of love and sacrifice.

Today is Passion Sunday. It is also known as Palm Sunday, because on this day we bless palms and process with them in recollection of Jesus' messianic entrance into the Holy City of Jerusalem, where he was to give his life as the Suffering Servant of God, the Paschal Lamb of the New and everlasting Covenant.

The First Reading at Mass is taken from the third of the four crucial Servant of the Lord Hymns, composed by the Second Isaiah. The Second Reading, from St. Paul, recalls that through suffering service—taking the form of a slave—Jesus was exalted as Lord, before whom all must bend the knee.

Jesus' identification with the Second Isaiah's prophesied Servant of the Lord is clear from several New Testament passages. St. Matthew, for example, from whose Gospel today's Passion narrative was read, used both the first and the last Servant Song of Isaiah to explain that Christ took away not only our sins, but also their physical infirmities (12:17-21 and 8:16-17). In today's account of the Last Supper, Matthew uses a concept from the Servant Songs when he refers to Jesus' Precious Blood as the "blood of the covenant . . . poured out for many . . . for the forgiveness of sins."

As Christ our Lord entered Jerusalem for the first Holy Week, therefore, he entered as God's Suffering Servant ready to go to the death that we—you and I—might be washed clean in his Precious Blood, thereby enabling us to enter into eternal life through his Resurrection. "Through Christ's dear sufferings," Archbishop John F. Whealon writes in *The Vatican II Sunday Missal* (St. Paul Editions, 1974), "our redemption was achieved."

Jesus' "dear suffering" included his betrayal by one of the Twelve, Judas Iscariot, and by the Prince of Apostles, Simon Peter, who, in fear, denied that he knew Jesus, not once but three times. They included, too, the Agony in Gethsemani, where he went to pray for strength and where he was abandoned by three chosen Apostles, who slept while he endured a bloody sweat.

Jesus' "dear sufferings" also encompassed an unjust trial, a cruel scourging and mock crowning with thorns, and condemnation to crucifixion, a horrendous punishment usually meted out only to slaves. Further, our Lord must carry his cross to the place of execution, just outside Jerusalem; and there be nailed between two convicts. As he hung suspended between heaven and earth, only one Apostle remained with him, along with his mother Mary, and a few committed women. Dying, he prayed for his persecutors, and said, "I thirst," as he had said to the Samaritan woman at the well. Thus in his last moments, his thought was of drawing mankind to the Father's loving forgiveness.

Today we recall these events of Holy Week; they constitute the crowning synopsis of how thoroughly Jesus, the Son of God Incarnate, became God's Servant for us. Through his Precious Blood we gain entrance into eternal life.

With hearts filled with loving gratitude today, we kneel in spirit before the Cross of Calvary.

3

HOLY THURSDAY (ABC)

The Lord's Supper

Exodus 12:1-8, 11-14; First Corinthians 11:23-26; John 13:1-15

Aim: to explain (1) the institution of the Eucharist; (2) the institution of the priesthood; (3) Jesus' command to us to love one another.

Today, Holy Thursday, the liturgy bids us ponder three mysteries: (1) the Eucharist, which was instituted in the Upper Room the day before the Savior suffered and died on the cross for us; (2) the New Testament priesthood, established by Jesus to ensure the Eucharist's re-enactment in the world to the end of time; and (3) the Mandatum, the law of Christly love symbolized by Jesus' washing the Apostles' feet. ("Mandatum" is the Latin for "mandate," a "commandment." "Maundy" is an old French derivative from "Mandatum"; this is why Holy Thursday is also known as Maundy Thursday.)

Jesus' command to love, as he loved us, thematically underlies both the Eucharist and the priesthood, for it constitutes a mystical sign of the all-embracing, disinterested love underlying the Incarnation. We recall this every year especially at Christmas when we read at Mass God's revelation as to his motive in becoming man for us; namely, the phrase: ". . . when the goodness and loving kindness of God our Savior appeared, he saved us. . . (Titus 3:4; Second Reading of Mass at Dawn).

Jesus is the Father's supreme and irrevocable Love-Gift. "God *is* love," the First Letter of John affirms (4:8). The New Testament tells us quite plainly that God encounters us as the Suffering Servant who came not to be served, but to serve; as the new and eternal Paschal Lamb, prophesied in today's First Reading.

Thus in the Eucharist, the celebrant says, as he rehearses the ineffable mystery of the Upper Room: "This is my Body, which will be given up *for you.* . . This is the cup of my Blood . . . it will be shed *for you* and *for all men* so that sins may be forgiven." The oldest written inspired record of this mystery is St. Paul's words to Corinth, from which today's Second Reading was excerpted.

That Jesus is the Father's Supreme Love Gift means not only that he pours out his Blood in the one eternal sacrifice of infinitely redemptive love, but also that he remains with us as the Sacrificial Victim and Priest, that he continues to stand between us and the Father even now, and pleads with the Father in our behalf.

Since there is no Eucharist without the New Testament priesthood, we recall the priesthood too, on Holy Thursday. It is the ministerial priesthood, inaugurated in the Upper Room, that constitutes the focus and the means of Jesus' love as concretized in the Eucharist.

The priesthood is the focus, because around it, as around the Lord himself, is formed the community of discipleship that constitutes Jesus' Mystical Body, the Church.

The priesthood—the presbyterate—is the means by which the Father's Supreme Love-Gift is realized through the ages, for without ordained ministers, men linked directly to the Upper Room, the Eucharist would not be. It was to his Apostles and their successors in the priesthood that the Lord said, "Do this in memory of me."

So today we pray especially in thanksgiving for God's great love for us in Jesus. We ask to be suffering servants in his footsteps, as symbolized by the Washing of the Feet. We intercede with him for his priests, to whom he has entrusted his word and his Body. Finally, we bow profoundly in gratitude for his Real Presence in our midst: the Eucharist.

GOOD FRIDAY (ABC)

How and Why Jesus Died for Us

Isaiah 52:13-53:12; Hebrews 4:14-16; 5:7-9; John 18:1-19:42

Aim: (1) to explain the Lord's death; (2) to teach the eternal benefits for us of that death.

The First Reading for this Celebration of the Lord's Passion was from the Second Isaiah's fourth (and last) Servant Song. Written six centuries before Christ, it foretells a mysterious Servant of the Lord who willingly suffers ignominious torture and death for us all.

This mysterious Servant, we know, is Jesus, who, because he is God, the Second Person of the Blessed Trinity Incarnate, became the source of eternal salvation for all who accept and obey him as Lord.

How Jesus, God-made-man, willingly suffered for us, is detailed in the Passion narrative from St. John's Gospel, just read.

One of the characteristics of John's Passion account, always reserved for the Good Friday liturgy, is that throughout the events— from Holy Thursday and his arrest, during his trial before those who sentenced him, right through his scourging, death and crucifixion— our Lord *was in complete control of his destiny.* He gave his life, freely; it was not taken from him. And through it all he gave it because he was the Suffering Servant who came to serve, not to be served; to ransom us, not to be given in ransom.

Thus, in the arrest scene, Jesus takes command immediately: "Who is it you want?" (18:4) he demands outright. Judas and the arresting officers are like secondary characters in a play; the spotlight is on Christ.

In the trial before Pilate, Jesus speaks directly of his own kingdom. And he tells Pilate in so many words that he would have no power over him except for the fact that he permitted it.

Even at the moment of death, Jesus remains in absolute control of his destiny; he is dying because he has a mission to accomplish. Notice how John's account says: "Jesus, realizing that everything was now finished, said to fulfill the Scripture, 'I am thirsty' " (19:28). And, at the final instant, what did Jesus say, in John's recollection? It was: "Now it is finished" (19:13).

What was finished? Jesus' atoning work, his making man and the world at one with God again; conquering sin; and, with it, sickness, ignorance and death; opening to mankind again the Gates of Heaven.

Toward the close of the St. John Passion, there is reference to the piercing of Jesus' side with the lance. John testifies—he is the only evangelist to witness to this (he alone of all the Apostles was there and saw)—that, at the lance thrust, blood and water poured forth.

Remember that Jesus once promised he would give us living water: that from him there would "flow rivers of living water" (8:38). These rivers of living water symbolize the waters of baptism, which bring salvation to all men. They are miraculous, though, precisely because blood poured forth too—the blood of Jesus on the Cross, who, in complete control of his destiny, handed himself over for us to save us from sin, and thereby *reigns* from the Cross.

THE EASTER VIGIL (A)

Jesus is Risen and We are Risen from Sin

Genesis 1:1-2; 22:1-18; Exodus 14:15-15:1; Isaiah 54:5-14; 55:1-11; Baruch 3:9-15; Ezekiel 36:16-28; Romans 6:3-11; Matthew 28:1-10

Aim: to explain (1) the history and meaning of the Easter Vigil; (2) our baptism, our rising from sin and living by faith; (3) and the expression of all this in renewing our baptismal vows.

Listening to the Old Testament prophecies, we have just kept vigil in the most ancient of Christian liturgical vigils anticipatory to the heart of the Good News of our faith; the Easter Gospel, just read. In the words of the angel: ". . . you are looking for Jesus the crucified, but he is not here. He has been raised, exactly as he promised. . . He has been raised from the dead and now goes ahead of you to Galilee, where you will see him."

The Old Testament readings this evening are especially instructive. One theme is sounded throughout; namely, God's deliverance of his Chosen People in the greatest single divine intervention of the Old Covenant; the Exodus: Israel's miraculous passing through the Sea and its final deliverance in the Promised Land.

The Epistle, from St. Paul's monumental Letter to the Romans, reveals how Jesus' followers pass through the everlasting liberating waters of grace through Baptism. And the Gospel, from Matthew, recalls the dawn of the day when this everlasting liberating exodus occurred; the dawn of Jesus' Resurrection. We dramatized this last motif this evening by the blessing of new fire, from which the Easter Candle, symbolic of Jesus, who fulfilled and gave meaning to the Old Testament, was lit to illumine this church.

In a few moments we shall bless baptismal water to be used here in our parish church. As we bless it, we shall plunge the Paschal Candle into it, as a sign of Jesus' death and burial; then raise the candle from the water, as a sign of Jesus' conquest over death in his resurrection.

These ceremonies remind us that our participation in the mystery of dying and rising in Christ begins in principle with our baptism. In his Epistle to the Colossians, St. Paul states that in baptism we were buried and raised to life with Christ because we believed in the power of God who raised him from death (2:12).

Our death and resurrection in Christ, we said, began in principle with baptism. It inaugurates an ongoing lifetime process, which we must personally ratify again and again in this pilgrimage below. This Easter Vigil Eucharist is one graced opportunity for such a ratification. In fact, this is why we shall renew our baptismal vows this evening following the blessing of the water.

Temporal life, we believe, is a continuous conversion Godward. The moment we are mature enough to reflect on the new birth we experienced in baptism, we begin to realize that life for us consists of immersing ourselves more and more deeply into the depths of death to self, and life to Christ. Physical death means for us the close of a period of trial in which we have buried ourselves with and in Jesus so that we achieve a new and eternal birthday with and in his Resurrection forever.

Easter tells us clearly that physical life, while a race toward a physical death, is nonetheless a process toward real and eternal life in the Lord, who bids his disciples to meet him forever before an empty tomb.

EASTER SUNDAY (ABC)

The Resurrection, Source of Our Faith

Acts 10:34, 37:43; Colossians 3:14 or First Corinthians 5:6-8; John 20:1-9

> *Aim: to explain (1) that the Apostles believed because of the Resurrection; (2) that we believe for the same reason; (3) the reason that we observe every Sunday as a Little Easter.*

Today is the Solemnity of the Resurrection of our Lord Jesus Christ, what in English we also call "Easter," reflecting an Old English word referring to the spring sun which brings new life.

By the Resurrection we mean that Jesus, following his true and actual death and burial, rose from the grave in his total and, consequently, physical reality, to glorified perfection and immortality. Thus, a mere figurative resurrection is ruled out by our faith. Jesus really and truly rose from the dead; Peter says this clearly in today's First Reading. As Peter and the Apostles believed, so do we.

There are two basic Traditions to Jesus' Resurrection on Easter morning: (1) the Tradition of the empty tomb, and (2) the Tradition of the risen Christ's various appearances.

Today's beautiful Gospel accents the empty tomb Tradition. It teaches us three lessons.

First, note that the Gospel relates that "Mary Magdalene came to the tomb" and "saw that the stone had been moved away" (20:1). What else can this mean but that the power of death, the power of Sheol—the Hebrew concept of the place of underworld darkness from which there is no return (Jb 7:9; Ps 63:10; Dt 32:22)—has been conquered? Tombs, by the power of Jesus' rising, can no longer be held shut; new life, risen life in Christ, literally bursts open every tomb's door. (All four evangelists note the fact of the rolled back stone; Mark adds that "it was very large" (16:4). Surely their intention was to accent Jesus' victory over death.)

Secondly, notice the reference to Jesus' missing body. The simple declarative, "He is not here," is recalled by Mark, Matthew and Luke. The meaning is that Jesus *is*; though he is not *here*. In other words, he lives; he is no longer in a state of death. Yet, "He is not *here*," opens up the quest for the living Lord: *certain* grounds for the hope for Jesus' appearing in our midst again.

A third lesson of the empty tomb is the symbolism of the burial linens, upon which today's Gospel dwells. Jesus had *passed through* the shroud. The Apostle John saw "the wrappings lying on the ground" (20:5). They had been discarded by Jesus; the new life to which he had risen rendered them irrelevant.

In his Resurrection Christ's body had attained the fullness of his existence. Pre-Resurrection things can now be put aside; the Lord must now be sought in a new form, not dependent on earlier habits or modes.

Our belief as Christians is of course not simply in an empty tomb; our faith is in the risen, living Lord Jesus, who really appeared to his disciples, as Peter recalls in today's First Reading.

Each of the two Traditions—the Empty Tomb and the apparitions—criscrosses and interpenetrates the other, confirming and enlightening both in the mysterious process.

By virtue of his apparitions, Jesus the risen Lord entered into our history and gives us the new life of which St. Paul speaks in today's Second Reading. We recall this especially today, Easter Sunday, and every other Sunday in the year, which for us is always a Little Easter.

SECOND SUNDAY OF EASTER (A)

Sin and the Forgiveness of Sin

Acts 2:42-47; First Peter 1:3-9; John 20:19-31

Aim: to establish (1) a sense of sin, in oneself; (2) the need for forgiveness of sin as essential to the Christian life.

Today's Gospel contains, in Thomas the Apostle's Credo, the most complete acknowledgement of Jesus' divinity found on the lips of anyone in the Gospels; namely, "My Lord and My God."

To grant that Christ was the greatest religious genius of all time is not too difficult for anyone who knows history. Nor is it difficult to admit that no human being has ever equalled his humanity. The key challenge put by Jesus is whether he is God—Lord. In this challenge, as Dostoevsky once remarked, lies the heart of the whole faith.

As Christians we believe that Jesus is Lord and God. And as Lord and God, he is our Savior—*my* Savior. In him I find forgiveness from my sins and the pledge of eternal glory in God's Kingdom. The very name "Jesus" means "God saves."

What was the very first command that Jesus uttered in his first recorded sermon? Wasn't it a command to repent? Mark, the oldest of the Gospels, tells us that after Jesus had fasted in the desert he appeared with the message: "This is the time of fulfillment. The reign of God is at hand! Reform your lives and believe in the Gospel!" (1:4).

Now, on Easter Sunday, this same Jesus, having risen from the tomb, says to his Apostles, "If you forgive men's sins, they are forgiven them; if you hold them bound, they are held bound" (today's Gospel).

Jesus announces a new birth to salvation, as Peter reminds us in today's Second Reading.

"A new birth to forgiveness:" this phrase is meaningless unless we are realistic enough to admit our sinfulness and our desperate need for salvation. The God who comes to save us—Jesus—is unrecognizable except to one who is willing to admit his or her sin. Today's First Reading recounts that day by day the Lord added to those "who were being saved." *Saved* from what? From sin, of course, from our—*my*—sin. Essential to salvation, essential to God's action in our lives, is a sense of our responsibility for guilt before the all-good God.

Today several factors are at work undermining the sense of sin. One is so called "situation ethics," which pretends to justify sinful actions on the theory that God's moral law is relative, and that circumstances can sometimes render evil good. Another is a prevailing secularism, which holds that everything in this world can adequately be explained without reference to the vertical dimension of reality—without God. A third factor is a false psychology which equates sin with emotional disorder or mental illness.

Not at all. Sin is a deliberate offense against God; it results in real guilt. It can only be taken away by our accepting Jesus as Lord and Savior in repentance and love. Which equivalently requires our saying, in the Sacrament of Confession, Thomas' words: "My Lord and My God."

Jesus is Lord and God. We confess this by acknowledging our sin and seeking the pardon only he can give us through "birth to an imperishable inheritance, incapable of fading or defilement," of which Peter in today's Second Reading writes.

THIRD SUNDAY OF EASTER (A)

At Mass We Recognize the Risen Christ

Acts 2:14, 22-28; First Peter 1:17-21; Luke 24:13-35.

Aim: to explain (1) the Mass as a special encounter with Christ; (2) the meaning of the Mass for the Lord's followers: "they knew him in the breaking of the bread."

The Jesus who died on Calvary and was buried in a tomb is the same Jesus who, risen from the grave, now walks with us, speaks with us, and helps us in our pilgrimage through this vale of tears. He is the same Jesus whom we learn to recognize at Mass.

Today's Gospel recalls an incident on the first Easter morning. The Old Testament paschal solemnities completed for another year, Israelites were beginning the homeward trek from Jerusalem. Among them were two of Christ's disciples, one named Cleophas. As they walked down the road, they were discussing the events of the week. Sadly they recalled how Jesus, in whom they had placed their trust and hope, was betrayed to his enemies and slain. Presently Jesus appeared and began to accompany them, but they failed to recognize him.

Our Lord questioned the men about their apparent despondency. He then began to explain how everything that happened during Holy Week had been predicted of the Messiah; he helped them review the Scriptures about his death and Resurrection.

Having arrived at their destination, the two disciples asked Jesus to stay with them. The Savior accepted their invitation. While at the table with them, he took bread; blessed it, broke it, and gave it to them. Immediately their eyes were opened. They recognized the risen Lord in "the Breaking of the Bread."

"The Breaking of the Bread" is one of the most ancient names for the Eucharist, or the Mass. And today's Easter Gospel is both a theological and a poetic description of the Mass, which emerged from the Easter event.

The first part of the disciples' journey is comparable to the Liturgy of the Word. Through the Bible readings and the homily, Christ the living Lord becomes present in our midst and teaches us how to recognize him.

The Liturgy of the Eucharist constitutes the recognized Christ's entering into our lives through our sincere invitation. And our union with him—our communion—is effected through our partaking of his Body in "the Breaking of the Bread."

No wonder that Peter, in today's Second Reading, refers to our life now as a "sojourn"—a kind of pilgrimage. This same Peter, in a sermon recorded by Luke in today's First Reading, adds that Jesus shows us the right "paths of life," leading to his real presence. Again, this is an allusion to the Mass, which is a Biblical journey leading to a banquet with Christ.

"Let us proclaim the mystery of faith"; thus the celebrant of Mass invites the acclamation of the congregation after he pronounces the words of the Lord over the bread and the cup of wine. Surely this means that the Eucharist is the divine, real, and effective Sign of all truth, the very sanctuary of all belief.

It is in the Mass that we, like the disciples on the road to Emmaus that first Easter morning, come to know infallibly that God is not dead, but *lives* (present tense indicative), *enters* into our lives, and *awaits* us at the close of this life's journey as Lord and Savior!

We too come to know Christ through "the Breaking of the Bread."

FOURTH SUNDAY OF EASTER (A)

Parish Life and Parish Membership

Acts 2:14, 36-41; 2:20-25; John 10:1-10.

Aim: (1) to explain what a parish is, and (2) to reiterate the importance of active parish membership as normative for Catholic living.

Today is commonly called Good Shepherd Sunday, since all the Bible readings, as well as the intervenient chant and Alleluia verse accent a pastoral theme. In fact, the word "shepherd" or "sheep" appears in all readings and verses except the first, where they are implied.

Our English word "pastoral" comes from the Latin by way of an Old English word pertaining to the task of leading, safeguarding and nourishing flocks, especially sheep. Early in Christianity, it was applied to the ministry of bishops, priests and deacons, the principal reason being Biblical use of this figure of speech, as evidenced in today's Scripture readings.

The local area of pastoral care—the local sheepfold in Biblical language—is what we call a parish. "Parish" is also a Latin derivative, though it reflects the Greek. The original meaning, interestingly, is "alongside one's house." The early Christians viewed themselves as strangers passing toward their true home, heaven, which is reflected in a unit of the Church in miniature; namely, a parish. The institution of the parish is at least 1500 years old, its structure dating from the emergence of the Church from the catacombs.

A parish is truly a spiritual sheepfold wherein the ministry of the Good Shepherd is carried out both by ordained and nonordained personnel. By its nature it reflects all dimensions of Jesus' loving care for us.

Thus, it is in a parish that Jesus says, as he does in today's Gospel, "I know my sheep . . ." and "I know my own . . ." For it is in a parish church, such as this, that we gather every Sunday as a whole; allow him to know us better through our presence and prayerful hearts, to nourish us, through his word and grace, and to lead and strengthen us so that we can help others, even those not of our flock, through our liturgical participation and communion.

Here, too, in our parish church, we first enter Christ's sheepfold, through the spiritual rebirth of baptism. Here we achieve maturity in faith, through confirmation. It is here that we come as prodigal children when we suffer an illness of soul—sin—so that we may experience his loving mercy. Here marriage vows are taken. It is from here that the oils of the Last Anointing are brought to the seriously ill.

Today's Second Reading recalls that though we were once scattered, we are now one; into this parish, in other words, Christ has gathered us. Here we find life, in terms of today's Gospel.

To bring all this down to a very concrete level, three basic expectations can be assigned to each member of a parish. They are: (1) registration; (2) involvement, and (3) support, spiritually and financially. Too, there should be concern for outreach; a thrust beyond parish limits can be implemented by social service, ecumenical activity, and education programs.

Archbishop John F. Whealon has written in his notes to *The Vatican II Sunday Missal*:

"The real purpose of a parish is, in fact, to develop saints who praise God together, who as a community carry out the two great Commandments. . ."

This is the purpose described in today's First Reading: the spirit of the first generation Christians. In a parish we and they are one.

FIFTH SUNDAY OF EASTER (A)

What God Looks Like

Acts 6:1-7; First Peter 2:4-9; John 14:1-12.

Aim: (1) to show that Jesus is the Father's revelation of himself. (An incidental commentary on the origins of the diaconate is presented.)

Today's First Reading, incidentally, is often read as depicting the origin of the diaconate, one of the three Orders in the Sacrament of Holy Orders. Today, following Vatican Council II, the permanent diaconate has been restored as a ministry. Deacons share with priests and bishops the power to preach the Gospel; they also can baptize solemnly, witness marriages, distribute Holy Communion and administer certain blessings. Besides such liturgical functions, they also may be assigned to teaching or catechetical roles and to charitable ministries. Underlying all diaconal activity is the premise that deacons help those who direct the Church.

Today's Gospel, however, is the main focus for our reflection. It reveals to us what God looks like.

In our striving to depict God we try so hard at times that we miss the obvious. For as Christians we affirm, at least in principle, that we *can* know what God looks like, that we *can* acquire an accurate picture of God.

How? Through Jesus, of course. We have but to contemplate Jesus of Nazareth to know what God looks like, how God acts. We have but to contemplate Jesus to know all we need to know about

God. "After I have been with you all this time, Philip," said Jesus to his Apostle, "you still do not know me? Whoever has seen me, has seen the Father" (Today's Gospel).

What is God like? Contemplate Jesus of Nazareth, who had compassion on the deaf, the lame, the blind. Contemplate Jesus, who brought a dead girl back to life, and who returned a dead youth to his widowed mother, and who summoned Lazarus forth from the tomb.

What is God like? Contemplate Jesus, who excoriated hypocrisy and insincerity; but who exalted the downtrodden, the alienated, the impoverished, the unconsulted. Contemplate Jesus, the Suffering Servant, who appeared after his Resurrection to the very Apostles, who, save one, failed to remain with him during his Passion and crucifixion.

The primitive Christian community had a profound grasp of God as revealed in Jesus. We detect this in today's First Reading, in which we recall the dynamic enthusiasm of the early faithful, committed to action as suffering servants in Jesus' footsteps.

We detect this, too, in St. Peter's First Letter, today's Second Reading, wherein Jesus is described as the keystone of our faith, the source of our life, the life of the soul; in effect, our way, our truth and our life.

To contemplate Jesus is not only to know what God looks like and how God acts. It is to contemplate God himself. Union with Jesus means union with God.

Last Christmas, in the Mass during the day we recalled, in the Second Reading, that Jesus Christ "is the reflection of the Father's glory, the exact representation of the Father's being" (Hebrews 1:3). In our faith we take these words literally; to know Jesus is to know the Father; to contemplate Jesus is to contemplate the Father.

SIXTH SUNDAY OF EASTER (A)

Joy and Courage in Living

Acts 8:5-8, 14-17; First Peter 3:15-18; John 14:15-21

*Aim: (1) to list some major problems in living; and (2)
to explore how a Christian faces life's trials that come
from the world, from others, from self.*

The "little while," about which Jesus speaks in today's Gospel,
refers to that era spanning the period from the Resurrection-
Ascension event until the Now—this current segment of history.

While physically here on this earth, Jesus did all that could be
done—or as Karl Rahner has put it, "what only *he* could do here."
Then, after his Resurrection, he returned in the flesh to the right hand
of his Father.

We ask (if we ponder Revelation at all): why not all at once? Why
did Jesus leave, return to his Father, his life's mission fulfilled in
principle only? This invites a re-questioning of such paradoxes as evil
still at work in this world: wars, racial hatred, widespread
abandonment of standards of human decency, abortion, rejection of
parental responsibility, deterioration of sexual mores, and so on.

And there are so many problems in day-to-day living: economic
problems, employment problems, educational problems, housing
problems, communication problems (sometimes within one's own
home).

We misread a great deal, really. Jesus did do what he could do
here. But he came to *draw* us, not compel us. He wants us as persons;

therefore, free. Freedom has no other principal purpose than to permit love. This "little while" in which we all now live allows us—each one of us—to exercise this love, to be *drawn* to Christ.

Again, according to Karl Rahner:

"It was not his (Jesus') affair that the Father, in his kindness, did not let the earth burst into flames immediately. That was his Father's business. He was pleased that we should still have something to say and do. Christ himself insisted on this delay for 'a little while' " (*The Eternal Year*: Helicon, 1965).

So that this "little while" in which we are now immersed, this brief moment in which we live and breathe, is our lone opportunity to say and to do something by way of witnessing to the risen Lord now living in our midst. As such, it is our opportunity to exorcise the evils that now plague mankind—to refer to today's First Reading.

Christ has trusted *us* with the responsibility of rendering such witness now, and for collaborating in his suffering service, as the Second Reading affirms. He has faith in us—faith that our living out this "little while" with which he had endowed us will be one of service to the Father and all mankind in accordance with the example of the Suffering Servant that he was.

Christ has trusted us to live in the conviction that life has profound supernatural meaning, and that we are essentially free agents, free to love and not to love, free even to affirm or to deny our dignity as human persons drawn to his eternal embrace (and not as robots whose fates are predetermined by calculations made with reference to the Signs of the Zodiac).

We must believe that our insignificant contribution can fulfill Jesus' trust in giving us this "little while."

Surely all these thoughts ensure the sheer joy of living. To be a Christian is to have eternal meaning!

ASCENSION (ABC)

The Ascension

Acts 1:1-11; Ephesians 1:17-23; Matthew 28:16-20 (A); Mark 16:15-20 (B); Luke 24:46-53 (C).

Aim: to show that (1) we too will rise and ascend to the Father after death; (2) we should live as people destined for eternity and not for this life only; and (3) our faith must be taught and witnessed to in the spirit of evangelization.

Today's First Reading, from Luke's Acts of the Apostles, is the most detailed Biblical account of the Ascension. Luke is writing to Theophilus, a Greek name meaning "one who loves God;" the name could designate you and me.

Luke suggests a 40 days interval between our divine Lord's Resurrection and his being taken up. It is a number we need not take literally. The rabbis in Jesus' time used 40 as a norm for completion. The Ascension marks the end of Jesus' public appearances in his risen body; now, until he comes again, Jesus reveals himself through his Spirit in his Church, his mystical body. Today's Second Reading, from Ephesians, focuses on this mystery of the Church, to which Christ calls all men, and which he safeguards until the end of time.

There are several key lessons of faith in today's liturgy.

One, obviously, is that there *is* another life, a higher life, to which we are called. And Christ is the only way to it, the only way. Christ's way means accepting Christ's word, following Christ's commandments, as Mark stresses in his account of the Ascension.

Another lesson could be gleaned from Luke's going out of his way to mention a 40 days interval between the Resurrection and the Ascension. Several commentators have noted that this interval constitutes a "grace period" for our advantage, to allow the events of Easter to penetrate more fully into our awareness. During the past several weeks we have had adequate time to ponder Jesus' death, Resurrection and apparitions. As a result we are ready now to approach, listen to, and touch him in his Church, through his sacraments. It is as if the entire Easter retreat has helped us assign experiential meaning to his words, "I am going to prepare a place for you" (John 14:3).

A third lesson today is that the "end time" in which we live should be dedicated to witnessing to Christ in Galilee—a symbolic word for the world. In Matthew's account of the Ascension, "You are to be my witnesses," he stresses the need for preaching and confessing the Gospel everywhere; Luke uses the word "witnessing." Christianity is not simply standing around, looking up to the heavens. It means bringing the light of Christ to the nations, by our example, words, deeds; by our prayers.

Another lesson. If we live in and for Christ, we shall join him in glory. The Ascension shows us our true goal in life: to rise with Christ through the power of his Resurrection.

Too, the Ascension teaches us what heaven really is. Heaven for us is where Christ is; heaven means—in St. Paul's phrase—"to be with Christ" (Philippians 1:23).

Finally, the Ascension is a dramatic reminder that Christ will come again—as the closing portion of today's First Reading affirms. The Lord Jesus will surely come again, to this world, as redeemer *and judge*. Hence we should live as persons destined for heaven, not merely for this passing world.

SEVENTH SUNDAY
OF EASTER (A)

Daily Prayer in Catholic Living

Acts 1:12-14; First Peter 4:13-16; John 17:1-11.

Aim: (1) to describe the various kinds of prayer; and (2) to give practical advice on how to pray.

Today's Gospel is taken from our divine Lord's High-Priestly Prayer, in which he consecrates those who will continue his work in this world. This Prayer was offered at the Last Supper, just before Jesus consecrated the bread and wine for the Sacrifice which he was about to institute, and which he was to empower his Apostles and their successors to renew until the end of the world.

The Gospels often depict Jesus in prayer, always at crucial moments of his mission: before choosing his Apostles, for example, before his arrest through Judas' betrayal in Gethsemani, and here, in the Upper Room, before offering the first Mass.

The Apostles, imitating the Lord, prayed constantly; today's First Reading depicts them in prayer with Mary, the Mother of the Lord. Incidentally, today's First Reading contains the final reference to our Lady in this life. This is significant in that Mary is a sign of the Church, the model of every person of faith. Seeing her for the last time waiting in prayer should remind us that we are called to follow her example.

The gift of the Spirit, whose coming is described in today's Second Reading, depends upon our constant and renewed prayer. This is especially true in times of distress, sorrow, or suffering of any kind, as the Second Reading suggests. (Peter wrote today's passage when it was rapidly becoming a crime even to be a Christian.)

Viewed in itself, prayer means communicating with God. This conversation can reflect one or several motives: thanksgiving, for example, or petition, penance, atonement. Viewed from another aspect, prayer is either liturgical or private. Liturgical prayer is the official prayer of the Church; "liturgy" derives from a Greek word signifying a public duty or work for the common welfare. Liturgical prayer includes first and foremost the Eucharist or Mass, as well as all the sacraments. It also encompasses public ritual, such as the Divine Office or the Liturgy of the Hours, traditionally recited daily by priests and religious, as well as many of the laity.

Private prayer refers to nonliturgical prayer offered either by individuals or by groups. Vatican Council II reminds that whereas the liturgy is, in a certain sense, endowed with a dignity higher than that of nonliturgical prayer, this principle does not minimize, much less dispense from, the obligation of non-liturgical prayer (*The Constitution of the Sacred Liturgy*, Section 12).

Prayer affirms faith, and faith is a gift from God. So that prayer itself is a divine charism. Indeed, we could not pray unless Jesus sent his Spirit to us to say, "Father" (Romans 8:15, 26-27). This also means that Jesus prays with us and for us.

Prayer, Christ told us, must be made in humility (Luke 12:22-31). And it must be persevered in; one cannot "give up" on prayer (Luke 11:5-13). It goes without saying, of course, that prayer must be sincere. As Shakespeare said, "words without thoughts never to heaven go" (Hamlet III:IV, 97).

We pray today, then, to realize more intensely the importance of constant renewed prayer. To this end we remember Mary, the Mother of the Lord, praying with the Apostles in that first post-Easter season.

PENTECOST
(VIGIL MASS) (ABC)

The Holy Spirit as Teacher, Guide, Unifier

Genesis 11:1-9; Romans 8:22-27; John 7:37-39.

Aim: to explain the role of the Holy Spirit (1) as directing the institutional Church now as in the time of Jesus; (2) as directing individuals; (3) as teaching, guiding and unifying all in truth.

The First Reading on this Vigil of Pentecost, the story of the Tower of Babel, records the tragic fragmentation of the human race following the sin of pride; this fragmentation was symbolized by a diversity of languages. At Pentecost, the very opposite happened. The first Christians, docile to the Holy Spirit's rushing upon them in the Upper Room, became one in spirit and—as the Acts of the Apostles reveals—(tomorrow's First Reading) were empowered to understand diverse tongues speaking in praise of God. Moreover, from the tragedy of Babel, confusion resulted. From Pentecost, courageous unity was born; the Spirit, sent from Jesus and the Father, helps us in our weakness (as St. Paul affirms in today's Second Reading). Within us, "rivers of living water shall flow," says our Lord in today's Gospel.

It was on the first Pentecost (the word is a Greek derivative meaning 50th, since today falls on the 50th day after Easter) that the confused, frightened Apostles and disciples of Jesus, huddled together for fear of the Temple police (whom they thought would come and arrest them now that Jesus was gone) suddenly became enlightened, courageous witnesses to the Gospel. And thus our Christian Church came into being.

We could go deeply into the subject of the Holy Spirit; how, for instance, he subsists as a Person, and what his relationship is with the Father and the Son. But after all our studying the subject, we would hardly have begun. For we shall never be able fully to understand the Third Person of God. Our intellects—even the most brilliant—are not capable of so great a mystery.

Besides, what is most important about the Holy Spirit, we *can* comprehend; namely, that he is God's own Spirit, sent forth by the Father and the Son. And when he comes he brings inspiration, peace, joy, fortitude, wisdom—all those wonderful qualities that come with divine life, and with which the Apostles and disciples were filled on Pentecost Day.

These gifts he brings of course to Christ's Church. Thus it is the Spirit who assures that the Church speaks for Christ, that the Church cannot err when it irrevocably commits itself in a statement regarding faith and morals. Too, it is the Spirit that quickens the Church, that breathes new life into it—as most of us witnessed in an extraordinary way during Vatican Council II, and as all of us are experiencing today, during the pontificate of Pope John Paul II.

This same Spirit comes to us, to individuals, teaching us, guiding us, unifying us as one people in the Lord. We know that the Spirit infallibly gives himself to those who have been baptized and confirmed within the Church.

He gives himself, we say. This does not mean that he comes regardless of our dispositions. No, as Jesus tells us in today's Gospel, we must thirst for God. The Spirit descends only upon those who are willing and ready to welcome him in faith, repentance, and love.

Thirst for God is impossible without suffering service in Jesus' footsteps. Had not Christ died and risen for us, the Spirit could not be sent to us. Hence only through our configuring ourselves to Jesus' passion and resurrection can we say that we thirst sufficiently for his Gift.

PENTECOST (ABC)

The Holy Spirit in Our Christian Lives

Acts 2:1-11; First Corinthians 12:3-7, 12-13; John 20:19-23.

Aim: to explain (1) the role of the Holy Spirit in the first generation Church; and (2) the role of the Holy Spirit in our souls and lives.

Sermons about Pentecost and the role of the Holy Spirit seem especially comfortable today, principally because they relate to our experience. Most of us vividly recall Pope John XXIII and the events of Vatican Council II; to have lived through those events was to have experienced the rush of the Holy Spirit descending upon us as really as he did on the first Pentecost Sunday, as recorded in today's First Reading. For a while we were all heady with the Holy Spirit, as we all plunged into the loving labor of *aggiornamento*—updating—and ecumenism—the quest for unity.

Since Vatican II we have seen further traces of the Spirit's breathing new life, enthusiasm, wisdom and joy into our midst. Witness for example, the growth of charismatic movements, of encounter groups. Witness, too, the sudden surge of new zeal that followed upon the election of Pope John Paul II: suddenly scores of confused or hiding Catholics came forth from the shadows, acknowledged their identity, and confessed their faith. (This situation was especially evident in Mexico, to which Pope John Paul II went for a meeting of the Latin American Bishops.)

The presence of the Spirit has been so detectable in our times that we would have to be spiritually blind not to notice. This is the same Spirit who descended in tongues of fire upon the first Christians gathered in the Upper Room; through the Spirit they became the nucleus of our Church, this Roman Church which has withstood storms and assaults from all sides down through the centuries; this Church which, like the mustard seed of which Jesus once spoke, has become a giant tree whose roots and branches spread to embrace all men.

The same Holy Spirit comes to us today, especially in baptism and confirmation, to steel us for discipleship in Christ's Church. It can even be said that the Sacrament of Confirmation exists to extend to the Church of every age and every place the Spirit given on the first Pentecost. Today's Second Reading affirms this. By this sacrament we are conformed to Christ in a special way; we are in fact sealed with a permanent character and become "temples of the Holy Spirit" (First Corinthians 6:19). By virtue of this sacrament, we are both deputed and strengthened for witnessing to Christ more than ever before. "Deputed," because we are configured to Christ more closely; "strengthened," because through confirmation we receive special gifts: wisdom, understanding, counsel, fortitude, knowledge, piety, and fear of the Lord. The fruits or rewards for using these gifts, we know from Scripture (Galatians 5:22-23), are charity, joy, peace, patience, benignity, goodness, modesty, continency, and chastity.

Again, we who are experiencing the Holy Spirit's breathing these days know so well that all this is real. We also know that the Spirit comes to us through Jesus, who died and rose that the Father and he might so grace us.

When Jesus promised to send the Spirit he did so in the context of today's Gospel, which focuses on forgiveness of sins. The Spirit can only be possessed by welcoming him in repentance, faith and love.

TRINITY SUNDAY (A)

The Trinity: The Revelation of God's Inner Nature

Exodus 34:4-6, 8-9; Second Corinthians 13:11-13; John 3:16-18

Aim: (1) to explain what the Church teaches concerning the Holy Trinity; (2) to encourage adoration of the Blessed Trinity.

Today is Trinity Sunday, a day set aside by the liturgy that we might intensify our faith in this great doctrine; namely, that in the one God there are three Persons: Father, Son, and Holy Spirit.

The Trinity, we affirm, is one of the four basic truths of Christianity. The first two, cited as such in the Epistle to the Hebrews 11:5, are (1) God exists, and (2) God rewards the just and judges the evil. The third and fourth, known only through Christian Revelation, are (3) the Blessed Trinity and (4) the Incarnation-Redemption (the Second Person of the Trinity became man, died for us, and rose from the dead that we might live with him forever).

That God is Tripersonal could only be known from Revelation; the greatest of human intellects before Bethlehem could not discover this truth from reason alone, not even the awesome intellects of ancient Greece, where the exciting adventure of the Western mind began. We could only have known about the Trinity from the Bible.

Moreover, the Trinity is a *Christian* Revelation. There is nothing in the Old Testament explicitly setting forth this mystery. Today's First Reading, from Exodus, for example, which reveals God's dominion, mercy and love, does not reveal his Tripersonal nature. Whereas the Israelites knew that God is one (the crucial doctrine of monotheism), and whereas they knew of God's readiness to forgive erring man because of God's overwhelming love for man, the Old Testament had no knowledge of the Trinity as such. This mystery was left to Jesus and his Apostles to announce; to Paul, writing to Corinth, for instance (today's Second Reading); or to John, recalling Jesus' own words (today's Gospel pericope).

What the Trinity really means to us is that God, who is outgoing, gives himself to us, that we might possess him and share his life forever.

God, the eternal and infinite Being, the Supreme Mind and Will who never began to be, manifests himself to us in his Son or Word, the perfect expression of which is Jesus Christ, God's self-manifestation in the flesh. But we could hardly recognize Jesus—as the Son of God Incarnate—unless we were drawn to this belief by God's own Spirit. Yet this Spirit—the Holy Spirit—only comes to us because the risen Jesus, having conquered evil and death through the cross, reigns with the Father; from Father and Son the Spirit is poured forth on us.

This means that—to refer to a statement by Karl Rahner—God is *ours*. He gives himself to us, only to draw us up into his very life, into the trinitarian community of persons he experiences from all eternity.

The doctrine of the Trinity is complex and profound. We shall never be able fully to comprehend it; our minds aren't strong enough (as our eyes are not strong enough to peer into space without telescopic instruments).

This prompts a final point for pondering today: the Trinity helps us remember how small and weak we are, really, relative to the Infinite God who never began to be.

Thinking about the Trinity should bring us to our knees frequently, in humble adoration.

CORPUS CHRISTI (A)

The Eucharist as the Bread of Life

Deuteronomy 8:2-3, 14-16; First Corinthians 10:16-17; John 6:51-58

*Aim: to explain (1) our belief in the Real Presence, and
(2) the word "transsubstantiation."*

Today is the Solemnity of Corpus Christi. *Corpus Christi* is Latin
for "The Body of Christ." It is a graced opportunity for renewing our
faith in, and deep appreciation for, the Real Presence of Jesus in the
Eucharist, which alone satisfies our deepest hunger.

The First Reading, from Deuteronomy, recalls that God provided
food—manna, a bread-like substance—for the Israelites of old,
wandering in the desert toward the Promised Land. In the Gospel,
from John, we are told that Jesus in the Eucharist is the real manna,
the eternal bread from heaven, by which we are sustained in our
journey here toward the eternal Promised Land. Today's Second
Reading reveals that this manna of the New Testament literally unites
us with Jesus, even now.

We describe the Eucharist as the Real Presence; we traditionally
capitalize the first letters of "Real" and "Presence." This is not to deny
that Christ is really present in his Word—the Bible—in all the
sacraments, in the Church, and in the assembly of the faithful. No; the
Eucharist is called the Real Presence not to exclude the idea of these
other presences, but rather—as Pope Paul VI taught in his encyclical
Mysterium Fidei—to indicate Jesus' presence par excellence, because
"it is substantial and through it Christ becomes present whole and

entire." In the Eucharist, we believe, Jesus' presence surpasses all other modes by which he is present.

This Real Presence is effected by a mystery which the Church calls "transsubstantiation" (also spelled "transubstantiation"). This is a strong and meaningful word for what happens in every Mass: bread and wine are changed thoroughly into the Body and Blood of Christ. The substances of bread and wine are no longer present after the consecration; only the accidents (e.g., quantity, quality, color, taste) of bread and wine remain. Thus a conversion (conveyed by the Latin word *trans*) of the whole substance (in Latin, *substantia*) of bread and wine occurs.

In *Mysterium Fidei*, Paul VI explained that down through the centuries, with the Holy Spirit helping, the Church has established a rule of language, a rule which "has often been the watchword and banner of orthodox faith." The word "transsubstantiation" is one such word. It explicitly and unequivocally describes a doctrine that is certain; namely, that in the Mass the elements of bread and wine are changed into the Body and Blood of Christ, the accidents alone remaining.

Hence this word leaves no room for allowing that, for example, Jesus' Real Presence merely co-exists with the bread and wine, or that Christ somehow manifests himself simply by rendering the bread and wine symbols of his power.

On the contrary, both the word "transsubstantiation" and the phrase "Real Presence" express in summary what Jesus meant when, in today's Gospel he said:

". . . I myself am the living bread. . .

"The bread I will give is my flesh. . ." (John 6:51).

This is our faith.

SECOND SUNDAY IN ORDINARY TIME (A)

The Baptism of Jesus and Our Baptism

Isaiah 49:3, 5-6; First Corinthians 1:1-3; John 1:29-34

Aim: (1) to explain what happened when we were baptized; (specifically, that God takes away our sin); (2) to present our baptism as a commitment for life to live in Christ and in grace; (and to note the Sacrament of Reconciliation as a "second baptism").

"Look there! The Lamb of God who takes away the sin of the world."

Isaiah—the Second Isaiah—prophesied about the sixth century before the first Christmas that the mysterious Servant of Yahweh depicted in his four Servant hymns (the second of which we read for today's first Bible lesson) would come to save all mankind—not only Israel, but also the nations: the Gentiles or non-Israelitic peoples.

When John the Baptizer first saw Jesus near the banks of the Jordan, John acknowledged that this mysterious Servant of God was Jesus: "Look there! The Lamb of God who takes away the sin of the world." In the Aramaic tongue John used the word "lamb" which can also be translated "servant."

"The Lamb of God who *takes away* the sin of the world."

Do we believe this great biblical datum? John the Baptizer's witness sounds so matter-of-fact; we are so used to hearing it, to repeating it even, as at Mass, just before Communion time. And in the Creed—the ancient Nicene creed whereby we affirm our historic faith every Sunday—we confess anew the doctrine of forgiveness of sins, a dogma we know is basic to our faith.

Do we really understand what this doctrine means? Is it possible that the mighty God whose voice thundered atop Old Testament Sinai, the mighty God who made the atom and the countless galaxies that brighten the heavens, the mighty God before whose holiness we are totally unworthy, is the same God who in merciful love for you and me wills to *take away* our sins?

To *take away* our sins? Yet isn't this what the Baptizer said of Jesus? Christ does not simply *cover over* our sins, as some theologians during the beginnings of the Protestant Reformation alleged; he does not merely whiten them over, leaving them underneath, as the first winter's snow blankets over the dark and muddy fields and lanes. The great composer, Amadeus Mozart, when arguing with Reformational theologians, used to emphasize that they did not appreciate the full meaning of today's Gospel acclamation, "Lamb of God, you *take away* the sin of the world."

This awesome favor is granted to us first in baptism, through waters sanctified by and empowered with new life by Jesus' death and Resurrection—the central event of our faith, accented by St. Paul in today's Second Reading. In our baptism, we were, in a mystical though real sense, born anew, endowed with a thoroughly new nature over and beyond our human nature, enriched with God's own life, which we call "grace," because it is gratuitously bestowed. By virtue of this new nature, we became children of God, his own adopted sons and daughters, heirs to his kingdom.

None of this could happen to us if God merely *covered over* our sins. To receive God's life, to be endowed with divine adoption, we must be free of sin. And this freedom is granted us through Jesus, who died and rose for us.

Surely this miracle, wrought for anyone who is baptized, requires personal response. And this response cannot be less than a commitment consciously to experience and to nourish the life of grace we have received through Jesus. At least we will take adequate means to manifest our appreciation for this life, through, for example, frequent recourse to the sacrament of forgiveness for the postbaptismal sins, Penance or Reconciliation. And if ever—God forbid—we should overturn the miracle of baptism through a mortal sin—we shall not hesitate to return to Christ in the Sacrament of Penance.

Again, we are reminded by today's liturgy, Jesus literally *takes away* our sins, if only we permit him to do so.

THIRD SUNDAY
IN ORDINARY TIME (A)

The Purpose of Your Life

Isaiah 8:23-9:3; First Corinthians 1:10-13, 17; Matthew 4:12-23

Aim: to show life's purpose as (1) to know God; (2) to love God; (3) to serve God in this world, and so to be happy with God for eternity. To encourage living by this purpose.

Maybe you recognize part of today's First Reading, from Isaiah. One of the sentences was read on Christmas; the one that begins, "The people who walked in darkness have seen a great light." In today's First Reading it appears as part of a larger oracle, one referred to explicitly by Jesus, in today's Gospel: "Land of Zebulun, land of Naphthali . . . heathen Galilee: a people living in darkness has seen a great light. . ."

Seven centuries before the first Christmas (in 734 B.C., to be as precise as scholars can let us be), Israel's ancient tribal cities of Zebulun and Naphthali, near the northern shore of the Sea of Galilee, were the first to fall to the Assyrian armies led by Tiglath-pileser III. Many of the inhabitants there were carried off into exile. With an influx of Assyrian immigrants, the cities became largely pagan, and were labeled by Israel as "heathen Galilee," or "Galilee of the Gentiles." Isaiah, the eighth-century prophet, foretold that just as the lands of Zebulun and Naphthali were the first areas of Israel to experience God's punishment in the Assyrian conquest, so they would one day be the first to experience God's word of salvation.

Thus it was that Jesus, about to inaugurate his preaching mission, left Nazareth, his home town, for Capernaum. Capernaum—archaeologists have identified it with the modern Tell Hum—was located in the midst of Galilee of the Gentiles, the land of Zebulun and Naphthali; in the midst, therefore, of a heathen setting. This fact, incidentally, fits in beautifully with one of several themes played upon by St. Matthew; namely, that Jesus came to save all men, Gentiles as well as Jews.

With what message does our Lord begin his mission? "Reform your lives," he says; "The Kingdom of Heaven is close at hand." "Kingdom of Heaven" is a favorite Matthean phrase meaning "Kingdom of God." So that Matthew here means that Jesus said, "Reform your lives. The Kingdom of God is close at hand."

God's reign, in other words, was initiated in Jesus of Nazareth. Jesus' ministry marks the beginning of the last age in mankind's history, when the dark powers of evil—illness, ignorance, death and sin—will be overcome.

This is, of course, what the Good News ("Gospel" comes from an old English word meaning "Good News") means. God's supreme power over the universe has been affirmed unequivocally and irrevocably in Jesus of Nazareth; the world and the cosmos are now at the first stage of that hour which will infallibly terminate in the scene of St. John's Apocalypse, when the Son of Man will come again, to this planet, as Lord of Lords and King of Kings, forever and ever.

But there is a condition for the Kingdom's advent in our lives; "Reform your lives." A fundamental sin is refusal to accept God's sovereignty over all creation in Jesus. Repentance is required because Jesus, God's only Son, effected the reign of God over creation by taking our sins upon himself and ascending to the cross. St. Paul, in today's Second Reading, expressly reminds us of this truth, a truth which, he humbly confesses, he was sent to preach.

Like Zebulun and Naphthali, we too were once under the punishment of sin; but like these cities we were graced by God through Jesus, who now announces the Good News of our salvation. Our acceptance of this good news depends on our acknowledging our sinfulness and embracing Christ as Lord; in confessing the truth that nothing is more important in life than knowing, serving, and loving God in this world, with an unreserved belief that final fulfillment can be realized only in God's eternal Kingdom.

Life's purpose, we reaffirm, is summarized in today's Responsorial Psalm, namely, "to dwell in the house of the Lord all the days of my life."

Faith is central to earthly existence; God and his word are all that really matter.

FOURTH SUNDAY
IN ORDINARY TIME (A)

The Beatitudes and Moral Living

Zephaniah 2:3, 3:12-13; First Corinthians 1:26-31; Matthew 5:1-12

*Aim: (1) to explain the spirit of the poor (Anawim)
whom Jesus declared happy in the Beatitudes; (2) to
encourage a similar spirit in ourselves today.*

The Beatitudes (today's list is from Matthew's account of the
Sermon on the Mount) dramatically reversed the values of the world,
and literally changed the world to its core.

Matthew recalls that our Lord went to the mountain top to
announce the Beatitudes. His ascent was symbolic. Moses received
the Law atop Sinai; so Jesus inaugurates the New Testament atop a
hill. Later he would also seal this new and everlasting testament upon
a height; his sacrifice would take place on a cross upon which he was
lifted up.

The symbolism inherent in the mountain setting has deeper
dimensions. For the Beatitudes tower by far above the most lofty
principles and values conceived of by the most brilliant of mortal
men.

The question to which the Beatitudes address themselves is the
age-old inquiry as to what, ultimately, constitutes peace and
happiness. To this problem Jesus says, in effect, that the answer does
not lie in temporal pleasure, or wealth, or power, or prestige, or even
health.

On the contrary, God's benediction is especially meant for the masses of God-loving men and women who hunger and thirst for justice, who must work hard for their bread, who are but pawns in power games played by kings, who believe in their heart rather than merely according to the letter of the law, and who must often suffer for their belief. St. Paul emphasizes this in today's Second Reading.

God's benediction is especially over these people, the poor, those whom the Bible refers to repeatedly by the beautiful Hebrew phrase, *Anawim Yahweh*; "God's Poor."

In one sense, the Sermon on the Mount should have come as no surprise. Again and again in the Old Testament, God manifested his preference for the oppressed and the downtrodden. Today's First Reading foretells that the humble and the obedient will inherit all.

True peace of soul, true happiness, Christ says, entails becoming as the poor of God are, the *Anawim Yahweh*—becoming so totally dependent on God that one literally requires nothing for oneself save to serve God's purpose for him. Specifically, it entails a spirit of poverty, of purity of heart, of reconciliation, of willingness to endure hardship, suffering, or death for the sake of Christ's values, a spirit that says, "I have God; therefore, I need nothing else."

This demands a radical change of heart, of course: what the Gospels call, in the Greek original, a *metanoia*. The Beatitudes point to a life-style so thoroughly different from that of even the finest humanists that they constitute one of the major turning points in the history of world civilization. From the moment they were enunciated a new kind of person began to walk the earth.

A person like St. Francis of Assisi, for example, demonstrated, perhaps more than any other saint, how the Beatitudes can be implemented in every dimension. A person like Patrick or Boniface or Francis de Sales, or Elizabeth of Hungary; or John Brebeuf or Vincent de Paul; or Mary Euphrasia or Peter Claver, or, closer to our own culture and times, a person like Elizabeth Seton or the Mohawk Indian Maiden Kateri Tekakwitha are good examples also.

These persons prove that the Beatitudes *can* be lived by mere human beings.

FIFTH SUNDAY
IN ORDINARY TIME (A)

The Beatitudes and Moral Living

Isaiah 58:7-10; First Corinthians 2:1-5; Matthew 5:13-16

Aim: (1) to show the impact on society which Christians in general should have, and to show the impact which each of us should have because of our (1) holiness, (2) simplicity, (3) peace.

"You are the salt of the earth . . . the light of the world."

Both metaphors are dazzling; they literally stagger the imagination. They are coupled in today's Gospel to stress both the privileged nature and the noble responsibility of Christian witness.

These metaphors sound strange today. Late-twentieth-century technological man is supposed to be but a number, a series of computerized squiggles on print-outs from highly sophisticated electronic machines that crazily click and whirl. To view the bits of data called man as potentially "the salt of the earth" and "the light of the world" seems myth.

But Jesus' metaphors are not mere poetic exaggerations: to understand discipleship at all, we've got to believe this.

We *can* season this world, render it a tasteful place to live; we *can* enlighten it, dispersing the black shadows of ignorance and superstition.

In our own times alone, look what discipleship has done to change the course of history. Recall the recent examples of Pope John XXIII, of Father Maximilian Kolbe.

Examples such as these tend to disconcert us; we think that they project models too heroic. Yet we tend to think too small in terms of our own witness. Meanwhile, those who would destroy Christendom, from the very great to the man-in-the-street, read and study and demonstrate with a passion in behalf of *their* premise. As the poet W.B. Yeats prophesied, many of the best today lack conviction, while the worst are characterized by passionate intensity.

"You are the salt of the earth ... the light of the world." We have a wisdom, the wisdom of God's Word as revealed in the Bible read within the body of the Church, that transcends by far the most refined of man's discovered sciences, a wisdom that gives us ultimate certainties which biology cannot offer (the ultimate reason for death, say), which psychological science cannot yield (that the human person becomes godlike through grace, for example), or which even philosophy, the queen of all human endeavor, cannot prove (that God is love, say). Yet how nonchalantly nonconcerned we are about adding the salt and light of Christianity to a secularist world which absurdly argues, for example, that direct abortion can be justified; or that business enterprise is not a moral issue; or that one's superfluous income is merely one's own concern.

In Anton Chekhov's famous play, *The Three Sisters*, one of the women, Masha, complains that her knowing three languages in their very ordinary town is a needless luxury, almost like a "sixth finger." Answering her, Vershinin, a military officer, argues that no knowledge is ever useless; that, in fact, the least intellectual refinement will have its effect on others and eventually leaven the entire environment by elevating it.

Surely this argument can be translated into terms of Christian witness. Even if there are but a few dozen in a parish who put their hearts into the Eucharist and in prayer in order to acquire holiness, and who live lives of Gospel simplicity rather than artificial sophistication, and who try to be peace-makers by their patience, kindness and humility, these few *can help form* a better world in and for Christ.

This requires a degree of self-crucifixion, of course. But God's wisdom, as St. Paul reminds us in today's Second Reading, is defined in terms of suffering service. To hand it down to us, Jesus underwent death on a cross. The light of the dawn prophesied by Isaiah—today's First Lesson—shines forth from the Mount of Calvary.

SIXTH SUNDAY
IN ORDINARY TIME (A)

The Beatitudes and Moral Living

Sirach 15:15-20; First Corinthians 2:6-10; Matthew 5:17-37

Aim: to show the new order of priorities in living as the basis for moral decisions—God first, then other people, then ourselves.

Whenever we read from the Old Testament Book of Sirach—today's first Bible lesson—we know immediately that the reading focuses on moral wisdom. Sirach, so called because its author was Ben Sira, the son of Sira, dates from about 190 B.C. In the Latin version, it is known by perhaps the more familiar title of *Ecclesiasticus. Ecclesiasticus* means "a church book"; it was used in the early Christian community as a manual for teaching morality to catechumens.

When we heard the lector reading Ben Sira today, here in this church, therefore, we were listening to the same book read for moral instruction in the early Church. And we were opening our minds and hearts to the same message to which the early Christians opened their minds and hearts; namely, that the only true morality is God's norm.

God's norm is summarized by Jesus, the Son of God Incarnate, in today's Gospel. It is amplified by the Apostle Paul, in his First Letter to the Corinthians, from which today's Second Reading is taken. It is a norm whose validity and application both are challenged and ignored today. But it is a norm on which we stake our lives in faith, because we know that the God who made us and redeemed us through his Son, Jesus, is all truth, who cannot deceive or be deceived.

In faith we try as best we can to understand, in accordance with our lights. To understand why dishonesty is ungodly, or discrimination, or hatred, or direct abortion, or contraception; to understand why there is no human activity—business included—that is not governed by moral principles reflecting God's will for mankind. To understand how marriage involves a covenant with Christ, why social justice is every man's apostolate, why one's superfluous income cannot be retained with absolute impunity, why war is no solution to human problems.

The first priority we must always remember is choosing to act by God's norm, therefore. Suffice it to say here that all morality must ultimately mirror God's wisdom. Where human wisdom, be it psychological, behavioristic, or ethical, is inconsonant with God's wisdom, it is not authentic wisdom, but error. Our commitment is to the wisdom of God as perfected in Jesus.

This is our faith. This is why we stand up to the world in the full assurance that the moral code we profess is the only moral code that can lead to peace and inner happiness.

Acting according to God's norm will not always prove the easier of alternatives, or the more personally comfortable. On the contrary, living by God's wisdom can sometimes be difficult, especially in a world that rejects the Gospel.

Nor is God's norm necessarily that which will cater to self as against neighbor. God's norm gives priority to reaching out to others prior to thinking of oneself, since God has told us we will find him in others.

Persons who act primarily with God and neighbor in mind lead the world in moral action. They are venerated as saints.

SEVENTH SUNDAY IN ORDINARY TIME (A)

The Commandments and Moral Living

Leviticus 19:12, 17-18; First Corinthians 3:16-23; Matthew 5:38-48

> *Aim: to give the Ten Commandments of God as a basis for moral living, expressing (1) love of God in neighbor (2) as implemented by overcoming feelings of hatred and by promoting unity.*

Today's Gospel, from Matthew, together with the First Reading, from Leviticus, presupposes the existence and the applicability of the Ten Commandments, also known as the Decalogue, from the Greek expression "ten words" or "ten statements."

As Catholics we hold in faith that the Ten Commandments are substantially part of the natural law; that, in other words, they are written by the Creator within the hearts of every creature. We also hold that these Ten Commandments were reaffirmed by God through a special Revelation in the Old Testament made to Israel through the great prophet Moses.

Finally, we believe that these Commandments, which exist for our welfare since they express what is advantageous for our nature as children of God, can never change, and that they bind all human beings everywhere and at every time.

The first three Commandments, as usually enumerated, focus on man's responsibilities to God in himself; the final seven, to God as he is seen and loved in one's fellow men.

Today's Gospel and First Reading obviously point to seeing and loving God in others. Specifically, we must honor and respect others, regardless of their adverse attitude—even hostility—toward us. This is not to say that we condone their actions; of course not. Nor is it to pretend that feelings of hurt—emotional traumas—may not be experienced by us when we are insulted by others, or rejected, or wronged in any way. That we invariably feel pain indicates that we are only human. That we can overcome these feelings by an act of the will aided by God's grace, indicates that we are Christians.

Today's Gospel and First Reading remind us not to allow ourselves to be governed by bitter or revengeful feelings against others, but rather to live by our higher faculties of mind and will, and with God's help, which he invariably grants to those who sincerely seek.

To live by these Gospel principles may seem like foolishness to those who do not know Christ; St. Paul, in today's Second Reading, stresses this. But, as St. Paul adds, so-called human wisdom is not wisdom at all unless it conforms to God's wisdom. And, again, God's wisdom is that our giving in to feelings of resentment, vendetta, or hatred, only separates us from God, and, consequently, weakens us as persons destined for his eternal embrace.

On the other hand, as St. Paul adds, fraternal respect, cultivated in Christ's name, helps strengthen one's own person. And not only this, it helps bind together the whole Christian community, from which we all derive strength. In this sense, it undermines factionalism, and serves as a spiritual cement joining us closer together, and to the risen Lord.

Thus the Ten Commandments are revealed as positive aids in helping us to conform to God's will that we be one in him—in his peace, in his happiness.

EIGHTH SUNDAY
IN ORDINARY TIME (A)

The Commandments and Moral Living

Isaiah 49:14-15; First Corinthians 4:1-5; Matthew 6:24-34

Aim: (1) to explain the Commandments, especially the last seven, as demanding a choice for God or against him; (2) briefly to explain conscience.

To live a Christian life means to choose; today's Gospel warns us that no man can serve two masters. God's commandments, expressing his will for us and for our welfare, constitute one choice. The alternative is to place ourselves under the mastery of the Father of Lies, Satan, who cares neither for us nor for our welfare.

The Commandments help us measure the rightness or goodness of our human acts; this is to say that they help us arrive at true moral judgments. Moral judgments safeguard the quality of life. Every immoral judgment, every judgment that cannot be sustained by reference to God's will for us, must be rejected as destructive of the quality of life. The Commandments—"You shall not steal;" "You shall not commit adultery;" "Honor your father and your mother;" "You shall not bear false witness;" "You shall not covet;" and so on— secure for us what is best for us by God's design. No authentic personhood can be achieved without their observance.

Again, to live as a Christian is to choose; our pilgrimage here, which though brief is nonetheless decisive, demands that we use the

God-given mystery of freedom to choose for God's will, and not against it.

In making our choices in life, we are aided by a mystery called conscience. St. Paul refers to it in today's Second Reading.

Conscience shouldn't be identified with a vague kind of feeling which renders us pleased about some actions and sad about others. Feelings can trick and mislead us; a right conscience cannot. Conscience is experienced in the depths of the personality, within the depths of the soul; it flows from man's mind and free will precisely in their reflection of God as he acts in the innermost center of the soul. In a sense, conscience is God's voice speaking to us in the depths of our personality and drawing us toward his way, and truth, and life.

Conscience *draws* us; note that it does not compel. Again, to live a moral life is to make choices. We must decide upon the master we shall serve.

However, even if we sin with our freedom—by, for example, paying more attention to the faulty judgments of our peers (as St. Paul warns against today) than the Commandments of God, the Lord still waits for us to forgive us and to start us on the right track again.

As God spoke through Isaiah in today's First Reading:

"Can a mother forget her infant?"

If God loves the birds of the air and the lilies of the field so much—today's Gospel—how much more does he love you and me, even if we stray now and then, but in our love, contritely return to him?

Today's Responsorial Psalm, incidentally, summarizes the purpose for which God has given us freedom; namely, to love him in whom alone our souls find rest and salvation. It was St. Augustine too who formulated one of the most famous variations of the theme of today's Responsorial Psalm. He said that our hearts are restless until they rest in God.

NINTH SUNDAY
IN ORDINARY TIME (A)

Faith Means Doing

Deuteronomy 11:18, 26-28; Romans 3:21-25, 28; Matthew 7:21-27

Aim: to explain that Christian faith means practicing what one preaches, relating this specifically to Sunday worship.

God's law—the Commandments—are not revealed to us simply that we might accept them intellectually. The Commandments are to be *obeyed*; today's First Reading, reflecting Moses' farewell address to his people, emphasizes this so eloquently. And Jesus, who brought Mosaic prophecy to perfection, tells us in today's Gospel that salvation is not assured us simply for our crying out, "Lord, Lord;" rather, the Lord's will must be observed. Our faith must be put into practice.

Christianity means *living* a belief, therefore. We must be *doers* of God's word, not simply *hearers*. The Gospel is a challenge to action, not merely the acceptance of certain truths. Implementing the Gospel is the only way we can build our homes on solid ground, where attacks from hostile powers can neithter destroy nor weaken.

We must practice what we preach. For a few moments, translate this principle into terms of the Sunday Mass context. It is one thing to sing a hymn, like, "Faith of Our Fathers;" another thing, to try to live by its spirit.

"Faith of Our Fathers, living still . . ." These words bring back memories of countless chapters of Church History filled with tales of courage and constancy in Christian witness—and, of course, martyrdom.

One thinks of the Apostles, all sentenced to death for the Faith they handed down to us, and their early successors who suffered so much for the same: St. Athanasius, who was hunted for his belief like a common criminal during the greater part of his episcopate; he was called "Athanasius against the world;" or St. Cyprian, the famed bishop of Carthage, exhorting his flock how to die in the Lord.

"Faith of Our Fathers" also means Jean Brebeuf and Isaac Jogues and their Jesuit colleagues in the 17th-century Canadian-American Indian missions.

"We will be true to thee till death." What about Margaret Clitherow, the protomartyr of her sex in Reformation England? She was accused of harboring Jesuits and seminary priests, alleged enemies of the queen. She was cruelly crushed to death.

"Oh, how our hearts beat high with joy . . ." Recall, too, the French Carmelite nuns during the Terror, in the summer of 1794. Before mounting the guillotine, they chanted Psalm 116: "Praise the Lord, all you nations."

"Our Fathers, chain'd in prisons dark, Were still in heart and conscience free . . ." How many countless Christians have been confined to sunless cells for the Faith down through the centuries to the present hour for *acting* on their faith?

"Faith of Our Fathers . . ."

Can really committed Christians file out of Church early while *this* hymn is being sung? Again, mark Jesus' words:

"Not everyone who says, "Lord, Lord . . .""

To practice what we preach also means to act in accordance with the hymns we sing at Mass.

TENTH SUNDAY IN ORDINARY TIME (A)

Interior Religion

Hosea 6:3-6; Romans 4:18-25; Matthew 9:9-13

Aim: (1) to emphasize Jesus' readiness to forgive even the most recalcitrant; (2) to cite the importance of acknowledging our sinfulness, primarily through the Sacrament of Reconciliation.

Christianity is primarily a religion of the heart. Not by externals are we saved, but by an interior commitment of faith, hope, and love. For our religion is but a response to God's love; our love in answer to the love of God, who always loves us first.

Today's First Reading, from Hosea, expresses this lesson in magnificent poetry. Therein God is portrayed as our loving parent who, regardless of our crimes, couldn't possibly think of abandoning us.

Hosea was the prophet who divorced his wife because of her infidelity to him, but eventually took her back because of his overwhelming love for her.

Hosea is the Old Law prophet to read and ponder for insights into the mystery of God's mercy and love. Again and again the lesson rings out loudly and clearly: God so desires man, every single human being for his or her own sake, that he will not cease to pursue even the most wayward or recalcitrant. Not even a multiplicity of infidelities, heaped one on another, will turn God aside from his loving quest for the person whom he brought into being to share in his timeless goodness, truth, and beauty.

Jesus demonstrates this in today's portion of St. Matthew's Gospel. "Go and learn the meaning of the words, 'It is mercy I desire and not sacrifice. I have come to call not the self-righteous, but sinners.' "

Christ is like the image projected in Francis Thompson's beautiful poem, *The Hound of Heaven*, relentlessly pursuing man with his mercy and readiness to forgive. That this promise will be met, that this pledge will be kept, is emphasized in today's Second Reading from Romans—though not because of what we may or may not do, but simply because God loves us infinitely more than a husband loves an errant wife, or a parent loves a rebellious child—to echo Hosea again.

Jesus' statement about coming to save sinners, not the self-righteous, ought to be pondered very carefully, lest we miss the nuance of his Revelation. Expressed bluntly, this statement means that any pretence to absolute innocence on our part literally impedes Jesus' saving action. If we are totally innocent, what need we of a *Savior*?

To avoid the Sacrament of Reconciliation—to avoid going to confession regularly—in the illusion that we do not need this Sacrament of Jesus' pardon, comes quite close, it would seem, to thinking oneself self-righteous. On the contrary, devotion to frequent confession—every month or six weeks, at least—is a sure sign that we understand today's Bible readings and Jesus' role as divine physician.

Only a realist can adequately appreciate the Sacrament of Reconciliation—confession. To approach this sacrament sincerely, one must know himself, and, consequently, his frailty and tendency to wrongdoing. Moreover, he must be a person of faith: a believer in Christ's saving action through the Church and the priest's words of absolution.

ELEVENTH SUNDAY
IN ORDINARY TIME (A)

Living in the Grace of God

Exodus 19:2-6; Romans 5:6-11; Matthew 9:36-10:8

*Aim: to give the teaching on (1) the life of grace in the
soul, and especially (2) the birth and growth, the
weakening and loss of the life of grace.*

The election of the Apostles, commissioned by Jesus to preach the
Gospel everywhere and to act in his name, is recalled in today's
Gospel from Matthew. God's election of Israel is the subject of
today's First Reading, from Exodus and both the first and the third
Scriptural passages today focus on God's having chosen us. The
Second Reading, from Paul's monumental Letter to the Romans,
assumes as a premise the mystery of our divine election in Christ, but
it goes on to stress God's love in having chosen us, as well as our
abysmal unworthiness for having been so chosen.

The phrase, "God's election," means, obviously, that our
salvation is not a matter of our pulling ourselves up totally by our
own bootstraps. In every case and always, it is God who first graces us
and enables us to make the pilgrimage to him, through the gift of faith
bestowed freely upon us in his loving mercy. Before we do, or can do,
anything in the order of our own salvation, and *while we are still in
our sin*—as today's remarkable Second Reading reveals—God seeks
us out to reconcile us with him through our Lord Jesus Christ.

By this divine election and our response in faith, hope, love, and repentence, we are graced by God with a mysterious participation in his own nature.

We call this gift, which elevates us above our own natures, "grace," because it is gratuitously given by God. Its portal is Baptism, by means of which we are reborn so thoroughly that we become God's children and heirs to God's Kingdom through the mystery of divine adoption. We call this gift "sanctifying grace" because our participation in the divine nature renders us holy.

As we progress in our years and days, we have the opportunity, in many ways, to strengthen and increase God's life—grace—within us. We realize this opportunity chiefly by meeting the living Lord Jesus in his sacraments, supremely in the Eucharist.

Grace, therefore, is, in Catholic belief, the very definition of life. Life means to exist with the very life of God within us, to experience to the hilt God's electing us and enabling us to share in his very nature toward a goal that is supernatural: namely, one day to possess God, and to rejoice fully in him.

The greatest tragedy that can befall us as disciples, therefore, is to opt against a life of grace; to choose not to share in God's incomparably rich gift of his very nature.

We opt against God, of course, by choosing to will or to act contrary to God's word; by choosing to commit serious sin, in other words. Through mortal sin—freely electing to turn from God and his gifts in serious matter and with full advertence the life of grace is cut off.

Venial sins do not of themselves constitute radical and essential barriers to life in God through grace. But they can, especially if deliberate and repeated, set the stage for a lethal spiritual disease such as a lack of vigilance, or of docility to the Spirit, or of constancy.

Through grace we have been made dear to God, a holy nation—to borrow those phrases from the First Reading. We have a treasure, therefore, to be safeguarded and—as the Gospel warns—to be witnessed to.

TWELFTH SUNDAY
IN ORDINARY TIME (A)

Original Sin

Jeremiah 20:10-13; Romans 5:12-15; Matthew 10:26-33

*Aim: (1) to give the Church's teaching on original sin;
(2) to show effects of original sin in the world and
ourselves; (3) to bring hope from our cooperation with
redemption.*

God has willed to save us despite our tendency toward sin,
inherited through Adam. This is one great Biblical theme crystallized
by today's liturgy.

Jeremiah, in today's First Reading, observes that we live in a
world tainted by evildoing. Paul, in today's Second Reading, focuses
on this human situation; doctrinally we describe it as original sin.

Original sin *is* a doctrine of our faith, and hence cannot be
rejected. It means, basically, that all human beings—save one, Mary,
the Mother of Jesus—first appear in this world in a situation of
inward alienation from God. It means, too, that human beings are
prone to evildoing, that we are all weak in the face of temptation,
complacent about our ignorance. Moreover, original sin is the lot of
humankind by virtue of generation; Adam's fall has somehow
affected all his progeny. Original sin is so basic a premise of
anthropology—the study of man—that only in its light can we
understand man's renewal by the Father through Jesus.

Jesus, we believe, is the new Adam, in whom all men are reconciled again to the Father. St. Paul emphasizes this doctrine in today's Second Reading. This reconciliation, Paul explains, belongs to the order of a gift. Though born into a world tainted by evil, though ourselves inclined to do evil, God of his own free and loving will comes to our aid so really that we can sing, as Jeremiah did, "the Lord . . . has rescued the life of the poor from the power of the wicked."

The dimensions of our Redemption in Jesus literally stagger the imagination. Ponder today's Gospel again: "Do not be afraid of anything . . . Whoever acknowledges me before men I will acknowledge before my Father in heaven." Here Paul is speaking to us—sinners, therefore. Baptized sinners, but sinful and weak persons, nonetheless.

Paul even goes a step further by asking whether backsliding on our part will cancel out, as it were, God's free and loving desire to reconcile us. The answer, Paul insists, is an emphatic No. For if the Father's first intervention in human history cost the life of his own Son, Jesus, how could one even suspect that the Father would not go to extremes to keep searching out Jesus' brethren, sinful though they may be, so long as their time of trial in this life remains?

Of course we don't presume on God's love and mercy. This would, in effect, be to turn one's back on him.

However, after reading Paul to the Romans in the light of Gospels such as today's, we can begin to grasp that Jesus' being the new Adam is for us one of the most consoling doctrines revealed.

Sometimes we tend to forget that the doctrine of original sin is taught by the Church in the total context of Salvation History. When we make reference to it, we should think at the same time about the universality of Redemption; of Jesus, who is our Savior. Though born into a situation of alienation from God, we nonetheless are *reborn* through a new Adam, in whom we find reconciliation with the Father.

THIRTEENTH SUNDAY IN ORDINARY TIME (A)

Reverence for Life

Second Kings 4:8-11, 14-16; Romans 6:3-4, 8-11; Matthew 10:37-42

*Aim: to explain (1) the human life as God's special gift;
(2) contemporary threats to human life in our society.*

In today's First Reading, from Second Kings, we read how God, in answer to the prophet Elisha's prayer, gave new life to a good woman; God graced her with motherhood. Reverence for life as a precious gift from God is one lesson we learn from the story.

The same lesson is there, implicitly, in today's Second Reading, from Paul to the Romans. Therein we are reminded of the awesome mystery of life in Christ which is inaugurated in us through baptism.

The Gospel today can be read in the context of this lesson. Helping others to live—by even giving a cup of water to another for the sake of the Kingdom of Heaven—secures for us a prophet's reward, which, we know is eternal life.

Shall we focus our reflections today, on reverence for life?

Today's First Reading emphasizes, as does the Book of Genesis, that the beginnings of human life mirror God's special intervention. Death, on the other hand, is viewed by the Bible not merely as a biological event. Rather, death entails God's withdrawing his life-breath, which he only can give and take (Cf. Jb 34:14 ff.; Ec 12:7).

Moreover, life as given by God is described as uniquely precious (Ec 7:17; 11:8; Ps 27:13; and today's First Reading, 2 K 4:8-11, 14-16).

In the New Testament, the unique value and holiness of human life are revealed in all their splendor. For one thing, life is destined to endure forever; death is absorbed by life. Today's Second Reading affirms this with forceful clarity. (See also 2 Cor 4:10, 5:4; or 1 Cor 15:35-55).

For Jesus, moreover, life is more precious than the Sabbath (Mk 3, 4), because "God is not a God of the dead, but of the living" (Mk 12:27).

In fact, Jesus *identifies* with life; he is the "Word of life" (1 Jn 1:1); as well as "the way, the truth and the life" (Jn 14:6); he is too the "resurrection and the life" (Jn 11:25). The perfection of this life will be attained only when the body becomes glorified. Then Jesus, "our life," will appear in the heavenly Jerusalem, where the river of life flows and the tree of life flourishes. (Read Col 3:4, and Rv 22:1 ff.; 22:14-19.)

Again and again, therefore, the unique value and sanctity of human life are cited in the pages of Holy Writ—from Gn to Rv. A believer cannot responsibly discuss the deliberate taking of human life—as in direct abortion or euthanasia—without reference to the literally scores of Biblical passages, from the Old Testament as well as the New, emphasizing the precious nature of human life—passages which culminate in Jesus' identification with life.

The same can be said, of course, for any act by means of which human life is demeaned or violated—or simply ignored, as sometimes happens in the case of the elderly, or the chronically ill, or the socially exiled.

Human life is precious; all human life must be revered in all circumstances. Where human life is, there God's creative act is mirrored, a creative act destined to render us alive in Christ.

FOURTEENTH SUNDAY IN ORDINARY TIME (A)

Childlike Faith and Joy

Zechariah 9:9-10; Romans 8:9, 11-13; Matthew 11:25-30

Aim: to explain how unreserved faith in God can effect a deep joy and, with it, inner peace.

Childlike faith and the joy it occasions make up one theme that rings out—like a refreshing Mozart melody—in today's Bible readings.

Most Christians today have at least read about, if not read, the Swiss theologian, Karl Barth, among the most famous Protestant theologians of the 20th century. (Barth insisted that it is wrong to try to remake God in the image and likeness of man; Barth argued eloquently for the "Otherness" of God.)

Barth had a recurring dream. It was about Mozart. Barth loved Mozart's music, and would play it every morning before he went to work on his great theological work, *Church Dogmatics*.

In his dream, Barth was appointed to examine Mozart on his theology. But Mozart kept answering the questions put to him merely by pointing to his joyful, childlike music: his famous Masses, for example. Mozart just pointed to his music and smiled.

Thomas Merton, the Trappist monk who died about the same time Barth did, mentions Barth's dream in *Conjectures of a Guilty Bystander*. Merton admitted that he was deeply moved by Barth's dream, and wanted to write him about it. The dream, Merton added, concerned Barth's salvation; the great theologian was attempting to confess that he would be saved more by the Mozart in himself than by his theology.

Don't today's Bible readings say the same?

Give one's heart to Christ, one's whole heart, and nothing else matters: joy and inner peace are thereby assured.

The saints were not all great theologians; there is nothing in the Church's canonization process requiring proof of a candidate's theological brilliance. St. Zita was a serving girl most of her life, St. Joseph Cupertino had a memory so poor that he had trouble remembering how to serve the bread in the monastery dining hall. St. John Vianney hardly got through the seminary because of his slowness of mind.

But even the great minds who became saints knew very well the meaning of Barth's dream about Mozart; namely, that intellectual brilliance does not effect holiness. St. Thomas Aquinas, whose genius still awes us, eventually dismissed all his books as "straw," when he succeeded in placing his heart totally in Christ.

Which is to say that the secret of Christianity, holiness and salvation, is in giving one's heart to Christ. As St. Alphonse de Liguori put it (in those traditional meditations on the Way of the Cross): "Lord, grant that I may love you always, then do with me what you will." We are creatures after all, totally dependent not only for existence, but for life, on God's bounty (as today's Second Reading warns). And any knowledge that we have is, after all, derivative. What else can we do but bow to the God who made us and who draws us to his embrace with words like those in today's Gospel: "Come to me . . . and I will refresh you."

The result is an inner peace and a joy that can't be achieved by worldly accomplishment. We are all saved primarily by the spirit of celebration (today's First Reading) in God's love for us, despite our unworthiness.

FIFTEENTH SUNDAY IN ORDINARY TIME (A)

Revelation the Basis of Our Faith

Isaiah 55:10-11; Romans 8:18-23; Matthew 13:1-23

Aim: (1) to teach how our Faith is based on God's Revelation, having come down to us through Scripture and Tradition.

Today's First Reading, from Second Isaiah (sixth century B.C.), is one of the most beautiful passages of the Old Testament. It views God's word as precipitation from the heavens.

Today's Gospel, from Mt, depicts in parable form God's word as seed in need of nourishment for life, for growth, and for fruit.

Juxtaposed, therefore, today's First Reading and the Gospel point to the mystery of Divine Revelation: God's word spoken through the Bible and Sacred Tradition.

"Revelation" comes from a Latin verb meaning "to unveil." Divine Revelation is our word for God's disclosing his will to us. As Catholics we believe that God has disclosed his will to us through the Scriptures and through Sacred Tradition.

Today's First Reading can be understood in the sense that every time the Bible is read, the Spirit of God speaks to us in a unique way. Just as the sacraments effect God-life (so long as the recipient is properly disposed), so Scripture brings about faith to one who opens his heart. It is so much like rain, which falls and waters an earth ready to receive its quickening capacity.

"To one who opens his heart," we said. God's word does not compel; Jesus said he came *to draw* us to him, not to force us. God desires us in our freedom; unless we embrace him in freedom our action cannot be authentically human.

Surely this helps explain why Jesus used parables in his sermons: parables like the sower and the seed, today's Gospel. As the French religious philosopher Pascal argued, parables let in just enough light for anyone who wants to believe to accept their meaning, but retain enough obscurity for those whose disposition is otherwise.

In a sense, too, a parable is a "gesture of mercy" on Jesus' part. It provides us with time to ponder God's word carefully, and with deference to our freedom to choose for him in our love. Someone has described parables as "periods of grace" during which we, having heard the word, sow them in the good soil of today's Gospel.

God's word, once received, is clearly a liberating word; it provides escape from the slavery of a world that "groans" (to use St. Paul's word in today's Second Reading) from the misery it still experiences until Christ comes again. So that neglecting to listen to it—which is the first stage of liberation—retards our escape from all that is not as yet aligned with Christ's Kingdom.

Which means, doesn't it, that the basic sin against the Gospel is, *not listening.*

The word cannot take root in our hearts—and, consequently, Jesus cannot draw us to him—unless we open our hearts by listening to his word, in the Scriptures, in Sacred Tradition.

Doubtless this was on Jesus' mind when he said in Mt's Gospel, of today's parable: "Listen carefully to this" (4:3); and, also in Mt, those haunting words: "Let him who has ears to hear me, hear!" (4:23).

St. Paul, in Romans, asked in the Spirit: "How can (we) believe unless (we) have *heard* of him (God)? . . . Faith, then, comes from hearing . . ."

SIXTEENTH SUNDAY IN ORDINARY TIME (A)

The Books of the Bible

Wisdom 12:13, 16-19; Romans 8:26-27; Matthew 13:24-43

Aim: (1) to explain the divisions of the Bible: Testaments, literary forms, books; (2) to encourage knowledge of the Bible in Church through the Lectionary selections.

"God's Word," the Epistle to the Hebrews reminds us, "is living and effective, sharper than any two-edged sword."

This means that the Bible—The Sacred Scriptures, Holy Writ—is dynamic, efficacious of faith, and the most keen instrument of all reality.

The term Bible is a general word; our English word derives from the Greek *byblos*, meaning *papyrus*, a loan word from the Egyptian referring to a marsh reed, abundant in the Nile delta, and processed as a material for writing. *Biblia* in Greek or Latin eventually came to mean "books."

Because of the unique position of the contents of what we call the Bible, they were simply described as "the books" (*biblia*). These "books" contain 46 writings that make up what we call the Old Testament—God's Revelation before Jesus' coming—and 27 that make up the New Testament.

Today's First Reading—as is usually the case on Sundays—is

from an Old Testament Book, the Book of Wisdom, also known as the Wisdom of Solomon, although it was written long after Solomon, about a century before Jesus was born in Bethlehem.

The author is unknown. Yet it seems certain that he was a refined, committed Greek-speaking Israelite, somewhat knowledgeable in Hellenic philosophy and culture; and an inhabitant of Alexandria, one of the greatest intellectual centers of the ancient world and a principal hub of the Jewish Diaspora (i.e., the Jews living outside the Holy Land).

Today's Second Reading, from Paul's Letter to Rome, is part of the New Testament; indeed, the most important writing in the New Testament outside of the Gospels.

The Gospel, too, is of course from the New Testament part of the Bible. It is one of four accounts of Jesus' life and ministry, the account according to St. Matthew, also called Levi. The other Gospels are those of Mark, Luke and John.

The Bible infallibly teaches wisdom, and is itself ultimate wisdom, for it is God's word. Thus, when we read about praying in today's Second Reading, we learn both that praying constitutes true wisdom, and that despite our weakness, the Spirit prays with us. Similarly, today's Gospel tells us, in the beautiful parable of the good seed and the weeds, that if we take God's word into our hearts and ponder it with his help, it will take root. Which means that the Bible will help us make our way safely through this confused world.

Curiously, the situation that prevailed when the Book of Wisdom was written—about the middle of the second century B.C.—is somewhat like that which prevails today. Once again, in our times, those who claim to believe in Transcendence are being attacked, confused, or ridiculed by innovative ideas, movements and fads. Some are abandoning the faith, even; others are so disoriented that they proceed almost as if in a state of panic.

The Christian's ready response to today's scene is, in essence, the response provided by the Bible. The Bible, God's revealed Word as read within the Body of his Church, is ultimate truth. And anything that contradicts, denies or casts doubt upon what is given biblically, is necessarily false.

SEVENTEENTH SUNDAY
IN ORDINARY TIME (A)

The Gospel and the Gospels

First Kings 3:5, 7-12; Romans 8:28-30; Matthew 13:44-52

Aim: to explain (1) the meaning of Gospel which preceded the four Gospels; (2) the characteristics of the Gospel according to Matthew, Mark, Luke and John; (3) the Gospel according to each of us.

One message that can be crystallized from today's Bible readings is the identification of true and lasting wisdom with God's word.

Solomon, today's First Reading recalls, prayed for wisdom; his prayer was answered in God's gift of understanding.

Paul, in the Second Reading, assures us that our belief that God will always provide for his disciples is not just a pious thought; on the contrary, it is true wisdom.

The Gospel, from one of Jesus' parables, emphasizes the wisdom that the Kingdom of God is a treasure—like a precious pearl.

God's Word is of course the fundamental, absolute and perennial wisdom. This wisdom reaches a summit of expression in the Gospels, the historical and divinely co-authored accounts of Jesus' life and ministry.

Our English word "Gospel" derives from the Anglo-Saxon "God-spell," meaning "good tidings." (It translates the Greek *euaggelion*.) "Good news" is one way the word can be understood. One is prompted to think of a herald, an announcer, proclaiming the "Good News" of Jesus' fulfillment of the prophecies by his life, death and resurrection.

This thought is apt, for the Gospel was originally proclaimed before it was written down. Which means that there was *a Gospel* before *the four Gospels*.

The oldest written Gospel, it now appears, is that according to St. Mark, which dates from approximately 70 A.D. Prior to Mark's account, the Good News was promulgated orally, chiefly in three contexts: catechetical instruction, the liturgy, and preaching.

Preaching—announcing the Word of God in its fulfillment—was a principal responsibility of Peter and the Apostles (Ac 2:22 or Ac 10:38).

Catechesis was another means of disseminating the Gospel (Ac 2:42, or Ac 8:26-40, or Lk 24:25-27). Catechesis focused on the key truth of Christian revelation; namely, that Jesus of Nazareth, who was foretold by the prophets and who rose from the death of the cross, freely accepted for the salvation of all mankind, is both Messiah (Christ) and Lord, who lives and reigns at the Father's right hand; and who will come again in glory as our judge.

The third context in which the Gospel was first proclaimed was the liturgy; for example, the Eucharist, called "the Breaking of the Bread" (Ac 2:42), or baptism (e.g., Ac 2:41, 8:36-39). Luke's Gospel manifests a strong liturgical character; his account of the Presentation of the Lord employs liturgical terms, for instance.

The Gospel according to Mk was probably written around 70 A.D. Mark was a disciple of Peter; the Gospel was written to show the Romans that Jesus is the Son of God.

Luke's Gospel dates from about 75 A.D. Luke was a highly cultured Gentile physician; his Gospel was meant for Gentiles, to show that Jesus is Lord and Savior of all men.

Matthew's Gospel is didactic. Written about 85 A.D., it was written to show the Jews that Jesus is the Messiah.

John's Gospel, finally, is theological and sacramental. Written perhaps about 90-100 A.D., it points to Jesus as the divine "Word" who became incarnate to be for all men the way, the truth, and the . life.

Again, the Word of God constitutes the treasure on which we stake our lives; there is no other ultimate wisdom. This is the Gospel we preach and live by.

EIGHTEENTH SUNDAY IN ORDINARY TIME (A)

God's Enduring Presence

Isaiah 55-1-3; Romans 8:35; 37-39; Matthew 14:13-21

Aim: to show that in Christ, made present to us through his word and the Eucharist, we experience God's loving, enduring presence, from which nothing can separate us, save our own sinful turning away.

"All you who are thirsty, come . . . You who have no money, come, receive grain and eat . . . I will renew with you the everlasting covenant . . ."

The author of these beautiful words was Deutero-Isaiah (Second Isaiah); the age, the sixth century before Christ. The Babylonian Captivity was ending; God had shown mercy upon his errant people, who had been deported to Babylon, modern day Iraq. Now a fresh invitation to the banquet of divine joy was being issued.

The perfect fulfillment of this banquet is of course realized in Jesus' giving himself to us in his word and in the Eucharist—a wonder prefigured by the multiplication of the loaves, recorded by Matthew in today's Gospel. Matthew stresses the hunger with which the Lord's followers sought him out; and that after finding him, and dining with him, they "ate their fill."

What the Hebrew exiles in Babylon longed for during their captivity, we now have: living water, eternal food, in an everlasting covenant. We have a Savior in our midst: the living Lord who brings us out of the slavery of sin, sustains us by his presence and continuous assistance, and safeguards us against another dread exile from the land of our heritage. And we know that he will never desert us; the only permanent exile now possible is one which we freely opt for through a sinful turning away from him.

No wonder that St. Paul, writing to the early Church of Rome, could exclaim: "Who will separate us from the love of Christ?" (Today's Second Reading). Christ's love for us will not be thwarted. Are we to assume that he who died for us will abandon us? Of course not.

How well Paul knew this. How well, too, the early Christians knew it: the countless persons who are buried in the Roman catacombs; women like Cecilia, Agnes, Felicity and Perpetua; men like Justin and Lawrence the Deacon.

How well believers have known this down through the centuries: the great bishop, Athanasius, an exile for his faith most of his life; St. Thomas of Canterbury—Becket—who was murdered in his cathedral; and that other Thomas, Thomas More, who died for his faith under England's King Henry VIII.

They knew, these heroes of faith, that death could not separate them from Christ's love; that, in fact, burying themselves in Christ's passion would secure for them an eternal covenant with God.

In this Eucharist we pray to appreciate more fully Christ's enduring love for us; to appreciate that all the evils of the world combined cannot remove the only treasure that remains forever: the divine invitation to joy.

The early martyrs made it a point to receive Communion before entering the area of torture and death. Steeled by the Eucharist, they could clearly understand the full meaning of prophecies like Isaiah's First Reading again:

"Why spend your (resources) for what is not bread? Come to *me* .. . that you may have *life*."

NINETEENTH SUNDAY IN ORDINARY TIME (A)

Christ's Presence in the Church throughout History

First Kings 19:9, 11-13; Romans 9:1-5; Matthew 14:22-33

Aim: (1) to show the Church's continuing existence as a sign of Christ's continuing existence; (2) to demonstrate this against the background of Church history.

Today's First Reading is the beautiful story of how Elijah the prophet found God. The scene was the ninth century B.C. The notorious Queen Jezebel had successfully thwarted Elijah's crusade to turn Israel back to God. The prophet was forced to take flight from the queen, who was determined to execute him, and he took refuge in a cave. There, he began to learn how God often works, how God enters into our world: not in spectacular commotions like earthquakes, raging storms, or gigantic fires, but in a quiet, subtle, unobtrusive manner, as Jesus himself came in a quiet, subtle, unobtrusive fashion.

Christ comes to us this way today, still, through his Mystical Body, the Church; this rather unspectacular community of believers without power or prestige in the worldly sense has survived the centuries.

The obituary of this our Roman Church has been written many,

many times; likewise, the obituary of the papacy. The Church, in fulfillment of Christ's promise (Mt 28:20), goes on, always.

From the very beginning, our Church was threatened with extinction. Peter, mysteriously drawn to Rome, was martyred there under Nero. For three hundred years, the Church was persecuted; it literally had to go underground—to the catacombs. It survived gloriously.

When the barbarians sacked Rome in 410, Christendom was reported at an end. The same report was circulated later when the barbarians swept throughout Europe, even to the British Isles. But the Church and the papacy survived.

The dawn of the Renaissance triggered new obituary notices for the Church and the papacy. When the popes went into exile in Avignon, France, in 1309, the Church's demise was thought by some as imminent. Later, when the Great Western Schism began in 1378, it was thought more imminent.

During the French Revolution in the late 18th century, the Church's death was announced anew. The name of Notre Dame of Paris was changed to the Temple of the Goddess of Reason. The Church and the papacy went on.

In more recent times, Josef Stalin once demanded to know, sarcastically, how many legions the Pope had. Today Stalin is dead, buried, and disgraced, even in the U.S.S.R. The papacy is alive; the Roman Church goes on.

Now other strident voices are heard, in fresh attempts to write the obituaries of the Roman Church and the papacy. Secularists charge that the Church has lost relevancy; dissidents claim the papacy has lost credibility. With Christ the Church of Rome endures.

In this Church founded on the Apostles he walks upon the stormy waters of this life: again, not spectacularly, but quietly, subtly, unobtrusively. And he brings with him, for those who recognize him in his Church, the covenant promises once made to Israel, of which Paul speaks in today's Second Reading: our divine adoption, our membership in his new Covenant, our sharing in his law, worship, and promises.

"Come," Jesus now says, to us, through his Church, as we falter on the rough seas of a confused world.

TWENTIETH SUNDAY IN ORDINARY TIME (A)

History of the Church Universal

Isaiah 56:1, 6-7; Romans 11:13-15, 29-32; Matthew 15:21-28

Aim: to explain that by divine will the Church is universal or Catholic; generally to cite some heresies which would narrow the catholicity of the Church as God's saving sign to all men.

Sometimes certain passing scenes in the Bible seem so unusual they tend to distract us from the total drama. Today's Gospel is a case in point, especially the account of the conversation between Jesus and the Syro-Phoenician woman. We don't quite understand it, and look for some help.

What is evidenced in Jesus' interchange with the non-Jewish woman is a kind of wit admired in the Orient: the matching of riddle against riddle; the turning of one wise saying into another, the conversion of an apparent rebuke into a commitment. Also, our Lord's reference to "dogs" is almost untranslatable in the English. The Greek word used by the evangelist doesn't really mean "dogs" in our sense of the term, but almost signifies—not quite, but almost— "pups." An attractive image is suggested, therefore. Besides, Christ sees the house pups eating at the same table as the children of the household.

However, all this is peripheral. Today's Gospel, like today's First

Reading, which prophesies an invitation to all humanity to the Lord's mountain, focuses on the universality of salvation. The same theme is sounded in today's Second Reading. The woman in the Gospel was a Canaanite; in his Gospel, Matthew bluntly describes her as a Syro-Phoenician. She was not a Jewess, therefore, but a Gentile. She nevertheless came to Jesus, and he graced her with the same benediction he imparted upon those whose ancestors had Isaiah for a prophet—the same prophet, again, who foretold the salvation of foreigners.

Today's Bible lessons, then, remind us of the great Catholic doctrine of the universality of salvation.

Indeed, our historic Roman Church founded by Jesus on Peter and the Apostles is described as Catholic (with a capital *C*) precisely because it is by nature universal. "Catholic" derives from a Greek word meaning "universal."

We know that Christ calls all men to salvation through his Church because divine Revelation says so. Reason alone could not tell us this with certainty. God's word is needed, and we have God's word in Bible readings such as today's.

As Catholics we reaffirm this doctrine at every Mass when, as the priest repeats Jesus' words over the chalice of wine, he says: "It (Christ's Precious Blood) will be shed for you and *for all men* so that sins may be forgiven."

Down through history there have been many attempts on the part of self-styled Christians to narrow the scope of Jesus' saving mission. The Church has consistently condemned these attempts as heretical. Pelagianism and Semi-pelagianism are two early examples. Another example, associated with the historic circumstances of the Protestant Reformation, is Calvinistic predestination: the theory that God chooses only a certain portion of mankind for salvation, while the others he rejects.

Again, we believe that Christ came to save all men. All men therefore are saved in principle. "In principle," we say, because Christ's saving will must be realized in each and every individual. While God's desire to save all persons is irrevocable (today's Second Reading), it has to be freely *ratified in love* by every person blessed by it.

TWENTY-FIRST SUNDAY IN ORDINARY TIME (A)

The Church and Peter

Isaiah 22:15, 19-23; Romans 11:33-36; Matthew 16:13-20

Aim: (1) to explain the importance of Peter in the Gospels, and (2) to explain the continuation of the Petrine Office relating to the Bishop of Rome.

Today's Gospel and First Reading—the familiar "Keys of the Kingdom" Gospel, and Isaiah's prophecy about placing the key of the House of David upon the Messiah's shoulder—point to the Church, our Church: this historic Roman Church founded by Christ upon the Apostle Peter.

As such, today's liturgy is helpful toward a better understanding of the Papacy. As Catholics we believe that the Papacy emerged from Christ's mission to Peter. The unique position of primacy that Peter enjoyed among the Apostles is especially evident from three Bible texts: Lk 22:31 ff., Jn 21:15 ff., and Mt 16:13-19.

The last text is today's Gospel. Therein we learn how our Savior changed Peter's name, by calling him *Kepha*, the Aramaic word for "rock," which in Greek is *petra*, from which derives the English "Peter." (Formerly Peter had been called "Simon.") By this symbolic act, the Lord meant to designate Peter as the foundation of the Church he intended to establish; Peter was to be the sign of stability, permanence and unity. Moreover, Peter is promised both the keys to heaven's Kingdom, and the power to bind and loose in Christ's own name.

In Jn 21:15 ff., Jesus fulfilled his pledge to give Peter the keys of heaven. This is the beautiful passage in which Peter is made shepherd of Christ's universal flock.

The Acts of the Apostles, St. Luke's inspired history of the early Church, shows us how Peter functioned in his role of Chief Shepherd. He is depicted as the principal spokesman for the Apostles; even though we read of Peter's "standing with the Eleven," Peter is the one who speaks. He is the principal preacher, the pace-setter for apostolic endeavor (Cf. Ac 1:15-26; 2:14-40; 3:1-26; 4:8; 5:1-11; 5:29; 8:14-17; etc.).

That Peter eventually went to Rome, and was martyred there, is part of our Catholic Tradition. One Biblical witness to his presence in Rome is from Peter himself, in his First Epistle, wherein he describes Rome, the place from which he was writing, in metaphorical language (5:13).

Our faith is that all Bishops of Rome—Roman Pontiffs—are Peter's heirs and "sharers of his see." Thus Vatican Council I declared:

". . . even to this time and forever Peter lives and governs 'and exercises judgment in his successors,' the bishops of the Holy Roman See, which was founded by him and consecrated by his blood. Therefore, whoever succeeds Peter in this Chair (i.e., of Rome) holds Peter's primacy over the whole Church according to the plan of Christ Himself."

One of the responsibilities of Peter and his successors, the Popes, is that of speaking for Christ. God's wisdom—referred to in today's Second Reading—is safeguarded and interpreted by Christ's Church, presided over by Peter and his successors.

This is what we mean when we speak of the Pope's teaching authority. We mean that the Pope speaks from the Chair of Peter. In Latin, chair is *cathedra*; hence, the expression, *ex cathedra.*

From his Chair in Rome Peter still speaks words of faith to guide and strengthen us in our belief.

Today we thank God for giving us the Papacy, a source of rock-like certainty in life's religious pilgrimage here below.

TWENTY-SECOND SUNDAY IN ORDINARY TIME (A)

The Importance of Being Catholic

Jeremiah 20:7-9; Romans 12:1-2; Matthew 16:21-27

Aim: (1) to show the uniqueness of the Catholic Church and (2) the importance of being a Catholic.

"Everyone mocks me," lamented the prophet Jeremiah in today's First Reading. For proclaiming God's word, he experienced derision and reproach. Yet prophesy he must. To him God's name was like a fire raging within his heart; overcome with zeal, he simply had to speak out.

To be a Christian is to be Jeremiah-like. St. Paul, in today's Second Reading, reminds us that as members of Christ's priesthood we must, despite the cost, offer ourselves as victims in a living sacrifice to God. And Jesus, in today's Gospel, from Matthew, crystallizes Jeremiah's role (and ours):

"If a man wishes to come after me, he must deny his very self, take up his cross, and begin to follow in my footsteps. Whoever would save his life will lose it, but whoever loses his life for my sake will find it."

Commitment to Christ—living out one's faith in the midst of a misunderstanding or even a mocking world—is *our* privilege, a privilege of self-oblation alongside the Lord Jesus, in whom we place unreserved faith, hope, and love.

Commitment to Christ means, for us as Catholics, commitment to his Church, founded on Peter and the Apostles. This Catholic Church is our Savior's principal sacrament in the world. It is here that the fullness of truth and grace are found. It is here that we meet, embrace, and hear the living Lord Jesus.

In the ancient Nicene Creed, we describe our Church as "one, holy, catholic, and apostolic." These are the four signs or marks by which the Church of Christ can be recognized. They are derived from Jesus' own will as learned from the Bible.

The Church is one; it is a living unity in communion with one head, the Bishop of Rome who succeeds Peter. It is holy, because within it we possess the Blessed Eucharist, Jesus' Real Presence, and the sacraments. It is catholic—a Greek derivative meaning "universal"—because its mission is to all people of all times. It is apostolic, because it is the same community of the apostolic era; there is a continuity between the early Church depicted in the Acts of the Apostles and our Church today.

Catholicism therefore is unique. There is an ancient adage: "Love Christ, love the Church." St. Cyprian (d. 230), in *De Unitate*, wrote that "one cannot have God for his father, if he does not have the Church for his mother." St. Augustine (d. 430), in a tract on St. John, argued that "to the extent that one loves the Church of Christ, one possesses the Holy Spirit." Both these fathers were quoted by Pope John Paul II in his opening address to CELAM in Puebla, Mexico, on 28 January, 1979.

Too, love Christ; listen to the Church. The Church speaks for Christ. "How could there be any authentic evangelizing," asked Pope John Paul II, "if there were no ready and sincere reverence for the sacred magisterium, in clear awareness that by submitting to it the People of God are not accepting the word of man but the true word of God?"

To be a Catholic—to return to Jeremiah—can be especially difficult today. But, as Jesus warns us, "What does it profit us to gain the world and lose ourselves?" For anyone truly committed, to abandon the Church is to abandon home and life.

TWENTY-THIRD SUNDAY
IN ORDINARY TIME (A)

The Mature Christian

Ezekiel 33:7-9; Romans 13:8-10; Matthew 18:15-20

*Aim: to hold up the Gospel ideal: (1) each of us another
Christ, (2) acting as Christ, (3) seeing Christ in others.*

Today's First Reading is from Ezekiel, in many ways the most
mysterious, yet, in a sense, one of the most familiar of Old Testament
prophets. He began to prophesy during the Babylonian Captivity
around 593 B.C. (The ruins of Babylon, to which the Israelites were
deported around 597 B.C., can still be seen near Baghdad, in modern
day Iraq.)

Ezekiel, incidentally, was the one who gave us the vision of the dry
bones, on which the Black Spiritual is based. He also gave us the
Good Shepherd allegory, wherein he foretold that one day God
himself would appear to shepherd his people. This great allegory was
clarified and amplified by St. John in the Good Shepherd passage,
wherein Jesus announces, "I am the Good Shepherd" (10:11).

The shepherd metaphor provides us with a link between today's
First Reading and the Gospel. Both have to do with fraternal
correction—the need for the mature believer to give sound witness,
guidance and direction. The underlying reason for this is God's will,
binding all believers, that his sheep should be protected through the
collaboration of all; and if, by chance, some should become

discouraged or confused, or should even scatter, they should have the good example of all, drawing them back to the true fold.

We *are* bound to one another by love, St. Paul reminded the early Roman Church in today's Second Reading. This clearly means that we do have a responsibility toward the Christian community, and to all those individually who constitute it. We are, in a sense, our brothers' and sisters' keepers.

As mature believers, we must realize that our faith can help support others. And, on the other hand, our lack of faith can be a factor in the falling away of others. There is need for us to develop and maintain an enlightened, enthusiastic, sound, and persevering faith so that our every expression or act of belief might reflect the interior commitment we treasure. In this way, we will fulfill our debt of mature faith-witness, and never, at least, occasion the spiritual decline or death of another.

Must we as mature, committed, Christians be reminded that sometimes even a hastily executed, matter-of-fact genuflection before the Blessed Sacrament can occasion another's turning from the Church; or a premature exit from Sunday Mass—before the Eucharist is even over?

Leo Tolstoy, surely one of the world's greatest novelists (*War and Peace, Anna Karenina*), and who had so intense a commitment to being his brothers' keeper that he turned over his estate to the serfs, made this last point in one of his short stories. Two brothers, while on a hunting trip, he wrote, stopped at a lodge where they put up for the night. When the younger brother knelt down to pray before retiring, the elder, watching him from a hay loft above, simply remarked: "So you still do that!" The brothers said no more to each other. Yet Tolstoy explained, from that night on the younger one stopped praying or going to church. The result was that he did not pray or receive Communion for over 30 years. The reason? Not because the younger brother decided anything in his own soul. But, wrote Tolstoy, "because the word spoken by his brother was like the push of a finger on a wall that was ready to fall of its own weight."

God forbid that our example might ever occasion anyone to stray. We must be, above all, persons of sound witness, encouragement and direction.

TWENTY-FOURTH SUNDAY IN ORDINARY TIME (A)

The Mature Christian

Sirach 27:30, 28:7; Romans 14:7-9; Matthew 18:21-35

Aim: to show how the mature Christian relates to others—always forgiving, always judging kindly, with the love of Christ.

Forgiveness, a sign of Christian maturity, is the focus of two lessons today, that beautiful text of Sirach (today's First Reading), and the Gospel pericope, from Matthew. "Christian maturity," we say, because we belong to the Lord, as St. Paul reminds us in the Second Reading, and the Lord is a Lord of mercy, forgiveness and reconciliation.

Overlooking faults, suppression of the revenge instinct, forgiving and forgetting, are Christian imperatives.

The Gospel today uses the example of a king's forgiving an official who, in turn, refuses to pardon a colleague. The official owed the king a huge sum; we are given the impression that it was so huge a debt as to preclude full repayment. Yet this extraordinary debt was cancelled out by the king; whereas that owed to the official by his colleague—a much smaller bill—was not.

Obviously the lesson refers to God and us; and in turn, to us and our friends and neighbors. Who of us can say—if the truth were known—that God has not forgiven us *so* many times, for *so* many faults, of *so* serious a nature simply because we begged him, with hearts filled with contrition and resolve, to receive us back into his mercy? Who of us can say that we never committed an infidelity against him, for which he graciously lifted our guilt?

Despite such generosity on God's part, how many of us are tempted to go right out—immediately after God has forgiven us, even—and adamantly refuse to forgive another—someone even, who has insulted us to far less a degree than we have crossed God?

Take the case of a woman who has committed an infidelity against her marital vows. She confesses to her husband; she asks his forgiveness. For love of her he receives her back with total pardon, and pledges not only to forgive but also to forget.

The following week this same woman, on a downtown shopping trip, passes her mother-in-law, whom she has avoided for years. (Perhaps the older woman was originally set against the marriage.) The mother-in-law is still shunned. "I still can't forgive and forget the way his mother treated me," the woman rationalizes.

Each Sunday—daily, in fact, in the Eucharistic Sacrifice—we pray, as Christ taught us to pray, in the Lord's Prayer: *not* simply, "Forgive us our trespasses," *period*; but, rather: "Forgive us our trespasses *as* we forgive those who trespass against us." Do not these words have meaning? Don't they help define the mature Christian?

God knows that we're only human: this is why he forgives us so readily. But he also knows that with his help we *can* forgive others, if we only make the effort to do so; otherwise he wouldn't have commanded us to do so. God never commands us to do the impossible.

And God also knows—as we all know if we are honest about it— that forgiving means *forgetting*.

Forgiveness, finally, should be a daily occurrence; so should forgetting. Doesn't God forgive and forget our weaknesses *every day*? We don't have to wait till Christmas to act like Christians; specifically, to judge others kindly, as God judges us.

TWENTY-FIFTH SUNDAY IN ORDINARY TIME (A)

The Mature Christian

Isaiah 55:6-9; Philippians 1:20-24, 27; Matthew 20:1-16

Aim: to show how the mature Christian relates to the things of this world; without attachment, with simplicity and generosity.

"My thoughts are not your thoughts, nor are your ways my ways," explains the Lord through the Second Isaiah in today's First Reading. While man must seek God, God's ways are beyond man's full understanding. Yet God's ways must be learned by man. God is transcendent, the eternal Other; yet he is close to us.

Today's Gospel concretizes these paradoxes. As God's ways are not man's ways, God's mathematics is not man's mathematics.

Regarding the Gospel, remember that it is a parable; our Lord's words about justice should not be interpreted according to the letter. Jusus had no intention of preaching that we—his followers—can ignore the dictates of justice. On the contrary, we must deem justice a sacred imperative.

In fact, today's Gospel holds many levels of meaning. One, surely, pertains to God's grace and salvation. We learn that God showers abundant graces on persons who, in our fallible estimation, have not lived especially good lives, individuals like the Good Thief, for example, who was crucified with our Lord. Even in cases of so-called "death-bed conversions," there is much *we don't know*; much that God alone knows. We never know, for instance, how difficult a struggle others must wage against serious sin.

In this sense, the Gospel provides hope for those who have idled even in the Lord's vineyard all their lives. It does not condone such idling; of course not. But can't the fact that those who were hired last were given the same recompense as those who were hired first, be translated into the principle that it is never too late for anyone to return to God's friendship?

At the same time, today's parable constitutes a caution for any of us who thinks he or she can stop laboring until others catch up to us, as it were. For—here is the main point—everyone is equally inefficient before God; all are equally unworthy before him. Our having borne the heat of the day any longer in terms of time cannot be used as an argument to the effect that we *deserve* eternal reward, or that we have won the race of life. Again, God's mathematics is not ours. To think otherwise is to manifest immaturity of soul.

Christian maturity demands that we face the world as St. Paul says we should in today's Second Reading. We "live for Christ," not in the sense that we wish a personal escape from this world, but rather that we see everything in this world and order everything in this world, in view of the mystery of Christ who is our final goal.

The Epistle to Diognetus, written about the year 200 A.D., describes Christians in these terms:

"They reside in their respective countries, but only as aliens . . . Each foreign land is their home . . . they marry like all others and beget children; but they do not expose their offspring. Their board they spread for all, but not their bed. They find themselves *in the flesh*, but do not live *according to the flesh*. They spend their days on earth, but hold citizenship in heaven . . . *They are poor, and enrich many* . . . They are dishonored, and in their dishonor find their glory . . ." (*Readings in Church History*, Volume I, ed. Colman J. Barry: Westminster, Md., Newman, 1960).

Again, to "live for Christ" is maturity as we see it. Our vision differs from; nay, transcends essentially, the weak and distorted vision of the world.

TWENTY-SIXTH SUNDAY IN ORDINARY TIME (A)

The Old Testament Prophets

Ezekiel 18:25-28; Philippians 2:1-11; Matthew 21:28-32

Aim: to teach (1) the meaning of "prophet;" (2) the major and minor Old Testament prophets; (3) how in a sense we are to be prophets, especially in the context of responsibility.

The Old Testament prophet Ezekiel, who lived in the sixth century B.C., focuses, in today's First Reading, on the mystery of responsibility.

This same theme—that of individual responsibility—resounds clearly in today's Gospel: the parable of the two sons, asked by their father to perform a certain task.

Responsibility comes from the two words, "response" and "ability." It means a capacity for replying to someone to whom a reply is due. For anyone with faith, for anyone who believes that man is God's creature destined to live with him forever, responsibility means reference to God's will for man. And God's will for us is not just a set of commands for command's sake, but a corpus of directives as to what is best conducive to our welfare, taken in its totality.

Christian responsibility is not always easy for the disciple of Jesus. Sometimes being responsible for right actions before God entails carrying a cross; martyrdom, even. Such is the thrust of today's Second Reading, from St. Paul to the Philippians. Here we are reminded that Christian responsibility is a service to others, a suffering service, in the footsteps of *the* Suffering Servant himself, Jesus of Nazareth.

Responsibility was a recurring theme not only of Ezekiel, but of all the Old Testament prophets. The word "prophet" refers to one who is called to speak for God.

Note that predicting the future is not essential to the concept of prophecy. A prophet is an accredited witness of the divine word in such a manner that he both experiences God's Revelation, and proclaims it accurately with the Spirit's guidance and confirmation.

Ezekiel is listed as one of the major prophets. Isaiah (724-701 B.C.) was another; the latter part of his book, from about Chapter 40 on, is attributed to a Second Isaiah (Deutero Isaiah), and perhaps to a Third Isaiah (or their disciples). Jeremiah (b. 650 B.C.) is a third major prophet. So was Elijah (869-850 B.C.), who, however, did not compose or inspire a separate book; he was not a writing prophet. The earliest writing prophet was Amos (786-746 B.C.). He is one of the 12 minor prophets, so-called because their writings are relatively brief. The others are: Micah, Nahum, Habakkuk, Zephaniah, Haggai, Zechariah, Hosea, Joel, Baruch, Malachi and Obediah.

The prophets all spoke to heighten the awareness of God's People to his word. They accented mankind's responsibility.

We too are, in a sense, prophets when we speak for God in this area: as responsible persons, by our witness and words of faith, we can help raise the consciousness of those who dismiss or ignore each person's accountability before God.

One speaks for God—truly prophesies—each time he affirms the holiness of God's name, for example, in the office or in the factory. One likewise prophesies every time one takes a stand, even in ordinary, everyday conversation, on reverence for life, or honesty, or social justice, or the sanctity of marriage.

TWENTY-SEVENTH SUNDAY IN ORDINARY TIME (A)

Appreciation for God's Gifts, and the Psalms

Isaiah 5:1-7; Philippians 4:6-9; Matthew 21:33-43

Aim: to emphasize (1) the importance of our appreciating God's gifts, lest they be taken from us; (2) the use of the Psalms as prayer-means to this end.

Today's First Reading is from Isaiah's celebrated Song of the Vineyard, written in the eighth century B.C. It is a sad song; Isaiah tells of God as a friend who carefully tended a vine, only to acquire bitter grapes.

A similar theme resounds in the Gospel: the tragic allegory about a vineyard's being neglected to those to whom it was given, and, consequently, handed over to others.

Do we appreciate the mystery we are privileged to experience in our Faith? This is one question we are challenged to face this Sunday.

Why have we come for Mass today, for example? Fundamentally, why? Is habit the main reason? A guilt complex, perhaps? Nationalistic or cultural background? How sincere are we, really? Do we go to Mass chiefly to fulfill a precept? Or are we profoundly aware that to assemble for the Eucharist on the Lord's Day is to witness to our total commitment to the Paschal mystery; to confess that Jesus is Lord, and to embrace him as he comes again into our midst to heal and encourage, and feed us; to steel ourselves to imitate Christ and thereby render our homes and environments more Christlike?

The answer to any one of these questions is personal; each must answer for himself or herself.

Do we appreciate our Faith? Can we present our needs to God in "prayer and petition full of gratitude?" (to cite St. Paul's phrase in the Second Reading).

If not, the key to a remedy is surely in prayer itself. Gratitude is born of petition for gratitude. And among the surest means to this goal is the prayer and petition we discover in the Psalms. Today's Responsorial Psalm is an excellent example; especially the incomparably beautiful lines: "Once again, O Lord . . . look down from heaven, and see . . . Take care of this vine, and protect what your right hand has planted. . ."

The psalms—there are 150 of them—are songs so constructed that they constitute God's Word in forms that can be used as prayers to God. Jesus prayed the psalms; as he was dying on the Cross, he was praying them. They speak of Christ, yet in a way that in them it is Christ who prays to the Father. And they cover all the possible situations, moods, and circumstances in which we can pray: sadness and joy, anxiety and confidence, night and day, loneliness and acceptance, hunger and plenty. There are psalms for depression (e.g., Ps 41); psalms for temptation (55), psalms for lack of confidence (26), psalms for a fear of storms (28). There are psalms for visiting the Blessed Eucharist (15, 19, 22, 41, 42); psalms for Holy Communion (25, 62, 110); psalms for evening prayers (3, 94, 95); psalms before confession (50, 78).

One way to pray the psalms is by reading them in *The Liturgy of the Hours*, the daily prayer book from which priests and religious pray daily, and which, in shorter forms, is generally available for the laity. Or, of course, the psalms can be prayed directly from the Bible—alone, or in a family group, each day.

The psalms *can* assist us appreciate the mystery we live in our Faith—the divine vineyard of today's Bible Readings.

TWENTY-EIGHTH SUNDAY IN ORDINARY TIME (A)

The Missionary Nature of Our Faith

Isaiah 25:6-10; Philippians 4:12-14, 19-20; Matthew 22:1-4

Aim: to explain (1) why our faith must have a missionary dimension; (2) how we should show our missionary or evangelistic spirit.

The literary form of today's Gospel is allegory, so that we needn't dwell at length over the circumstances of etiquette detailed in the narrative; specifically, the problem of a wedding garment. Besides, it is quite likely that in accordance with the manners of the day in the Biblical context, wedding garments were available in the anterooms of reception halls, much in the same way that dinner jackets today are available in some restaurants (usually on highways) for the man who inadvertently comes sans coat and tie, yet would prefer not to dine out on the patio with the golfing crowd.

In the historical context, the wedding feast symbolizes the New Covenant, to which the Israelites—God's elect people—had first been called. Viewed in its full theological dimensions, the banquet represents the life of grace here and now with culmination in eternal glory. The feast, we are told, and the life of grace, will be opened up to all men. Today's First Reading, from Isaiah, dimly foresees this universal messianic banquet.

Among several themes sounded in the readings today, one is that of the Church's missionary vocation. Faith is not inherited; nor is it acquired simply by cultural or social assimilation. On the contrary, faith must be preached in every age; the invitations to the universal messianic banquet must be delivered and announced.

There can be no doubting this theology. Missionary endeavor is perennially important and relevant. We are in possession of an explicit mandate from Jesus to preach the Gospel to all nations (Mt 28:19, 20).

Besides—and this helps explain Jesus' mandate—we are certain that this Church of Rome founded on Peter and the Apostles has been entrusted with the fullness of God's redeeming word and grace. That men may come to the fullness of grace and truth in this our historic, one, apostolic, Catholic Church, is the desire underlying our missionary commitment and labor.

Indirectly, in a sense, today's Second Reading reminds us of the Church's perennial missionary thrust. It was written by St. Paul from prison, to Philippi. Philippi was the first European city to hear the Gospel. Before arriving there, Paul had been in Asia Minor, preaching to cities in the mideast, where Christianity was born and cradled. But Paul had a vision; a Macedonian stood before him and pleaded: "Come over to Macedonia and help us" (Ac 16:9). Paul lost no time in replying. Taking passage from Troas (near ancient Troy, the city of the famed Wooden Horse), he sailed across to Macedonia, in northern Greece, where he soon reached Philippi. At Philippi he found a group of women praying at a river bank; he preached the Gospel to them. So the faith of most of our ancestors—those of us whose roots are in Europe—began with St. Paul's Second Missionary Journey and his sermon to a women's prayer group in Philippi.

Voices of men and women yearning to be invited to Jesus' messianic banquet can still be heard throughout the world, in every age. Today we pray for more vocations to the missions: for priests, brothers, sisters, lay missionaries. And we pray for those who are now delivering and announcing Christ's Good News invitations in fields afar. God grace their efforts.

TWENTY-NINTH SUNDAY IN ORDINARY TIME

Church and State

Isaiah 45:1, 4-6; First Thessalonians 1:1-5; Matthew 22:15-21.

Aim: to explain the relationship between Church and State, and to accent our responsibilities to our nation.

In the age in which today's Gospel was written, the axiom, "Render to God what is God's, and to Caesar what is Caesar's," was probably a reminder that one's loyalty to civil authority need not contradict his obedience to God. This principle must have been embraced fervently by the Roman Christians during the persecution under Nero, in 64 B.C.

This is one way the text has been read through Christian history. Today's Gospel has made for, if not actually made, many a martyr: Becket, for example, St. Thomas of Canterbury, who refused to compromise religious truth under challenge by Henry II; and Thomas More, that Man of All Seasons, whose clear and steadfast commitment to it drew the wrath—and the death sentence—of Henry VIII. It is a Gospel that stirs anew memories of Bohemia's great St. Wenceslaus (after whom the popular Christmas carol is based), Poland's St. Stanislaus, the Martyrs of Uganda (whose shrine Pope Paul VI visited during his trip to Africa), and the French Carmelite Nuns during the Revolution.

No; a man's loyalty to the state need not contradict his obedience to God. All authority derives from God. Yet what if Caesar begins to play God? Historically, we know, this happens, and not infrequently.

Sometimes, however, perhaps more often, the "Caesar or God" dilemma is posed in a context of priorities. Here is where contemporary man living in the free world is most likely to experience it.

As Christians we affirm in faith that man is a son of God before he is a citizen of the State. Hence he has certain innate rights—"inalienable" rights, said America's founding Fathers—which take precedence over the State's jurisdiction: life, liberty, the pursuit of happiness in one's chosen vocation. None of these rights can be preempted by the State.

Even if one lives in a graced society such as ours, where the benediction bestowed on rulers in today's First Reading almost seems renewed, right priorities can occasionally be challenged. And here it is important to keep in mind that our form of government imposes upon *us*, the People—from the national to the local level—the task of observing correct priorities. *We* are Caesar; it is *we* who must render to God what is his. We are the ones who, in providing for the common welfare in terms of the State, must strive always to defer to God's law respecting man's dignity, equality, and the general good (e.g., God's law regarding discrimination, abortion, euthanasia, dishonesty).

As Vatican Council II stated:

"Human institutions . . . must labor to minister to the dignity and purpose of man. At the same time let them put up a stubborn fight against any kind of slavery, whether social or political, and safeguard the basic rights of man under every political system. Indeed human institutions themselves must be accommodated by degrees to the highest of all realities, spiritual ones. . ." (*Pastoral Constitution on the Church in the Modern World*, No. 29).

(Here, if election day is near, the homilist can encourage use of the voting franchise.)

Remember, again, that though we are members of a great nation, we primarily belong—as today's Second Reading declares—to God the Father and the Lord Jesus Christ. Christ is our King.

THIRTIETH SUNDAY
IN ORDINARY TIME (A)

Love of God

Exodus 22:20-26; First Thessalonians 1:5-10; Matthew 22:34-40.

Aim: (1) to explain the two principal commandments as interrelated, and (2) to stress the first as basic to the second.

To love the Lord our God with our whole heart, soul and mind; and to love our neighbor as ourself: those are the two primary laws of Christian discipleship.

Today's Gospel centers on these commandments. Today's First Reading prophetically accents the second; love of God in others. Today's Second Reading, from Paul's First Letter to the Thessalonians (the oldest of the 27 New Testament books, written only about 20 years after Jesus died and rose) accents love of God in himself, specifically as he revealed himself as a model for us in Jesus.

Love of God in himself and love of God in neighbor; the two go together. For some reason today, curiously, love of God in neighbor often overshadows the first commandment, as if it were possible to practice the second without reference to the first.

Writing in the London *Tablet* in the summer of 1968, Yvonne Lubbock observed that today the holy area in which men feel compelled to "take off their shoes" and kneel down in loving adoration of the Supreme Creator and Father, is rapidly shrinking. A sense of awe for the sacred is weakening; sacred ground is disappearing. What is needed most of all today is a reaffirmation of God's very *Godness*.

Baron Frederick von Hügel once suggested that the Christian's stance in the world must be cruciform. The vertical stake points Godward; while the horizontal beam extends to the suffering brotherhood of man. If the two parts of the cross, the vertical and the horizontal are inseparable, then the horizontal beam cannot exist without the vertical. Christianity is not simply a fraternal organization, a "society of friends," in which our relationship to God is either nonessential or nonrelevant. Not at all. As the writer in the London *Tablet* argues:

"The worship of God in his holiness has a timeless precedence in importance and is a constant orientation of the human toward the divine in a desire to love and know God, while the helping of the afflicted fellow-being must take precedence in time not only for his own sake but because God has ordained that men serve him by being witnesses to the divine concern for all that he has created."

The Christian is one, therefore, who in time embraces all persons in God, while gazing upward toward God's timeless being, in whom all persons find the source of their brotherhood.

True and effective humanism is Gospel-inspired and sustained. This is why there have been no greater humanists in history than the saints: Francis of Assisi, whom all men venerate, or Vincent de Paul, who was at the beginning of all modern social service work; or, in our own country, Mother Frances Xavier Cabrini and Elizabeth Seton. Though the way to God is through humanity, humanity cannot be embraced perfectly without embracing God in himself.

In the Our Father, the perfect prayer and model for prayer, don't we say, "Hallowed be thy name," before we petition the advent of Jesus' Kingdom? The base and purpose of all religion viewed as love for our fellow man is the theocentric or vertical beam rising upward. In simple language, we recognize our brothers in the one Father.

THIRTY-FIRST SUNDAY
IN ORDINARY TIME (A)

Precepts of the Church

Malachi 1:14, 2:2, 8:10; First Thessalonians 2:7-9, 13; Matthew 23:1-12.

Aim: (1) to explain in general the seven Precepts of the Church and (2) why the Church has Precepts; and (3) to encourage their faithful observance.

"You have turned aside from the way," God warns Israel through the prophet Malachi in today's First Reading. (Malachi means "God's Messenger;" the author of this book, written about 440 B.C., is referred to as "the last of the prophets.")

Paul, in today's Second Reading, the oldest New Testament Biblical work, reminds us that Christians must be willing to share not only the Gospel, but their lives.

Jesus, in today's Gospel, tells us directly that discipleship means acting on one's sincere belief: practicing what we preach.

The interlinking theme of all Bible lessons is so clear, then. We must *be* what we say we are; *act* in accordance with our profession.

Christianity, St. Paul says in another place, is like running a race. Being a Christian doesn't mean, simply, that one has signed up for a race. Being a Christian doesn't even mean running a race. Rather, discipleship in Christ means running as if to win.

Surely one of the attitudes we must avoid is that of drifting. To drift is to be passive. We must deliberately determine to run: to participate actively in the race to eternal life. And we must determine to run—as Lewis Carroll puts it in *Alice in Wonderland*, twice as fast if we want to get somewhere.

To act in accordance with one's belief means, of course, that we observe faithfully God's word: the moral law, the Ten Commandments as expressed in our Christian faith. There are, too, what we traditionally call the Precepts of the Church, certain observances which witness to our being what we say we are. Among these are seven specific responsibilities:

1. To keep holy the day of the Lord's resurrection; to worship God by participating in Mass every Sunday and holy day of obligation; to avoid those activities that would hinder renewal of soul and body on the sabbath (e.g., needless work and business activities, unnecessary shopping, etc.).

2. To lead a sacramental life; to receive Holy Communion frequently and the Sacrament of Reconciliation regularly—minimally, to receive the Sacrament of Reconciliation at least once a year (annual confession is obligatory only if serious sin is involved); minimally also, to receive Holy Communion at least once a year, between the First Sunday of Lent and Trinity Sunday.

3. To study Catholic teaching in preparation for the Sacrament of Confirmation, to be confirmed, and then to continue to study and advance the cause of Christ.

4. To observe the marriage laws of the Church; to give religious training, by example and word, to one's children; to use parish schools and catechetical programs.

5. To strengthen and support the Church—one's own parish community and parish priests, the worldwide Church and the Pope.

6. To do penance, including abstaining from meat and fasting from food on the appointed days.

7. To join in the missionary spirit and apostolate of the Church.

In a Christian's striving to be what he claims he or she is, lies the key to his identity. Many an "identity crisis" on the part of a Catholic has had its origins in failure or neglect to keep in mind the laws of God and of his Church.

THIRTY-SECOND SUNDAY IN ORDINARY TIME (A)

Preparation for Death

Wisdom 6:12-16; Thessalonians 4:13-17; Matthew 25:1-13.

Aim: to describe (1) the importance of dying well and (2) the way to prepare for a good death.

What more meaningful topic to preach on today than preparation for death. The Gospel, from Matthew's celebrated 25th chapter, focuses on the Last Judgment, which each one of us must one day experience. In the Second Reading, St. Paul sings of Jesus' Second Coming. Today's First Reading, from Wisdom, written in Greek around a century before the first Christmas, reminds us to seek truth, which of course means living with an eye toward Jesus' Second Coming and his judgment.

God has entrusted us in this life with the power to make of ourselves what we aspire to be forever. We do this by virtue of our free will; to live is to make choices. We can either choose God and his word as our ultimate wisdom; or, in our God-given freedom, we can place our highest priorities somewhere else. Death marks the final free choice in a pilgrimage of choices leading to a future—with God or without God.

Our faith as Catholics tells us that life without God is meaningless. We were created by God for God; our destiny is to be with him forever. Outside of him there can be no personal fulfillment, no lasting peace, no real happiness. In fact, all other goals, attractive as they may seem to the senses, and even at times to the intellect—will shatter and vanish forever like so much cheap broken glass swept away for disposal.

Since death is the last free choice in our journey to God—a journey during which the living Lord Jesus is constantly at the side of anyone who sincerely calls on him—it represents the summit of a series of elections taken Godward; hence, is both anticipated and prepared for throughout life.

This is to say that, when we are about to die, we will be the kind of persons we have aspired to be at the moment of death. Thus, the way we have lived our commitment as Christians made in baptism and confirmed later in life, describes in general the way we shall die. Specifically, the way we have participated in Sunday Mass, received the Eucharist; the way we have tried to remain faithful to our state of life—in marriage or vows or ministry; the way we have tried to share our faith; the way we have seen Christ in others—today's Gospel: in this same way we shall die.

The early Church Fathers used to emphasize that the moment we are born, we begin to die to this world in order to be born again to eternal life. One might say that in death we finally achieve the ceramic mold we cast *for* ourselves, *by* ourselves, through roads freely traveled, graces embraced, hopes grasped, despite the difficulties.

In a sense we are like chalices for a royal table; St. Paul used the metaphor in Romans 9:20. The great English poet, Robert Browning, borrowed the thought in his poem, *Rabbi Ben Ezra*. In medieval times chalices were engraved on the outside with a traditional hierarchy of images: beginning at the base, the images were of youth; around the brim of the cup, they depicted age and death. Isn't a chalice meant to slake the Master's thirst? Didn't Jesus, atop Calvary, cry "I thirst?"

We are living chalices meant for Christ our Lord. We pray today that we might come to believe this more firmly. We pray that God will perfect the cup he has made, that he will help us get ready for our death-day. In Browning's words:

"So, take and use Thy work: Amend what flaws may lurk—My times be in Thy hand! Perfect the cup as planned."

THIRTY-THIRD SUNDAY IN ORDINARY TIME (A)

The Purpose of Life

Proverbs 31:10-13, 19-20, 30-31; First Thessalonians 5:1-6; Matthew 25:14-30

Aim: to show (1) the inequality among people in this world and (2) the equal goal of sanctity for each one of us.

Today's Gospel looks forward to Jesus' Second Coming, as Judge and Lord. So too does the Second Reading. St. Paul's warning to his converts at Thessalonica that the date of Christ's Second Coming is not only *not* known, but in all probability is not imminent. Some of the Thessalonians had actually given up their jobs to await the world's end. Paul had to tell them to get on with their lives here below. But he urges the Thessalonians to stay wide awake and keep spreading the light of faith against the day when this world will end.

The key truth sounded in both readings is that we live now with an eye toward our final goal: the possession of God in heaven. Remember how simply the basic catechism puts this: we are created to know, love, and serve God in this world, and to be happy with him forever in the next.

Today's First Reading says the same, although it is directed primarily to women, and expressed in a woman's idiom. (St. Paul injects another feminine point in today's Second Reading; that comparison between the end of the world and childbirth.) It's the celebrated "valiant wife" passage from Proverbs, wherein we are reminded that physical beauty and charm, as noble as they may be, are nonetheless passing; what endures forever is spiritual attractiveness. For men, this passage could meaningfully be translated into terms of physical strength or vigorous youth: both of these fade away as age progresses; what remains forever is strength and vigor of soul.

Reference to a woman's physical beauty, or to a man's strength or vigor, also prompts some reflection on physical inequalities; some people seem to be gifted less than others in this world's attributes, physical as well as psychological and intellectual.

What matters, again, is a person's spirit. What will remain is a person's beauty and strength of soul. And beauty and strength of soul necessarily reflect one's priorities in this brief pilgrimage to our only real and everlasting homeland: heaven.

How do we achieve beauty and strength of soul so that we will be recognized by Jesus our Judge and Lord at his Second Coming?

Today's Gospel reminds us that living here below means making the most of the talents God has given us for his greater honor and glory. Simply for trying to do this, we are assured of being rewarded a hundredfold.

This means, of course, that we should not live our lives in a constant process of demanding things of God. On the contrary, we should try to use all that we have of God's worldly gifts to increase our investment in heaven's riches—the only treasure, Jesus reminded us, which will never diminish in value.

Essential to this way of life is that we always keep before our minds and hearts the Gospel vision of the Lord Jesus, seated as Judge before us at the Last Day, and asking of us what we did with the talents he gave us.

If we live, however, as if this world were its own goal; if we live merely to acquire all the pleasure and satisfaction this world alone can give—always a transient pleasure or satisfaction; if we live merely, as the saying goes, to eat, drink, and be merry since tomorrow we shall die; then we will have squandered all our talents and must appear before Christ our Judge and Lord without anything to show for having lived. *Without anything to show for a life's opportunity, which once given, is never given anew.*

THE SOLEMNITY OF
CHRIST THE KING (A)

The Last Judgment

Ezekiel 34:11-12, 15-17; First Corinthians 15:20-26, 28; Matthew 25:31-46.

Aim: to give the Church's teaching on (1) the Particular and (2) the General Judgment.

Today the liturgical year comes to a resounding conclusion—like the close of a Beethoven symphony—with the Solemnity of Christ, King of the Universe.

When the Archangel Gabriel spoke to Mary the Mother of the Lord he announced that the Child of her womb was to be a king (Lk 1:33). Later, Jesus, standing before the judgment seat of Pontius Pilate, clearly affirmed his kingship (Jn 18:37). And in the Book of Revelation, St. John sees Christ wearing a mantle inscribed with the words, "King of Kings and Lord of Lords" (19:16).

As Catholics we believe—today's Second Reading states—that the hour of Christ's reign is now. Until the Lord's Second Coming, when he will deliver his Kingdom to the Father (First Corinthians 15:20-25), God's action in our world is through Christ—as we commonly say in the conclusion of our prayers.

Today's Bible readings, especially the Gospel and the opening lesson from Ezekiel, portray Christ the King as a shepherd. Since he is God, he fulfills perfectly Ezekiel's prediction that God himself would come to shepherd his people. The Gospel, which reflects the ancient pastoral custom in Palestine of separating the sheep and goats each evening because while the sheep are strong enough to remain outside all night, the goats required shelter, interprets Jesus' rule as one of loving judgment. Hence this aspect must be emphasized today.

From the Bible as read within the Church, we know that we shall be summoned to two judgments after death intervenes.

One occurs when we cross the threshhold of this temporary life into the endless corridors of eternity. At that moment the last opportunity to make of ourselves what we want to be forever has passed (Jn 9:4). We stand before God with our entire history, of merits as well as failures. And there we are judged by the Shepherd-King of Kings. (Read Lk 16:19-31; 2 Cor 5:6-9; Ph 1:21-23.)

The General Judgment—the one immortalized in art by Michelangelo behind the altar of the Sistine Chapel in Rome—occurs within the context of the Resurrection of the Dead at the end of time. The Bible reveals this Judgment explicitly; today's Gospel is one instance. Another is Mk 13:14-27.

Belief in the General Judgment is part of the Creed we recite at Sunday Mass. The Particular Judgment was witnessed to by the Ecumenical Council of Florence (1445), and earlier by Lyons (1274).

The relationship between the first or Particular Judgment, and the General Judgment at the end of time, when all Jesus' disciples will be raised in the flesh, is especially mysterious. But we know in faith that judgment—*my* judgment and *yours*—will be cosmic as well as individual; personal as well as universal. To minimize the importance of the Particular Judgment would be to minimize each man's individual responsibility before God. On the other hand, to play down the General Judgment would be to downplay man's responsibility to find Christ in his neighbor and all mankind—a duty dramatically stressed in today's Gospel.

A final note could be added here in view of some false ideas current; namely, that we will *be judged* by God. Man does not judge himself. I—you and I—must one day stand before the Lord of Lords and *be judged* for this precious life given to us that we might participate in God's reign forever.

SOLEMNITY OF ALL SAINTS
(1 November)

The Beatitudes

Revelation 7:2-4, 9-14; John 3:1-3; Matthew 5:1-12.

Aim: to explain that the saints lived the Beatitudes, to whose spirit we are also called.

Today, on All Saints' Day, we recall the greatest heroes of our Catholic faith, those men, women and children who as today's First Reading says—"washed their robes and made them white in the blood of the Lamb." The Lamb is, of course, Jesus, *the* Lamb of God who takes away the sins of the world; their robes symbolize their souls. Conscious of their divine adoption as children of the Father in Christ Jesus—as today's Second Reading notes—they have followed Christ the Lamb in his sacrificial pilgrimage of suffering service, a service detailed in incomparable terms in today's Gospel, the Beatitudes. Now, the reign of heaven is theirs.

"How blest the poor in spirit." Think of St. Elizabeth of Hungary, and our own Elizabeth, the first native-born American saint, Mother Seton, both of whose lives literally represent a story of riches to rags in the worldly sense, but rags to riches in the lasting sense.

"Blest too are the sorrowing: they shall be consoled." St. Rita of Cascia bore the cross 18 years of a husband who was dissolute, and who mistreated her. Her two sons had learned to imitate their father's ways. Rita was able to save all three; in fact, each one died in her arms reconciled to God.

"Blest are the lowly." St. Vincent de Paul was kidnapped and enslaved. After his escape he ministered to slaves, to prisoners, to the ignored of this world: widows, the aged, the orphaned, the poor. A dying king of France begged him to come to help him die, and all modern social service can be traced to his efforts.

"Blest are they who hunger and thirst for holiness; they shall have their fill." Thomas Aquinas, one of the most brilliant minds who ever lived, eventually experienced God so really that he dismissed all his theological masterpieces, before which the world still stands in awe, as so much "straw."

"Blest are they who show mercy . . ." As a nurse during World War I, Bertilla Bouscardin used to move among the wounded soldiers as an angel of mercy during shellings and bombardments. In 1952 she was raised to the honors of the altar by Pius XII.

"Blest are the single-hearted . . ." Maria Goretti, hardly 12 years old, was stabbed to death in 1902 by a 20 year-old youth when she resisted his advances with the single-hearted plea: "It is a sin. God does not want it." In 1950 her mother, then in her 88th year, was present at her canonization.

"Blest too the peacemakers . . ." Think of Peter Claver meeting the slave boats alone year after year in Colombia, to minister to them with food, medicine and grace; to atone for "white man's crime."

"Blest are the persecuted for holiness' sake . . ." Think of Isaac Jogues, the North American Martyr, who after being tortured by the Mohawks, returned to serve them, only to be slain by them.

The saints are blest because they lived these Beatitudes. They gave the Beatitudes highest priority in their lives. With God's help, they maintained this priority. So can we—if we try.

SOLEMNITY OF THE IMMACULATE CONCEPTION (8 December)

Mary, Immaculately Conceived

Genesis 3:9-15, 20; Ephesians 1:3-6, 11-12; Luke 1:26-38

Aim: to explain (1) the dogma of the Immaculate Conception; and (2) its meaning for all human beings.

Today's First Reading, from Genesis, constitutes the drama of the beginnings of original sin. In it we are given a hint as to the opposition between Eve's descendant and Satan—the first implicit reference to the promised Redeemer, Jesus. Today's Gospel is the story of Mary's election by God to be the mother of the Redeemer, Christ our Lord. And the Second Reading, from Ephesians, is a profound revelation as to how God elected Mary—and us, too,—from all eternity.

"As to how God elected Mary"—there's a key phrase to ponder today. That Mary was from the first moment of her conception preserved free from original sin, in view of the foreseen merits of her Son, Jesus, and because of the redemption wrought by him (which is what today's dogma means), was an act of God's free will. All righteousness is God's gift, which no human being, howsoever extraordinary, could acquire for himself or herself.

As Pope John Paul II said in an Angelus message on 8 December 1978:

"Hail, full of grace." What do these words mean? The Evangelist

Luke writes that Mary (Miriam), at these words spoken by the Angel, "was greatly troubled . . . , and considered in her mind what sort of greeting this might be" (Lk 1:29).

"These words," Pope John Paul II once explained in an Angelus address, "express a singular election. Grace means a particular fullness of creation through which the being, who resembles God, participates in God's own interior life. Grace means love and the gift of God himself, the completely free gift ("given gratuitously") in which God entrusts to man his Mystery, giving him, at the same time, the capacity of being able to bear witness to the Mystery, of filling with it his human being, his life, his thoughts, his will and his heart" (From *Osservatore Romano*, English Edition, 11 May 1978).

Mary's election was of course unique. She alone was called to be Mother of the Incarnate Word; for this, God graced her with freedom from original sin from her very origins. But Mary's election and ours both belong to the same mystery of God's love that of the Redemption. By preserving Mary from sin, God wished to show us that we too could be freed from sin. And although our freedom occurs after our birth through the rebirth of baptism, both what happened to Mary, and what happens to us, reflect God's overwhelming, gracious love for mankind.

Too, the Immaculate Conception is a sign of God's fidelity. Karl Rahner argued, in his *Mary, Mother of the Lord*, that God, once having given the beginning of holiness to our blessed Lady, undoubtedly had her glorification in view. So, too, as regards man in general: having bestowed his forgiveness, God will be faithful, in the logical consequence of forgiveness freely granted; which means that to all men God has, in principle, pledged eternal glory. Because of the Immaculate Conception, we have "become the blessed prisoners of God's fidelity . . . because (we) always move into the limitless domains that are his" (*Ibid*).

Today, therefore, is a day of celebration not only for Mary's privilege, but for us—for *all* human beings. For whatever God wills for one human being—Mary—God also wills for all human beings.

THE ASSUMPTION OF THE BLESSED VIRGIN MARY (VIGIL MASS)

On The Assumption and Us

Chronicles 15:3:4, 15, 16; 16:1-2; First Corinthians 15:54-57; Luke 11:27-28

Aim: to explain that Mary is a "sign" as to how God deals with us.

In today's First Reading, we are reminded of the Ark of the Covenant, a mysterious chest in which the tablets of the Ten Commandments and other holy items of the Old Testament were kept. To the Israelites, it was a sign of God's presence. When Jerusalem and the Temple were destroyed by Babylonian invaders around 587 B.C., the Ark of the Covenant disappeared. It has never been seen since—in *this* world, that is. The Ark of the Covenant is now seen only in heaven. Thus the Apostle, in a vision, writes:

"Then God's temple in heaven opened and in the temple could be seen the Ark of the Covenant . . ." (11:17).

Mary, the Mother of the Lord, is invoked in the Litany of Loreto as the Ark of the New Covenant. Gone from this world, she (to borrow a beautiful thought from Monsignor Ronald Knox's *Pastoral Sermons*), is seen again, but now she is seen in heaven.

Nowhere in Christian literature or art can one find an authoritative reference to Mary's tomb or grave. And although churches and shrines dedicated to her are countless throughout the world, none has ever responsibly maintained possession of her relics.

The Church's faith that Mary was assumed into heaven is an ancient faith. In theological language, today's liturgy emphasizes that Mary the Mother of the Lord, after her pilgrimage of faith in this life was completed, was assumed—taken up bodily—into heaven. This woman's flesh, from which Jesus, the Son of God made man, was taken, was not allowed by God to return to dust in an earthly tomb. This, again, is what the Assumption means in theological language.

To understand what the Assumption means *for us*, it is necessary to emphasize that Mary's role in Salvation History is what theology calls a "sign" role. Mary indicates what God has in store for all persons who respond in love to his election by hearing his word and keeping it—as today's Gospel explains.

Like Mary, therefore, we too are called by God to be exalted. This flesh of ours, this mortal flesh, is destined to share in Christ's victory over death—which St. Paul writes about in today's Second Reading. This is what the Assumption means for us.

Thus, when we say, in the Creed of Mass, "We look for the resurrection of the dead," we know that God can never go back on his word to make this word come true of us. For already there is one human being, albeit the perfect human being, Mary, who is already assumed in the flesh. And what God has in store for one human being, he has in store for all.

Mary the Mother of Jesus was blessed in a unique way, of course. She alone was chosen to be Mother of the Word Incarnate. But in her election and in her exaltation all humanity was meant by God to share. Today's Gospel makes the point that in the final analysis it is in our spiritual relationship to Jesus—through faith, hope and love—that our election in God is perfectly realized, and that our glorification is assured.

On this Solemnity of Mary we pray that she might help us understand, appreciate and live this truth.

THE ASSUMPTION OF THE BLESSED VIRGIN MARY
(Mass during the Day)

Mary Assumed, and We

Revelation 11:19, 12:1-6, 10; First Corinthians 15:20-26; Luke 1:39-56

Aim: to explain the meaning of Mary's Assumption and its relevance to us.

The doctrine of Our Lady's Assumption is reflected in Scripture implicitly rather than explicitly. So that the texts indicating that Mary was taken up bodily into heaven are (1) those which tell us that she was a uniquely privileged person—a creature who alone was "full of grace" (today's Gospel for instance), and (2) those which teach us that the flesh will resurrect and be glorified (today's Second Reading is a classic example).

To hold that a truth is implicitly revealed is not saying that it is simply a theological conclusion drawn from a major premise from the Bible, together with a minor premise from reason.

No; a Biblical implication results from searching the Scriptures and "putting two and two together." Theologian Bernard Lonergan makes this point well in his *Collections* (Herder and Herder, 1967).

Take St. Luke's story about the two disciples returning home to Emmaus on the first Easter Sunday (24:13-35). As they walked along, they evidenced sadness of Jesus' passion and death. Then a stranger appeared—Jesus himself, whom they failed to recognize. Slowly, he began to "put two and two together" for them, by citing the Old Testament messianic prophecies. Finally they began to see more deeply into the prophecies than they had ever seen before; and realized, for the first time, that the mystery of the suffering and crucified Lord is contained within the Old Testament.

This is how the Assumption of Our Lady is revealed in Scripture.

Thus we find out about the Assumption by first rereading Genesis and the story of Adam's fall. Then we study texts like today's Second Reading, and those passages wherein Jesus is set forth as the new Adam who will conquer death and bring all men to immortal life in the flesh.

Next, we study texts relevant to Mary, such as today's Gospel, and consequently view her as a person of unique privilege. She is "blessed among women" (Lk 1:42); to be invoked as "blessed by all generations" (Lk 1:48); and again, "full of grace." Then we review Genesis 3:16, wherein a woman is said to crush the head of the serpent (i.e., evil), and visions such as today's Second Reading.

Here we ask such questions as: Can we admit that Mary was free of the dominion of sin (which is clear from the Bible), yet not free of the dominion of death (which after all is but a consequence of sin—a fact which is revealed)? Or: Can one call Mary "full of grace" and deny that the Assumption is a grace?

Our conclusion will be that, as England's great poet, Francis Thompson sang in *Assumpta Maria*, if Mary were not assumed into heaven, heaven would have been assumed to her—so deep was God's love for her.

What does the Assumption mean in practical, everyday, language? Simply, that Mary is a sign of how God deals with us— with you and me. Like Mary, we too are destined for glory before God. Moreover, like Mary, our flesh will one day be glorified, as Mary's flesh is now glorified. The Assumption of Our Lady means that what happened to Mary is meant to happen to us.

CYCLE B

FIRST SUNDAY
OF ADVENT (B)

Preparing for the Lord's Coming

Isaiah 63:16-17, 19; 64:2-7; First Corinthians 1:3-9; Mark 13:33-37

Aim: (1) to contrast commercial preparations for Christmas with our spiritual Advent preparation; (2) to encourage prayer, penance, Advent devotions, Bible reading.

In today's first Bible lesson, from Deutero-Isaiah—the Second Isaiah (about the sixth century B.C.)—the prophet cries aloud for divine intervention, specifically for a manifestation of God more wondrous than his appearance to Moses atop Mt. Sinai. God alone saves wretched humanity; God alone can make man wholesome and clean and hopeful for the future; so we acknowledge in the responsorial psalm.

What a meaningful Advent theme this prophecy is: a theme played upon again by St. Paul, in his First Letter to Corinth (today's second Bible lesson); and again by Mark, recording Jesus' warning us always to be ready for his Second Coming (today's Gospel). "Be constantly on the watch!" our divine Lord tells us.

Advent has to do with waiting, of course. The word "advent" derives from the Latin for "coming," and implies a kind of arrival for which a welcome is due—like the arrival of an invited guest for dinner.

Advent, in other words, is a special season of anticipation: (1) anticipation of yet another Christmas, the annual commemoration of God's being born among men, at Bethlehem; (2) anticipation of Christ's coming again to this world, though not as an infant, but as Lord of Lords and King of Kings; and (3) anticipation of Christ's being born anew in our hearts through a revivified eucharistic encounter, especially on Christmas Day. The purpose of this season then is primarily spiritual, not material.

In fact, an overemphasis on Christmas shopping and Advent partying can undermine the spiritual anticipation which lies at the heart of Advent.

In some parts of the world, such as the Northern parts of America and Europe, Advent coincides with a drear, cold season of the year; the coincidence helps us reflect. Thus, the world seems grey (spelled with the "e," not even with the "a," so as to exclude more light). And it is rather a melancholy time, ushered in not only by the weather (cold or rainy) but everywhere in the world it is also the beginning of the close of a long year, a year almost worn out, as it were. And beginnings of ends are usually reflective times, occasions for pondering.

Thus Advent comes at an opportune moment, a time to reflect, prayerfully, on what Christmas really means, and to prepare for a good Christmas.

Reflect on what? One thought we could ponder is how drear and dismal our world would still be without Bethlehem; how every December would really be an ending, not only of a year, but of all our hopes.

A second thought might be how empty our own hearts might be without our faith in the living Lord Jesus, in whom we have been baptized into a new birth, and through whose Precious Blood we have been ransomed from our sins. To us who believe, doesn't Advent essentially mean going to Confession—approaching the Sacrament of Reconciliation—with renewed fervor, and receiving our divine Lord at Christmas Mass with freshly intensified devotion?

Shouldn't we begin to make preparations now to make sure that this melancholy season of anticipation is not lost forever— preparations including some self-penance and a renewal of commitment to the Sacraments of Penance and the Eucharist?

SECOND SUNDAY
OF ADVENT (B)

Simplicity and Prayer in Our Lifestyle

Isaiah 40:1-5, 9-11; Second Peter 3:8-14; Mark 1:1-8

Aim: (1) to describe the desert as the place of simple pioneer, quiet, prayerful living; (2) to encourage preparing for the Lord in our desert.

Today's Advent readings—all three of them—focus on the absolute necessity of our readying ourselves for the Christ-event by penance and contrition. And this message, prophesied by Isaiah of old, echoed by St. Mark, in the first written Gospel (Peter's Gospel, in a sense, since Mark was Peter's companion and scribe) is summed up in the person and preaching of John the Baptizer.

Baptizer often seems preferable to *Baptist*. Our Bible translations give both. In contemporary English, the *izer* nouns are frequently more active than the *ist* nouns. *Baptist* can sound rather passive. There was nothing passive about Zechariah's son; he was fiery zeal personified.

And so was his preaching. "Make ready the way of the Lord," he proclaims. "Clear him a straight path."

John's preaching, too, was—still is, of course—a summons, about which there is also nothing passive. His words are like whipcords; they sting. Phrases like "You brood of vipers" electrify us. We shudder when we hear him say that our penance has not been penance enough, but that more is needed. He makes us ashamed of ourselves—the little we have done, the little we do. But, as Monsignor Ronald Knox once observed, John was a bulldozer, and bulldozers aren't subtle. His business was to help us steamroller the rough roads.

John learned his vocation and acquired the wisdom for his preaching in the simplicity and hardships of a desert experience. Away from the artificial lights and the empty noises of a world wrapped up within itself, he was able to ponder the Scriptures and pray without external distractions, and thus learn to see the divine light and to hear God's voice in this world. Too, we are told that he fasted; he took means to ensure that his hunger for material food did not distract him from becoming aware of a deeper hunger still, a hunger we all experience but sometimes tend to deny; namely, a yearning for the substantial bread of the soul which only God can provide.

"Make ready the way of the Lord. Clear him a straight path." We can establish desert experiences like John the Baptizer's in our small worlds this Advent. We can turn off the television, for example, especially when it is just empty noise, and no more. We can seek to avoid, inasmuch as possible, the artificial lights: stores accenting the commercialization of Christmas—especially on Sundays—in order to give ourselves time to search with the real light of faith into the inner recesses of our souls, thereby preparing for a good confession. The fact is that we all have little areas that we would rather not search out; didn't St. Augustine admit, in his *Confessions*, that he once dared to pray, "Lord, make me chaste, but not yet?"

The divine-gift giver, Jesus, has already pledged to embrace us with forgiveness; repentance is the attitude by means of which his encounter with us can only be realized.

Desert-like simplicity and prayer can help us experience the vision today's Second Reading places before our eyes:

"What we await are new heavens and a new earth, where, according to his promise, the justice of God will reside. So, beloved, while waiting for this, make every effort to be found without stain or defilement, and at peace in his sight."

Again, there is nothing passive about Christianity.

THIRD SUNDAY
OF ADVENT (B)

How Christ Comes into Our Lives

Isaiah 61:1-2, 10-11; First Thessalonians 5:16-24; John 1:6-8,19-28

> *Aim: (1) to show that Jesus Christ comes to us in many ways; through the word, especially in the Sacraments of the Church; (2) to encourage Penance and Communion as making for a holy Christmas and a true Christian life.*

Today's First Reading, from the second part of the Old Testament Book of Isaiah, is the Bible text which Jesus himself chose to read one day in a synagogue at Nazareth.

On that occasion, recorded in Luke's Gospel (4:18 ff.), Jesus was asked to read the Scriptures. He stood up, opened the scroll to Isaiah 61, and began to read where today's First Reading begins:

"The Spirit of the Lord God is upon me, because the Lord has anointed me; He has sent me to bring glad tidings to the lowly, to heal the brokenhearted."

St. Luke also records Jesus' sermon after he finished the Isaiah text. In this sermon, Christ said: "Today this Scripture passage is fulfilled in your hearing. . ." (4:21).

The Second Isaiah, in today's first lesson (written in the sixth century before the first Christmas) is searching for a key to the mystery of man and the universe. The priests and Levites who went to

St. John the Baptizer in today's Gospel were searching too for a key. John said he was not the key. But, he added, he was the precursor of the key.

I use the word "key" because the Book of Isaiah, in another passage, prophesies this about the Christ:

"I will place the key of the House of David on his shoulder; when he opens, no one shall shut; when he shuts, no one shall open" (22:22).

The Book of Isaiah foretold only that at some time in the future the family of David would again emerge gloriously in the person of one who could finally unlock the dark, cold, labyrinth-like prison cells of human existence. The key of David would be a person with answers, *ultimate* and practical answers, to the great enigmas of life and death.

If there is any one aspect of Advent today that parallels closely the reality of human existence during the long centuries spanning the Sin of Adam to the Cave of Bethlehem, it is the dimension of quest. As yesterday, every mature man who thinks is still engaged in a life-and-death search, a pilgrimage of the heart reaching out for answers to life's most basic questions such as, "Who am I?" "What is my origin and destiny?" "What must I do to achieve my identity and fulfill my purpose?"

Inevitably, if we are true to ourselves, the quest will impel us to ask questions of modern day prophets such as those asked of John the Baptizer in today's Gospel; inevitably the quest will engender a holy curiosity that will draw us to the Church's word and its preachers.

Philosophers, those men who probe life's problems to the depths of human wisdom, can only lead us so far. In this pilgrimage, Revelation alone can give us the keys we seek at the most fundamental levels of existence. Moreover, Revelation alone can provide absolute certainty.

By the graciousness of God, moreover, the key to ultimate wisdom is not reserved exclusively for the most intellectual or sophisticated of men. On the contrary, it is provided to lowly and mighty alike. In plain language, the key to God's wisdom, the key to the secrets of life, are provided to *me*—to *you* and *me*. The key is Jesus, pointed to with a plea for repentance, by John the Baptizer.

We find Jesus in his Church, in the sacraments. But this means the sacraments sincerely experienced. Advent is an opportune time to ready ourselves to receive Penance and the Eucharist more sincerely, and thereby to find, for ourselves, the basic answers—the keys—to existence.

Our faith is that a true human life is a true Christian life. The principal key, once again, is Christ, whom we find and embrace in the Sacraments of Penance and the Eucharist.

FOURTH SUNDAY
OF ADVENT (B)

The Meaning of Messiah

Second Samuel 7:1-5, 8-11, 16; Romans 16:25-27; Luke 1:26-28

Aim: (1) to explain the word Messiah and the Messianic Prophecies; (2) to show Jesus as the Messiah, fulfilling the Old Testament Prophecies.

Prophecies, like deep, bass chords on an organ, vibrate to rest in today's Gospel, St. Luke's simple yet awesome account of the annunciation: what Catholic doctrine describes as the virginal conception of Jesus, in the womb of Mary of Nazareth.

And as Old Testament prophecies are fulfilled—today's text from Second Samuel, for instance, promising that the house of David, Jesus' house, would emerge into an eternal kingdom—an entirely new world is begun. A fresh creation is inaugurated.

It is not by chance that the first key word of the Gospel is the same as the first key word of the Old Testament: that word is *beginning*. Just as the world and man were created by God in the first creation, so through Jesus, born of the race of Adam and Eve, God would re-create the world and man.

This is why Jesus was virginally conceived; namely, to emphasize that God was giving us all a fresh start, and a new covenant.

This is why, too, it apppears, that Mary the Mother of Jesus was visited by the Archangel Gabriel in her town of Nazareth. Nazareth is never mentioned in the Old Testament. Bethlehem, yes; Jerusalem, of course. But Nazareth is a fresh name; it emerges as something entirely new, pointing to an entirely new world.

Finally, this is why Gabriel was chosen to tell Mary of her divine election. He was the angel who, in a famous passage in the Old Testament Book of Daniel (chs. 7, 8, 9) foretold the end of the old covenant and the anointing of a most holy one—the Messiah—who would "ratify" all former prophesies, and "introduce" a new and everlasting Kingdom.

The word *Messiah* is a Hebrew derivative; it means "the anointed." In Greek, "the anointed" translates into *Christos,* from which our English word "Christ" comes. "Christ" therefore means "the anointed one." the Messiah.

Throughout the Old Testament individuals inspired and authorized to speak for God—prophets—fired and kept alive the hope of future salvation to be accomplished by an anointed king of the family of David. Even such details as the place of the Messiah's birth—Bethlehem—were foretold by the prophets, who gradually unfolded the divine secret in their utterances and writings—a fact to which St. Paul, in today's Second Reading, alludes.

This Messiah, this Christ, is of course, God-made-man, Jesus of Nazareth, the Eternal Word of God, born of the Virgin Mary. He is the fulfillment of all the prophecies pointing to the Savior of the world; he is the one anointed by God to reconcile sinful man with God.

Born of the Virgin Mary, he is the one who re-creates the world and gives us all a new beginning, regardless of our past. All, that is, who acknowledge him as Lord in loving repentance and believe the Good News he announces to the world.

Like Mary, in today's Gospel we have all found favor with God through Jesus, her Son, our brother. In him we *can* begin anew, no matter how far behind we have fallen in our religious life, no matter how poorly we have lived the life of grace given us.

Clearly, this is an overriding theme of the Advent season: in Jesus we have a Messiah, a Savior, who grants us a new start. As Christmas approaches, we are reminded that God has willed to take away our past—*my* past—and to allow *me* to begin anew in his merciful love.

FIRST SUNDAY
OF LENT (B)

Lent and Self-Discipline

Genesis 9:8-15; First Peter 3:18-22; Mark 1:12-15

Aim: to show that we also are (1) strengthened by overcoming temptation; (2) strengthened by self-imposed hardships.

When the world was first destroyed at the time of Noah (today's first Reading), God permitted a remnant of mankind to survive; the name "Noah" derives from the same Hebrew root as the word for "remnant."

As a sign of his covenant with Noah and his successors, God pointed to the rainbow. For the ancients, the bow, without an arrow, was a sign not of war, but of mercy. By pointing to the rainbow, God was expressing his mercy.

We, of course, are part of the People of God upon whom God showered mercy. The remnant who survived the flood are our ancestors in salvation history; their story became the foundation for the New Covenant, the New Testament, in which we live. As they were saved from the waters of the flood, so we are saved (as today's Second Reading recalls) by the waters of baptism. This is of course the deepest theological meaning of the rainbow.

In today's Gospel we see Jesus of Nazareth inaugurating the New Testament with the statement which the liturgy uses as an alternate form as ashes are placed on our foreheads on Ash Wednesday, the beginning of Lent: "Reform your lives and believe in the good news." ("Turn away from sin and be faithful to the Gospel.") According to Mark, the first of the Gospel writers, these words were spoken by our Lord after his temptation by Satan in the desert.

Are we not invited to consider that, and how, we can be strengthened by life's "desert" moments, as well as by the experience of having sucessfully overcome temptation?

Jesus' reply to the first temptation was, "Not on bread alone." Don't we discover, through corporal fasting, what spiritual hunger really is? And by this discovery are we not strengthened to resist the need for material bread as an end in itself instead of simply a means?

Satan's second temptation was one of tempting God: presuming that God will jump to do our needs, as it were, especially by miracles. Hardships, voluntary (such as fasting) or imposed (such as illness) but borne with resignation, strengthen us to accept the truth that sets us free.

Satan's third temptation was an attempt to subordinate God's Kingdom to the kingdoms of this world. Again, it is only when we withdraw (momentarily, even, as during Lent) that we can acquire a realistic perspective regarding earthly kingdoms and how they cannot endure, cannot fulfill. So that, again, our vision is strengthened by our "putting some distance" between ourselves and this passing world.

As children of Noah, we have seen God withhold the arrow from the bow, as a sign of his mercy. To experience this sign in our lives, a retreat into the desert of Lent is most helpful.

The symbol of the beginning of this retreat has been that of the ashes of Ash Wednesday, a symbol dating from the early Church. Thus four truths are kept clearly before our minds: our mortality, our humility as creatures, our need for contrition, and our need for repentance.

God grant us the perseverance to live by this symbol for the next forty days.

SECOND SUNDAY OF LENT (B)

Transfiguration: How to Understand Jesus

Genesis 22:1-2, 9, 10-13, 15-18; Romans 8:31-34; Mark 9:2-10

Aim: (1) to show Jesus in the Gospels as human but also divine; (2) to explain the Church's definition of Jesus as possessing a divine and human nature; (3) to stress the need for unreserved faith in God through Jesus Christ our Lord.

God saved Abraham's son from death; so today's First Reading reminds us. But, as Paul recalls in today's Second Reading, the Father did not spare his own Son, the Eternal Word, from death. Jesus, whose identification with the Father's glory is revealed so clearly in the Transfiguration event (today's Gospel), must carry a cross to the death.

Isaac, whose sacrifice was aborted, prefigured Jesus, the Son of God incarnate. We learn this from St. Paul's Epistle to the Galatians (3:16).

Why, we ask, did Abraham unhesitatingly follow God's command to take Isaac's life? Surely it was because Abraham believed that God is powerful enough to bring Isaac back from death.

Isaac of course did not die. At the last moment, God stayed Abraham's sacrificing hand. This happened because, again, Isaac was the forerunner of Christ. As the early Church Fathers loved to emphasize (e.g., Tertullian), the real sacrifice was to occur later, in Jesus. Incidentally, concerning that curious reference to the wood on Abraham's altar Genesis tells us that Isaac carried it there: the Church Fathers used to see in this a beautiful allusion to Jesus' carrying the wood of his cross to the altar of Calvary.

Spiritually, we are children of Abraham; in the Roman Canon we speak of him as "our Father in faith." But we know, as he did not, that faith in God is faith in Jesus. Abraham knew that God is so powerful that he can bring the dead back to life. But Abraham did not know that God's only Son, Jesus, would conquer death by his own sacrificial death, foretold in the Isaac event, and, risen from the tomb, would live forever in our midst.

Jesus, we believe, is true God *and* true man, as we affirm in the Creed of Mass. Like ourselves, he walked and slept and ate and wept. But this Person, Jesus, who lived a fully human life, is the Second Person of the Blessed Trinity, whose glory was seen atop the Mount of the Transfiguration.

Jesus, we profess, is not only the supreme teacher and perfect model for man; Jesus is God-made-man, Lord and Savior, sent by the Father for our salvation. The Person born of Mary at Bethlehem is therefore the only Person who ever had a prehistory. Though Jesus began in time as a human being, he is without beginning as Son of God. Before his earthly existence, Jesus *is* God, existing from all eternity. The Person who is Jesus Christ did not begin to be at Bethlehem; rather, the Person who is Jesus Christ never *began to be*; he *is* from all eternity. He is God. A glimpse of his divinity is seen atop the Mount of the Transfiguration.

Abraham never knew about the Transfiguration. Yet *how he believed!* What of *us*, who have seen what Abraham and the prophets longed to see.

As we recall Abraham's faith in the Eucharistic Prayer today (we shall use the old Roman Canon), we shall make an attempt to intensify our faith commitment in the risen, living Lord Jesus.

THIRD SUNDAY
OF LENT (B)

Redemption through the Passion of Christ

Exodus 20:1-17; First Corinthians 1:22-25; John 2:13-25

Aim: (1) to describe the Passion of Christ as Christ's willing acceptance of sufferings; (2) to show this attitude of Christ as our model for living.

All four Gospels record Jesus' driving the money-changers from the Temple; today's account is from St. John's Gospel.

Jesus' action, the Gospel notes, prompted his disciples to remember the psalm, "Zeal for your house consumes me" (69:10). This psalm appears more often in the New Testament than any other, and always refers to the coming Messiah—the Christ. In fact, the Old Testament prophet Zechariah had prophesied that the Messiah would cleanse the Temple and render it pure again (14:21).

Thus, for anyone at the time who knew the Scriptures, as they should have (and as *we* should), Jesus' driving the money-changers from the sanctuary—a dramatic act—was a sign that he was the promised Messiah who would redeem Israel.

Jesus was repeatedly asked for signs of his mission, as St. Mark's Gospel (8:11) reminds us; "Give us a sign," was a recurring demand. St. Paul recalls, in today's Second Reading, that this question continued to be asked in post-Resurrection times. "Jews demand 'signs,' " he writes, "and Greeks look for wisdom" a reference to Greek philosophies and their intricate arguments.

The sign that Christ gave to the money-changers was the supreme sign of his commitment to be the Suffering Servant of God: the sign of the Cross from which his conquest of death was achieved. The same sign is given today to those who challenge the Christian premise.

To many of Jesus' nation who were looking for a Messiah to lead a crusade against Rome and to initiate a new political empire centered in Jerusalem, the sign that Jesus gave was incomprehensible. Later, at his trial, some were to interpret Jesus' words in today's Gospel simply in material terms, as if he were speaking simply about the stones of the Temple.

What Christ meant, of course, was that he was about to lay down his life to create a new holy People of God, a living Temple not of stones, *but of people*, called to follow him through suffering service to eternal life: a mystical Body more glorious and lasting than Jerusalem's magnificent sanctuary.

When we follow God's law—reflected in the Ten Commandments, today's First Reading—we are in effect following Jesus with the psalmist's words, "Zeal for your house consumes me." Our house, again, is Jesus' Mystical Body, the Church, which he bought by his Passion, Death and Resurrection. As his disciples, we strive to remain worthy of membership in this Body through a commitment to suffering service in his name, knowing that this wisdom—his wisdom—is the only true wisdom, although it is seen either as a scandal or foolishness by the world of unbelievers.

When we say that the wisdom of the Cross and Resurrection is the only true wisdom in the light of observing God's commandments, we mean this concretely. Thus, in our effort to follow Christ in this world we should not be surprised to discover that there will occur agonizing moral situations to which there is literally no other answer but to kneel and embrace the Cross of Jesus. Despite the contradictions of a confused and often errant world, kneeling and embracing the Cross *is* an answer; and, in the long run, the only enduring one.

FOURTH SUNDAY
OF LENT (B)

The Meaning of the Crucifix

Chronicles 36:14-17, 19-23; Ephesians 2:4-10; John 3:14-21

Aim: (1) to explain the familiar crucifix; (2) to encourage its understanding as a constant reminder of God's love and of our reconciliation with God.

The raised, bronze serpent, referred to by Jesus in today's Gospel, is what Christian Tradition calls a "type." A type is a person, object, or event in Old Testament history that mysteriously points to the New Testament. In a sense, it is a dim prophesy about the future.

Christ in today's Gospel, had in mind, an Old Testament incident found in the Book of Numbers, 21:4-9. During a plague of poisonous serpents in the desert, Moses raised on high the symbol of a bronze serpent; simply by looking at it, the Israelites were cured. In today's Gospel, Jesus tells us that Moses' bronze serpent prefigured, or was a "type," of himself. Specifically, it foreshadowed Jesus crucified, bearing the burden of the sins of the world, represented by the serpent.

This sign was intensely loved by the early Church Fathers. Tertullian, the second century lawyer-apologist, wrote:

"Why is it that when all images had been forbidden, Moses should provide as an object of salvation the brazen serpent lifted up like a man on a cross? Surely it was because he saw in it the power of the

Lord's cross, which revealed the Devil as a mere serpent, and all who were bitten by spiritual serpents; and at the very same time proclaimed the cure of these wounds of sin and salvation to all who looked upon it."

There is an apparent paradox here, of course; namely, that in the sign of our serpentine evil, we should also see the sign of God's love. But our faith is replete with paradoxes. Today's First Reading is an example; Cyrus the Great, though a pagan conqueror, was allowed by God to be the instrument of God's mercy to his Chosen People, an overpowering mercy, concerning which Paul writes in today's Second Reading.

To look upon the Cross of Jesus, therefore, is to see the ugliness of our sins. Contemplating it, we see what our sin can do. Perhaps we have grown too used to looking at a crucifix, so much so that we have begun to forget its real meaning. Lent is an opportune time to contemplate the Cross of Christ as a stark reminder of sin—again, *my* sin—as disease and death.

At the same time, however, like the bronze serpent Moses raised, the Crucifix is a sign of healing and reconciliation. To look at a Crucifix is not only to stare at the ugliness of sin, but also to see—in the most concrete form possible—the enduring sign of God's love and mercy for *me, a sinner.*

That we might not succumb forever to the serpentine evil with which we have been infected, the Word of God made flesh, Jesus of Nazareth, ascended to the cross for us—out of love for us, as St. Paul reminds us in today's Second Reading.

Lent is an opportune time to get to know the Crucifix in our lives. Surely there should be a representation of the cross of Jesus in our homes, in some prominent place, so that it will be noticed, at least, every day. And when it is noticed, some prayer should spontaneously come to our hearts, a prayer acknowledging what my sin has done, and thanking God for being so merciful to me, a sinner. A good way to start this devotion is by contemplating the crucifix on our Rosary for a few minutes daily, perhaps before retiring.

7

FIFTH SUNDAY
OF LENT (B)

Dying to Sin

Jeremiah 31:31-34; Hebrews 5:7-9; John 12:20-33.

Aim: to show (1) that sin, though it presents itself as attractive, is nonetheless heinous; (2) that we must eliminate sin from life by dying to self in the footsteps of Jesus the Suffering Servant of the Lord.

Today's First Reading is from Jeremiah. His obedience to God's will under hardship foretold Jesus' obedient suffering service, summarized in today's Second Reading, from the Epistle to the Hebrews. Jesus buried himself perfectly within his Father's will.

This relates quite beautifully to today's Gospel, from John. Therein we read that a delegation of Greek-speaking individuals once sought an interview with our Lord. They went to Philip (because he had a Greek-sounding name?); Philip referred their request to Andrew, who arranged for the audience.

The question these Greeks put to our Lord is not recorded. (One theory is that they asked Christ to become a teacher in an academy, to be an intellectual leader, like Socrates or Aristotle, perhaps.)

If the question is not in the scriptures, Jesus' answer is. We just read it, in the Gospel: "I solemnly assure you, unless the grain of wheat falls to the earth and dies, it remains just a grain of wheat. But if it dies, it produces much fruit. The man who loves his life loses it, while the man who hates his life in this world preserves it to life eternal."

What priorities have we to assign the various activities and endeavors of a lifetime? To amass knowledge or friends? To secure the adulation of the crowds? To take from life everything we possibly can in the premise that to live here below is a one-time opportunity?

Jesus, who is Wisdom incarnate, tells us that supreme wisdom is to bury oneself in God's will so thoroughly that nothing else matters in life. To bury implies crucifixion, of course; at least the acceptance of suffering. Yet the person "who loves his life will lose it."

Obviously this means following God's law; avoiding sin, in other words, and if serious sin is committed, approaching the Sacrament of Reconciliation as soon as possible. We cannot fulfill our destinies as sons and daughters of the Eternal Father while sin separates us from him and his love.

Burying oneself in the divine will also means not living simply for ourselves, but for others; by trying to find Christ in others, especially those who are unconsulted or rejected.

Burying oneself in the divine will also means being instruments for Christ in grace: by witnessing to him for example, in our everyday conversation, as well as by our attending Sunday Mass. It also means avoiding not only sin—which is never right or good, which is always wrong and ugly—but also the occasions of sin; the persons, places or things which set the climate for temptations against God's will to emerge, albeit subtly.

Being a Christian then is discovering how our identity—my identity—can conform to Christ, without whom I have no meaning, or real life, or any future, through burying myself within him.

This is not impossible to do when we keep in mind, as today's Second Reading bids us, that Jesus, who went before us in this life, knows our plight as poor pilgrims wandering here below, and intercedes with the Father for us always.

PASSION (PALM) SUNDAY (B)

How to Spend Holy Week

Isaiah 50:4-7; Philippians 2:6-11; Mark 14:1-15:47.

Aim: to explain (1) the liturgical and (2) the personal observances of Holy Week in the life of a follower of Christ.

The first two Mass lessons today emphasize that Jesus came to serve, not to be served: to give his life as a ransom for us all. The First Reading is from the Second Isaiah's third Servant Hymn, which looks forward to the day when a mysterious Suffering Servant of the Lord would appear. In the Second Reading, Paul stresses that Jesus' suffering service even to the Cross ensured his exaltation as Lord.

In the Passion narrative this year, from Mark—we followed Jesus, the Suffering Servant of God as he fulfilled the Old Testament prophecies, giving up his life for us. And in the blessing (and procession) of the palms, we remembered and dramatized the Lord's entrance into Jerusalem to inaugurate the first Holy Week, when the events recounted in the Passion Narrative took place.

Today marks but the beginning of the most sacred week in the Church year, what we call Holy Week, the last three days of which constitute an inner sanctuary, known as the Paschal or Easter Triduum. ("Triduum" is a Latin derivative meaning "three days.") As Christians, we are invited to participate in the liturgy of this Triduum. The invitation is a graced privilege; the ceremonies are especially instructive and devotional.

The principal Holy Thursday parish liturgy is the afternoon or evening Mass of the Lord's Supper. Just before this Mass, Lent ends, and the Easter Triduum begins. The Eucharist is offered in white vestments. During the Gloria, the church bells are rung and the organ played for the last time until the Easter vigil. In the homily we are reminded of the three great Holy Thursday mysteries: the institution of the Eucharist, the institution of the New Testament priesthood, and the promulgation of Jesus' commandment to love one another as he loved us.

Following the Mass, a procession begins; the Holy Eucharist is borne by the celebrant to a place of reposition. For the remainder of the day—until midnight if possible—the faithful are invited to pray before the tabernacle-shrine in praise, joy and thanksgiving for the three mysteries recalled at Mass.

On Good Friday there is no Mass, but a beautiful afternoon or evening Communion service is enacted. Wearing red vestments, symbolic of Jesus' Precious Blood, the celebrant presides over (or reads) a series of three Bible lessons; the last ending with St. John's Passion account. The ancient Prayer of the Faithful comes next, then the Veneration of the Cross. Finally, Communion is distributed.

On Holy Saturday the Church in spirit waits at Christ's tomb and contemplates his death. With the first hour of evening, a magnificent vigil, anticipatory of the Easter Mass, commences in darkness. A new fire is struck and blessed. The Paschal Candle, signifying Jesus, the Light of the World, is blessed, lighted, and borne into the sanctuary, where the beautiful *Exsultet*, an ancient Easter Hymn, is proclaimed. A series of insightful Bible readings follows. Then the Gloria is intoned again, for the first time since Holy Thursday, and the bells ring loudly. The Gospel is the Easter story.

Following the homily, the parish baptismal water is blessed and, if scheduled, baptism administered. Next, everyone in the congregation, led by the celebrant, joins in the renewal of baptismal promises; then sprinkled with "Easter" water, reminiscent of baptism.

Make an effort this Holy Week to attend the liturgy. Being here in church to follow Jesus in prayer empowers us to follow him as suffering servants in the world: to help transform our lives, our families, our neighborhoods.

This is our most precious week. It sould not be wasted.

EASTER VIGIL(B)

Easter, the Greatest Christian Feast

Genesis 1:1-2:2; 22:1-18; Exodus 14:15-15:1; Isaiah 54:5-14; 55:1-11; Baruch 3:9-15; Ezekiel 36:16-28; Romans 6:3-11; Mark 16:1-8.

Aim: (1) to explain Easter as the fundamental Christian feast because Christ's resurrection is the reason for our faith, our joy, our hope.

Contemplate the Easter Candle burning here in the sanctuary; it is a symbol of Jesus, light of the world.

Earlier this evening, in darkness, we lit this Candle with new fire, and we carried it down the aisle of the church; during the procession we stopped to exclaim three times, "Christ, our light."

Later, we listened to a series of Old Testament readings. These prophetic texts were fulfilled when Jesus of Nazareth, the Son of God Incarnate, the promised Messiah, conquered death and sin by rising from the grave of Good Friday. And because Christ rose from the dead, all those who believe in him—all who accept him as Lord and are baptized—can experience freedom from sin and death. As St. Paul puts it in today's Epistle:

"His death was death to sin, once for all; his life is life for God. In the same way you must consider yourselves dead to sin but alive for God in Christ Jesus."

Easter—the Resurection of Jesus—means that all the Old Testament prophecies are true, that God exists, that he reveals himself in his own Son, Jesus of Nazareth, who, having assumed our guilt for sin, went to the Cross for us, rose from death, and now *lives,* intervenes in our lives, and awaits us at the close of earth's pilgrimage, to embrace us forever.

Easter is a day of faith, then, because we know that even though we cannot fully understand God's words, we know with absolute certainty that they are true, so true that we can fearlessly stake our lives on them. The words of the angel in the tomb refer to *us* in our belief: "Do not be frightened . . . He has been raised from the dead and now goes ahead of you. . ."

Thus founded on the rock of Jesus' Resurrection, our faith assures hope, and consequently, joy in living. For so many people who do not know Christ, the world is empty, a meaningless labyrinth, even a morgue. Easter—this Easter—the annual commemoration of the Resurrection of our Lord and Savior Jesus Christ from the dead—serves to remind men again that even the spiritually dead can rise to life: to a real consciousness of life's nature and goals. Easter can literally fire the forces of God-life within us again, can ignite relevancy; can burn away the stains of sin, the wounds of wrongdoings, the remnants of earthly, stupid attitudes consciously sought after or adhered to.

Easter is not just a date on a calendar, but a living event; Jesus is both the model and the efficient cause of our resurrection here and now, as well as at the hour of bodily death.

Life, after all, consists of many grades. Eternal life begins here below, now; our rising to God's summons today is, in effect, a will to live forever. Easter allows us to feel the breath of immortality so that we will be empowered to arise above our weakness, ignorance and wretchedness. In St. Paul's words to the Colossians:

"Since you have been raised up in company with Christ, set your heart on what pertains to higher realms where Christ is seated at God's right hand. . ." (3:1).

SECOND SUNDAY
OF EASTER (B)

Living Lives of Faith
in the Christian Community

Acts 4:32-35; First John 5:1-6; John 20:19-51.

*Aim: to describe (1) the ideal parish and Church, that
which we are trying to reach in faith.*

Faith in Jesus, the living Lord; a dynamic faith in Jesus, a faith
which impels us forward in this vale of tears, that draws us together
on this common pilgrimage, that allows us to see the goal ahead of us,
even though we do not fully understand: this, in summary, is the
grand theme of today's Bible readings.

Faith in Christ as Lord and God is the first and basic posture of
the Christian soul: faith that Jesus is God's own Son, sent for our
salvation and given us for our sanctification.

Faith means believing—believing unreservedly in God's word—
despite one's inability fully to understand. Faith can entail
difficulties, but difficulties should never be allowed to deteriorate
into doubts. A hundred thousand difficulties should never even add
up to a single doubt. Difficulties can be good for us; they can awaken
and sharpen our minds; they can test our commitment. But they
should never undermine our willingness and readiness to say, with
Thomas, "My Lord and My God."

Pope St. Gregory once said that our faith owes more to Thomas' problem in today's Gospel than to the faithfulness of all the other Apostles put together. For if it hadn't been for Thomas' questioning, we wouldn't have the ninth beatitude, enunciated by Jesus in behalf of those of us who do not see Christ present physically, yet believe nonetheless: "Blest are they who have not seen and have believed" (today's Gospel).

Three categories of immediate rewards for faith in Jesus are reflected in today's lessons. One is peace and pardon from sin: the Gospel affirms this in Jesus' words granting his first priests the power to forgive sins. A second encompasses freedom from fear and superstition. That faith bestows such freedom, is stressed in today's Second Reading, from John's First Letter.

A third reward of peace is outlined in today's First Reading, from Acts, the earliest inspired history of the Church. Therein we see the Christian community of faith depicted as a sign of fraternal charity.

It is faith in the risen living Lord, therefore, that is at the foundation of this parish, which can be described as the Church in miniature. We are gathered here today, for example, because every Sunday is a little Easter, the day, we believe, that Jesus, who is God, rose from the tomb and entered our lives with his Spirit. We are here primarily because we believe that God is here present in the assembly, in the word proclaimed and preached, and supremely in his Body and Blood, the Eucharist. We are here because we know that as we leave this Mass we will be strengthened to renew our practice of Christian principles throughout the week, to renew our attempts in Christ to help make our homes, our neighborhoods, our cities, better places for all.

As descendants of the first Christians depicted in today's First Reading, in faith we relate to one another, reach out to those here in need, and encourage each other by our prayers, witness, service, brotherhood.

In faith, we say. Without it, our parish would be simply an organization, not an organism alive with the life of Christ. With faith, God will not only bless our lives, but will—as today's First Reading pledges—add to our number those who are saved. Others will follow us if only we keep faith.

THIRD SUNDAY
OF EASTER (B)

The Bible in Our Lives

Acts 3:13-15, 17-19; First John 2:1-5; Luke 24:35-48.

Aim: to show (1) the meaning of Biblical inspiration; (2) the importance of the inspired Bible, in Church and at home; and (3) the importance of the teaching Church as interpreter of Sacred Scripture.

The reference in today's Gospel wherein we see the newly risen Savior dining with his Apostles on the lakeshore should whet our curiosity as to why it appears in the Bible. Why does the evangelist go out of his way to say that Jesus asked for food, and that his Apostles obliged with a piece of cooked fish, which, St. Luke carefully records, Jesus took and ate in their presence?

Is it really so significant, this reference? How slow of mind we sometimes are. Isn't everything in Scripture there for a reason?

A person who partakes of food is *alive*. Not dead; alive. This is the point of it all. It is the point of all today's readings, in fact. "God raised him from the dead," Peter says of Jesus in today's First Reading.

Jesus was dead. He had died on the cross on Good Friday. He had been buried in a tomb. But now risen, he appears to his disciples. Simply an apparition? A product of the Apostles' imagination? Do apparitions dine at table?

No wonder that the Apostles were so certain they had seen the risen Christ. This Jesus, the Lord who had died and was buried, now *dines* with them.

A Christian is one who believes with all his heart that Jesus *lives*— the risen Lord is present, here, now, really. He meets us in our lives, he inspires us, forgives us, guides us, awaits us, helps us.

We know all this from the Bible as it is read within our Church, to which the Scriptures were bestowed by Christ. Our faith is that God is the principal author of the Bible. The process by which God accomplished this is called "inspiration," meaning God's action in the composition of the various books of Scripture. Second Tm 3:16 tells us that all Scripture is inspired by God through his Spirit. The Epistle to Hebrews tells us that the Bible is "living and effective, sharper than any two-edged sword" (4:12). Because God is its principal author, the Bible is dynamic. Vatican II reminds us that Christ is really present in his word; "it is he himself who speaks when the holy Scriptures are read in the church" (*Constitution on the Sacred Liturgy*, No. 7). Because God is the author of the Bible, too, it is a graced word, effective of faith to anyone who opens his or her heart.

To know the living Lord better—to know his cleansing power, described in today's First and Second Readings—we must return to the Bible, not only here at Mass, but at home—family Bible reading in union with the Church, to which the Scriptures were conferred by God.

Faith generated through the Bible helps us dine with Jesus too— in this Eucharist, for it leads us to the knowledge that Christ *lives*. This is the reason why the second part of Mass, the Eucharistic Prayer by means of which Jesus becomes really present under the appearances of bread and wine, is preceded by Bible reading. Before we encounter Christ in the Eucharist, we confirm and nourish our faith in his Real Presence by listening to his living word.

FOURTH SUNDAY
OF EASTER (B)

Priestly and Religious Vocations for the Church

Acts 4:8-12; First John 3:1-2; John 10:11-18.

Aim: (1) to explain what a vocation to the priestly or religious life is, and (2) to encourage a positive response to such a vocation.

This is Good Shepherd Sunday; today's beautiful Gospel depicts Jesus carrying the one lost sheep, for which he is ready to die if need be.

One lesson we learn from today's liturgy is that whereas we are not saved in isolation—like sheep we tend to stray even in groups—neither are we saved (to use a common expression) "by the barrel load." God's love for us is personal; he carries each of us as he carries the one lost sheep; he knows *me*, and invites *me* to know him, personally.

Christ's personal approach is emphasized repeatedly in the Scriptures. Surrounded by crowds, remember, Christ was aware of the lone woman who touched his cloak (Mk 5:25-34). Jesus gave Nicodemus an audience at night, so that he might talk to him personally (Jn 3:1-21). Jesus waited at the well of Samaria to talk with that beautiful woman who came to draw water (Jn 4:4-42).

A good shepherd, Christ calls us all by name, as a Father calls his children, according to today's Second Reading. To this end the Good

Shepherd summons men—ordinary flesh and blood people—to follow in his footsteps: to exercise his personal care for souls now and until the end of this world, to minister in his name, as Peter stresses in today's First Reading. He configures these men to himself by sealing them with the sign of his own priesthood; by empowering them to prophesy, to renew his Eucharistic Sacrifice, and to forgive sins by his authority.

These men are the priests of the New Testament, ordained to minister God's word and grace. We pray for them especially today. We ask the Good Shepherd to protect them, to enlighten them, and to raise up others to take their place in manifesting Christ's personal concern for individuals everywhere. We likewise pray for the deacons of our Church, also ordained to minister at the altar and in our midst for Christ's sake.

Today, too, we pray for all those men and women who, by means of vowed commitment, collaborate with the eternal Good Shepherd in calling and caring for each sheep by name, lest any stray. Hence we pray for nuns and monks, cloistered in solemn vows; for Sisters and Brothers, vowed to the active apostolates in various congregations and communities. We pray for all engaged in Christ's ministry: lay missioners, for example, and catechists.

Prayer is the basic necessity. In the final analysis, the priesthood, diaconate and religious state are all faith-concepts, totally incomprehensible outside of reference to the Good Shepherd, Christ our Lord. And prayer is an affirmation of faith. As no one could accept Holy Orders unless he had faith; so no one could experience concern for priestly or religious vocations unless he or she believed sufficiently to pray: to pray to the Good Shepherd (Lk 10:2).

Specifically, our prayer should be that God might grace us by calling more men and women to his special service. It should also be that those whom God calls might be open to his invitation, accepting it with love. Finally, it should be that believers in general may encourage and facilitate, not discourage or impede, vocations to the ministry or vowed commitment.

FIFTH SUNDAY
OF EASTER (B)

Living in Christ

Acts 9:26-31; First John 3:18-24; John 15:1-8.

Aim: to show the importance of (1) imitating Jesus Christ and (2) living in Christ.

Today's Gospel is taken from Jesus' homily to his Apostles in the Upper Room on the first Holy Thursday. Its key lesson is that our faith involves life, eternal life, and that this life is found in Jesus, the true vine. St. Paul once wrote: "For to me, 'life' means Christ..." (Ph 1:21).

"I am the vine, you are the branches," Jesus said. Think about this metaphor. Don't we tend to view the vine as the basic reality, and that it was rather convenient that our Lord chanced either to see or to imagine a vine when he was explaining the mystery of life in union with him? Yet shouldn't we rather think the opposite; namely, that life in Christ through union with him is the fundamental reality, while vines are the metaphors, but shadows of the real substance?

Monsignor Ronald Knox, in one of his pastoral sermons, once made this very point; specifically, that for Jesus the vine was not the basic reality, but only a shadow. In other words, the unity of the Church is the basic reality; vines only exist because eons and eons ago in the divine mind the unity of all men living in Jesus was conceived by the Father.

To live in Christ is to remain in him, as today's beautiful Second Reading describes our existence; to live in Christ is to enjoy the consolation of the Holy Spirit as the early disciples depicted in today's First Reading enjoyed peace in fraternal charity.

Christ is the vine; we, the branches. Surely this means, first, that Christ is the efficient cause of all grace, or God-life. He is not simply a model of perfection, such as the artist contemplates or the poet sings of. No; all the holiness—God-life—which God has destined for us he has placed in his Christ. To touch God, therefore, we touch Christ. It is upon Christ's humanity that the ladder between heaven and earth dreamt of by Jacob in the Old Testament rests. Jesus himself told us that Jacob's ladder, upon which the angels ascend and descend, is his sacred humanity (Jn 1:51).

St. Augustine, interpreting today's Gospel, remarked that it is precisely as man that Christ is the vine. As God, one with the Father he is the vine dresser who labor interiorly to increase the divine life within our souls.

Concretely, how do we experience Christ's life pouring into us? How do we encounter Christ's Sacred Humanity, the cause of all God-life?

In this post-Pentecostal age, the Vine of which we are branches is Jesus' mystical body, the Church. In this Church our union with the eternal Vine is secured primarily through the seven infallible signs of God-life which Christ left us: the seven sacraments.

Each and every time we receive one of the sacraments, therefore, we either receive of Christ's life, or receive it more abundantly. This is especially true of the Eucharist, the sacrament of union with Christ par excellence, as Jesus told us (Jn 6:57).

Christ is the vine. Without him, nothing good is possible (Jn 15:5, Mt 8:2-3, Mk 7:32-35). We must believe in his name, as today's Second Reading insists—and love one another as he loved us.

SIXTH SUNDAY OF EASTER (B)

The Greatest Love, the Sacrifice of One's Life

Acts 10:25-26, 34-35, 44-48; First John 4:7-10; John 15:9-17.

Aim: to explain and encourage the virtue of love as (1) self-forgetfulness and (2) total dedication.

In Willa Cather's classic volume, *Death Comes for the Archbishop* (the story of Archbishop Jean Baptiste Lamy, the first bishop of Santa Fe, about whom Pulitzer Prize-winner Paul Horgan wrote a history in 1975), there is a scene about a Mexican bondwoman named Sada. Unable to sleep because of the cold one snowy night, she sought shelter inside the church. The valiant bishop found her in the courtyard; she was shivering from the cold. He took his old, furred cloak from his shoulders and gave it to her. The scene is one reason why the book has been described as a golden chalice of Christian love.

As disciples of Jesus we are called to be persons for others, especially in their need. The new commandment that Christ gave us is to love others *as he has loved us.*

We do not help others simply out of pity. Pity implies a feeling of compassion for others, because they are not quite so fortunate as we are. Peter, in today's First Reading, told Cornelius, the Roman, to get up, for he—Peter—was only a human being. Peter remembered Jesus' mandate to see the Lord in others, to love God as he has loved us.

How does Christ love us? As today's Second Reading testifies, he gave his life as an offering for our sins; he gave his life that we might be free from sin and death, and that we might live forever in him.

The greatest love is therefore the sacrifice of one's life, after the example of Jesus of Nazareth. In this context one immediately thinks of the great martyrs. One thinks of men like Father Maximilian Kolbe, who died in the Nazi prison of Auschwitz after voluntarily taking the place of a fellow prisoner condemned to execution. One thinks, for instance, of St. Isaac Jogues and the North American Martyrs, who labored here in New York State and Quebec over a century before 1776: of how they were tortured and slain by the savages.

But sacrificing one's life for Christ can also be implemented on a less heroic scale. Take the sacrificial example of mothers, for example, or fathers who labor so hard in love for their families. Take nurses, or physicians, or teachers, or social workers. Take factory workers or clerks or service personnel who gladly bear the contradictions or ridicule of a godless world in order to witness to Christ by their everyday lives: in their example, speech, even in the kind of entertainment they enjoy.

In 1951 Cardinal Francis Spellman of New York blessed a plaque in old St. Patrick's Churchyard at the burial site of a black hairdresser who died in 1853. His name was Pierre Toussaint. Once a slave, he operated a hairdressing salon in Old Manhattan, to which the socially elite would gather as to a holy person, for wisdom and spiritual direction. After work he nursed the sick and dying, fed the hungry, counseled the confused. His whole life was a life of loving others as Christ has loved him. Totally dedicated to helping others, he hardly ever thought of himself. For it, he was acknowledged as close to God.

As today's Second Reading tells us:

". . . everyone who loves is begotten of God . . . for God *is* love."

SEVENTH SUNDAY OF EASTER (B)

Apostolic Mission And Grace

Acts 1:15-17, 20-26; First John 4:11-16; John 17:11-19.

Aim: to explain (1) that God first chooses us through his ministers, and (2) that his gift of grace must be guarded.

In today's Gospel, a segment of Jesus' Last Supper sermon, Christ our Savior sends—missions—those he has chosen, and consecrates them in truth. The theme of consecrated mission is accented, therefore.

The same motif is sounded in today's First Reading, from Acts, St. Luke's inspired history of the primitive Church. There we read how Matthias was selected to take the place of Judas in the Apostolic college. The theology of priestly vocation is contained herein, for we read that Matthias was chosen by God, in the Church.

Today's Second Reading rings with a note which St. Paul also dwelt upon often; namely, to know God is to know his love for us so intensely that we are literally impelled forward, not only to perfect this love within ourselves by union with God, but also to testify to it through and for others (Cf. 2 Cor 5:14).

Thus the entire theme, fleshed out, of today's readings, is Christ's consecrated mission of love.

Jesus had come into the world to reveal his Father, to point the way to him, and to ensure us the possibility of knowing this revelation. Now, as he is about to cross the threshhold leading to his glorification as the great High Priest returning to his Father, he utters an awesome prayer of intercession for his ministers, those who will continue his work in the world when he returns to the Father's right hand. Through these ministers sent in his name, men down through the ages will come to the truth.

In fact, though, it is not man who seeks God; *rather it is God who seeks man.* He stands there in our pilgrimage toward truth, beckoning us onward, in the paths of history, in the paths of inner experience, through grace. Pascal once said: "You would not seek him, if you had not found something of him already."

Each of us, after all, was conceived in a state of alienation from God: original sin. (Among creatures, Mary is the sole exception.) Yet in his mercy and kindness, God gratuitously willed to deliver us from sin, and to call us to his own divine life through the mystery of adoption (Cf. Rm 6-8, and Ep 1). He does this through grace—so called because it is gratuitously given us. Grace—sanctifying grace— is really God-life; the very divine life given to us, by which we partake of the divinity of the Son through the Spirit of adoption and enter to intimate union with the Holy Trinity.

As Christians we have a serious responsibility not only to retain, but also to develop, this relationship to God. Only while in the state of grace can we merit further blessings and eternal life, as, for instance, when we receive the Eucharist or sacramental absolution. So precious a gift is grace that we should keep constant vigil never to lose it by deliberate mortal sin.

Which brings us back to the opening point, pertaining to apostolic mission. Jesus' ministers help us maintain and develop grace, principally through their preaching and the sacraments, if only we allow them to do so, if only we cooperate with their ministry.

Today we could pray not only that we may persevere and progress in God-life, but that Jesus' priests will be allowed to help us, and others.

TRINITY SUNDAY (B)

The Sign of the Cross

Deuteronomy 4:32-34, 39-40; Romans 8:14-17; Matthew 28:16-20.

Aim: to explain (1) the Sign of the Cross; (2) to understand it as a traditional and public sign of our belief in the Holy Trinity.

Today is Trinity Sunday, a liturgical opportunity for reflecting on the doctrine that in the one God there are three Persons, distinct but equal, whom we invoke, as the Bible bids us (today's Gospel, for example) as: Father, Son and Holy Spirit.

Every time we make the Sign of the Cross we affirm our belief in this doctrine, one of the four basic truths of our faith. (The others are (1) God exists; (2) God rewards and punishes; and (3) the Second Person of the Trinity, God the Son, became man, died for us, and rose from the dead to redeem us and draw us into the very life of the Trinity forever.)

The words of the Sign of the Cross are words taken directly from today's Gospel, in which Jesus sends forth his Apostles to preach and baptize everywhere until the end of time. The action accompanying these words—tracing the hand from the forehead, to the breast, thence to the left and right shoulders—reminds us that it is through the Cross of Jesus—the Son of God made man—that the life of the Trinity is opened to us, and that the Cross is the only means by which we can follow Christ our Savior and Lord to enter into the eternal life of the Trinity.

Because of the Cross of Calvary we can possess the Spirit of adoption, by which we can really call God "Father," as St. Paul states in today's Second Reading. We can only be heirs with Christ if we are willing to suffer with him, for his sake.

The early Christians had dramatic experience of this truth. For them making the Sign of the Cross meant signaling their willingness—and readiness—to go to a dungeon, to torture, even to death. Countless martyrs have surrendered their lives in flames or by the sword after making the Sign of the Cross. In the Tower of London, for one historic example, the pilgrim can still see the Sign of the Cross scratched into the stone walls by Catholics condemned there to suffer or die for the Faith; a reminder of endless Signs of the Cross made by martyrs down through the ages on their persons.

In pondering the Sign of the Cross, sometimes the words are minimized. This tendency is unfortunate. On God's side, signs are expressions of his love for us, as today's First Reading says. On our side, signs must also be manifestations of love—of love fixed in the heart. Otherwise they are mute, meaningless, sterile.

Thus, when we make the Sign of the Cross, our hearts must be in what we do. Which means, first, that we must be aware of what we are doing and saying. What we are doing is recollecting the Cross of Calvary, on which Jesus our Savior, the Son of God Incarnate, died that we might have life through him with the Triune God forever. What we are saying is that we believe that in God there are Three Persons, Father, Son and Holy Spirit.

To relegate this sacred sign to a superstitious symbol is, it goes without saying, sacrilegious. To make the Sign of the Cross half-heartedly is to make no true sign at all; under such circumstances, it expresses nothing. To rush through the Sign of the Cross mechanically, as if it were something simply to be *done with*, is to forget that its real meaning is derived from three hours of agony on Calvary.

CORPUS CHRISTI (B)

The Eucharist as a Sacrament

Exodus 24:3-8; Hebrews 9:11-15; Mark 14:12-16, 22-26.

Aim: to encourage (1) frequent reception of Holy Communion; (2) this receiving of Holy Communion in an understanding, reverent fashion.

Today is *Corpus Christi*; the Latin phrase means "the Body of Christ." It is a day for pondering, with heartfelt thanksgiving, Jesus' supreme love-gift to us: the Holy Eucharist, which alone satisfies our deepest hunger.

The Eucharist began over 19 centuries ago, in the Upper Room of Jerusalem. The altar was a table; the celebrant, Jesus of Nazareth, Eternal High Priest—as today's Second Reading acknowledges him—whose Precious Blood, poured forth once for all, was foretold by the countless Old Testament sacrifices recalled in today's First Reading.

The event in the Upper Room was the first Mass, offered, as Vatican Council II reminds us, to perpetuate the Sacrifice of the Cross throughout the centuries until Jesus, now risen from the tomb and ascended to the Father's right hand, comes again. This first Mass, we believe, was entrusted to Jesus' spouse, the Church, as the sacrificial memorial of his death and resurrection, as a sacrament of his love, as a sign of Communion, and as the paschal banquet of the New Testament.

To this day we, Christ's disciples, like the Apostles of old, assemble to renew this mystery wherein the elements of bread and wine are changed into Jesus' Body and Blood in remembrance of him; and depart from the altar recommitted to intensify our efforts to help transform the world in his name, through his grace.

Our participation in Mass, from listening to the Bible readings to joining in the hymns and prayers, culminates in communion—our embracing Jesus as the Bread of Life.

The Mass is a sacrificial *meal*; Jesus bade us, "Take and *eat*;" not simply, take and contemplate. The Eucharist is spiritual nourishment; it is analogous to food. Holy Communion completes the eucharistic sacrifice for us. Eating means just what the verb connotes: consuming what Jesus himself told us is true food, his Body and Blood.

Normally speaking, therefore, communion is integral to one's attendance at Mass; it should not be the exception. This means that so long as one is in the state of grace (i.e., not conscious of an unconfessed mortal sin), and has the right intention (e.g., to worship God, not to please others), one should not hesitate to receive the Eucharist frequently: monthly, weekly; daily, if possible.

"Without the Eucharist we are dead," the Martyrs of Abitinia exclaimed many centuries ago as they prepared for martyrdom. Our martyrdom today is witnessing to Christian values in the midst of a world which dismisses faith as nonrelevant. Without the Eucharist we too could be dead—dead to Christ, that is, in a world which doesn't acknowledge, which doesn't even know, in large part, that *he lives*.

And the struggle today is undeniably intense; so intense, in fact, that the Christian who fails to give at least Sunday Mass and communion highest priority is placing himself in eternal jeopardy.

Are we stronger than the Martyrs of Abitinia? Was Jesus serious or not when he said:

"If you do not eat the flesh of the Son of Man and drink his blood, you have no life in you. He who feeds on my flesh and drinks my blood has life eternal, and I will raise him up on the last day" (Jn 6:52-54).

SECOND SUNDAY
IN ORDINARY TIME (B)

The Baptism of Jesus and Our Baptism

First Samuel 3:3-10, 19; First Corinthians 6:13-15, 17-20; John 1:35-42

Aim: (1) to explain what happened when we were baptized (specifically, our being personally called by God); (2) to present our baptism as a commitment for life to live in Christ and in grace.

That God calls us in the Spirit by name—provided that we try to listen to his voice and reflect upon his call in an effort to know him—is a principal lesson of today's Bible readings.

The Old Testament story of the call of Samuel—perhaps one of the first Bible stories we read in our childhood—witnesses to this lesson in a beautiful, dramatic fashion. Today's Gospel, about Andrew's vocation, is in a sense even more beautiful and dramatic. In fact, the total message of today's Bible texts is encapsulated in the story of the Apostle Andrew. Focus on him for a few moments.

Andrew is recalled regularly in the Mass; in the Roman Canon his name occurs directly after that of Peter and Paul. The insertion, which dates perhaps from the fifth century, seems to have been occasioned by deference to the Eastern Church. Even today Andrew is one of the two patron saints of Russia.

Andrew, today's Gospel reminds us, was the first Apostle called by Christ. Moreover, he was the one responsible for bringing his brother Simon to Jesus. Simon of course became Peter; our Lord changed his name. Peter means "rock." Andrew said to Peter: "We have found the Messiah."

Andrew, we know, was a deeply religious person from early adulthood. As a youth, before Jesus' public preaching, Andrew had been a disciple of John the Baptizer; we know this because Andrew is mentioned among those in the company of the Baptizer's followers that historic day when St. John first glimpsed Jesus coming toward him near the Jordan and exclaimed in the Spirit: "Look there! The Lamb of God who takes away the sin of the world."

Today's Gospel records Andrew's reaction to John's pointing out Jesus as the Lamb of God. Without delay he rushed up to our Lord and asked to speak to him—alone, in the home at which Christ was staying. Jesus granted the interview. All that Andrew needed was a few hours (it was four in the afternoon, the Gospel tells us) to make his total, permanent, and irrevocable commitment to discipleship.

Capernaum, Andrew's city, later became one of Jesus' favorite stops in his continuous journeying for souls. Doubtless one of the reasons was that it was Andrew's home.

In Andrew's story—as well as in the Old Testament prophet Samuel's—we can see the genesis and anatomy of God's election, which comes to us through our baptism; and we are reminded of the only response that matters: commitment of life in Christ and in grace.

First, God's election follows upon sincere, humble curiosity; a *holy curiosity* about the mystery of life and death, our identity and goals. Like Andrew, we must all put aside the distractions of this world and seek out an interview with Jesus, who lives as risen Lord in our midst.

Secondly, there is need for some hours of contemplation. We must try to remain open to the Spirit, to say with Samuel, "Speak Lord, for your servant is listening." (This requires turning off the television occasionally, and putting aside the daily newspaper.) Otherwise, God's personal call to us cannot be heard.

This means prayer, of course. No Christian can live without it. God's calling us by name and his speaking to us can be detected only if we occasionally halt our routine worldly pursuits to make contact with his living presence.

Following Andrew, therefore, with holy curiosity about Christ, and with personal prayer, we can keep hearing God's calling us, by virtue of our Baptism, and can—as St. Paul puts it in today's Second Reading—bring our total persons, body and soul, under the Lordship of Christ.

THIRD SUNDAY
IN ORDINARY TIME (B)

The Purpose of Life

Jonah 3:1-5, 10; First Corinthians 7:29-31; Mark 1:14-20.

Aim: to show life's purpose as (1) to know God (2) to love God (3) to serve God in this world, and so be happy with God for eternity (for this world is transitory). To describe (1) What a saint is, and the purpose of life as becoming a saint.

Today's First Reading is from the Book of Jonah, surely one of the most fascinating and comforting of all Biblical stories.

Some people particularly like that passage toward the end, remember, when Jonah literally sulks under the shade of a gourd plant because God has decided to forgive the city of Nineveh for its sins.

Nineveh of old was a city of sin: godlessness and immorality were commonplace. So that when he was called by God to preach repentance to the Ninevites, Jonah declined to accept the mission. He even tried to hide from God so that God wouldn't ask him again.

Besides, there was another reason for Jonah's reluctance. Jonah knew only too well God's readiness to forgive sin at the first sign of repentance. Jonah argued that he would extend himself preparing sermons, traveling to Nineveh, preaching the word of God; yet, after all this work, God would forgive the Ninevites at the first sign of their repentance. God forgives too readily, Jonah thought; so he'd rather not play the prophet for God. He took flight, like the soul in Francis Thompson's *The Hound of Heaven*. And he was swallowed up by a big fish (the Hebrew means a big fish, not a whale), and literally was stopped in his flight away from God.

Jesus told us, remember, that the only sign he would give us would be the Sign of Jonah (Mt 16:1-4; 12:38-40). The Sign of Jonah is fundamentally the sign of Jesus' resurrection from the dead, by means of which we sinful people are reconciled to the Father.

Christ's Resurrection means that there can be no other purpose in life but getting to know God through Jesus Christ our Lord, so that we can live and serve him in this life and be happy with him forever. Taking Jesus as our Master and guide, as the Apostles did, summarizes our goal.

Like Jonah, though, in our sinfulness, we frequently find ourselves drifting—or even running—away from Christ, misusing our lives for unimportant, certainly not lasting pursuits; confusing life's priorities, in the contemporary idiom. For instance, we interpret the importance of personal fulfillment selfishly, without reference to Jesus' admonition that pesonal fulfillment necessarily entails the sacrifice of taking up our cross and following the Savior. Or we are tempted always to do the "practical" thing in life, forgetting that the most practical stance of all is the stance of faith, since it alone prepares us for life beyond the grave.

If we really believed in Jesus' Resurrection, then, we would sincerely pray, in response to today's opening Bible reading, that God will send us a "whale" to stop us in our worldly escape attempts, as he did Jonah; and set us on the right path again, as he did for Jonah and the Apostles.

Isn't this what the saints all did? Isn't a saint a person who cares nothing for this world, and whose only purpose in life is to embrace God's pardon and direction in a lifetime pilgrimage to him—and who does this without losing any time, as St. Paul warns us to do in today's Second Reading, since "the world as we know it is passing away?"

Every saint—meaning, of course, anyone who embraces, and is embraced by, Christ forever—has experienced the whale of God's mercy and direction in his or her life, and has lived by this experience.

FOURTH SUNDAY
IN ORDINARY TIME (B)

Sexual Morality For a Christian

Deuteronomy 18:15-20; First Corinthians 7:32-35; Mark 1:21-28.

Aim: to teach (in view of the reality of Jesus' exorcizing evil spirits) the norms of Christ that (1) deliberate sexual pleasure is lawful only in valid marriage; (2) therefore solitary pleasure, fornication, adultery are immoral and wrong.

Today's Gospel is from St. Mark's account, which is commonly regarded as the oldest of the four Gospels, written, probably, as early as 70 A.D.

One of the truths about Jesus' ministry especially evident in the Gospel of Mark is that Jesus was an exorcist; Jesus drove out devils.

For some reason—diabolic?—the existence of the Devil and his angels is not universally accepted today within Christianity; while, ironically, the opposite is true among many nonbelievers, as witness current interest in witchcraft and the occult. Pope Paul VI thought it pastorally necessary on more than one occasion to emphasize the existence of the Devil and his fallen angels.

In the New Testament evil spirits emerge as the cause of possession and illness again and again. Moreover, they epitomize what is un-Christly so much so that they are in a state of continuous combat with Jesus and with Jesus' disciples. Read for example, Ac 16:16.

A certain influence of Satan over sinful man is acknowledged by the Church. Vatican Council II restated this tragedy: "Although he was made by God in a state of holiness, from the very dawn of history man abused his liberty, at the urging of personified Evil" (*Pastoral Constitution on the Church in the Modern World*, Section 13).

Satan cannot coerce man; of course not. But the Spirit of Evil can, by virtue of those who elect to be deceived by him, so taint the very climate of an age that even those committed to Christ and his Kingdom must be vigilant lest they too are swayed by the Father of Lies.

One matter in which satanic deception can (and, we know so well) does occur is that of sexual morality. Today's Second Reading, from St. Paul, discusses some aspects of this subject.

We have God's own word—for which we must one day answer in judgment, as today's First Reading prophecies—that human sexuality has no valid meaning unless it is related to married life in a family. For a disciple of Christ, sexuality cannot be viewed outside the perspectives of the marriage covenant, which involves three persons: a man, a woman, and the living Lord Jesus.

Because of this faith the disciple of Christ knows that extramarital, premarital and solitary sexual experience must be repudiated; such actions cannot be related to the marital covenant of spouses with Christ, to which human sexuality is ordained.

Again, there is an attitude abroad that condones the opposite. "Living together" is treated as morally indifferent in society at large, even celebrated on television shows; adultery and fornication are also viewed as at least ethically neutral.

Our determination to live by the Gospel in this area canot be expected always to draw a popular response. When Jesus drove out the devils in the Land of the Gerasenes, the townspeople asked him to leave. Then, as today, those who would label evil for evil and reject it as such, are not always widely appreciated.

But, to return to the thrust of today's First Reading, we do have a responsibility to witness to the truth of God's Word; and, by virtue of that resposibility, to help others from being deceived by the Father of Lies.

FIFTH SUNDAY
IN ORDINARY TIME (B)

The Sacrament of the Sick

Job 7:1-4, 6-7; First Corinthians 9:16-19, 22-23; Mark 1:29-39.

Aim: to show (1) the need for this sacrament when in danger of death; (2) how and when to celebrate this sacrament in one's own case and to help others receive it.

Today's magnificent First Reading is from Job, one of the finest poetic books of the Old Testament, and, indeed, one of the most respected literary works of world literature.

The subject of the Book of Job is the perennial inquiry as to why God permits suffering in this world.

Not that this problem is defined in so many words, however. The Book of Job is not primarily a theological argument, but rather the record of a personal experience. This great poem ends with Job's reaffirmation of commitment that faith alone allows one to stand up straight despite suffering and proceed as surely as ever in the confidence that God can make man equal to any task. Moreover, God orders suffering to the greater good of the sufferer. God can, in fact, bring good out of the apparent evil.

As Christians we know that what Job prophesied has been fulfilled in New Testament Revelation. As Christians we speak of the doctrine of redemptive suffering; meaning, of course, that our pain, our agonies physical, emotional or mental, can mysteriously be united with the sufferings of Jesus in his Passion and Crucifixion, and by this union, can become blessed and spiritually advantageous for us and others.

There is, in fact, a sacramental means by which this is accomplished: the Sacrament of the Sick, or Extreme Unction, by which Jesus' healing mission, so beautifully recounted in today's Gospel, is celebrated to the present day through the anointing of the forehead and the hands, together with certain prayers said by the priest in the name of the Church.

The Anointing of the Sick is a sacrament of faith—of Job-like faith. We have two key Biblical revelations on this subject: Jm 5:14-15, and Mk 6:13. It is a sacrament which may be received by anyone who is dangerously ill owing to sickness or old age.

The proper time to ask to be anointed is when one *begins to be* dangerously ill.

This means that a sick person may be anointed before surgery, if a dangerous illness is the reason for the surgery. It also means that an aged person may be anointed if he or she is in a weak condition.

It is important, therefore, that Catholics think of the Sacrament of Anointing not as a last-minute measure, to be put off until the final moment when death looms imminent, but rather as an extraordinary, graced opportunity to encounter the Lord Jesus precisely in one's dangerous illness.

By the Anointing of the Sick, the sickness of the recipient is mysteriously immersed in the victory of Christ. Thus, sickness is transformed into a saving situation leading to salvation; it becomes an occasion for uniquely and infallibly encountering the risen Lord.

This meeting of Christ occurs through the Church, especially in the person of the priest, who is charged with the conferral of this Sacrament as one of the services he must render—to recall St. Paul's words in today's Second Reading. One who receives the Sacrament of the Sick with the right disposition is assured that Christ is standing by his side in his Bride, the Church; that the Church is holding on high—as Karl Rahner has put it—the lamp of faith as night begins to fall on one's own passing world.

Today we pray that as the sunset of our life on earth approaches, we will line up with the crowds in today's Gospel to seek Jesus' healing embrace in Job-like faith through the Sacrament of the Sick.

SIXTH SUNDAY IN ORDINARY TIME (B)

The Imitation of Christ

Leviticus 13:1-2, 44-46; First Corinthians 10:31-11:1; Mark 1:40-45.

Aim: (1) to picture the perfect life and character of Jesus Christ and (2) to encourage the Imitation of Christ as our key to living.

Purity of soul, which comes not primarily from man but from God, is the dominant theme of today's Bible Readings. Such purity, symbolized by freedom from leprosy in today's First Reading and Gospel, is of course a goal of Christian living. We are called to rid ourselves of all that is not Godlike—sin and its affection.

Again, though, this cleansing process begins with God and his grace. We are all desperately in need of a Savior. Jesus, the all-pure victim for our sins, is both the key and the model for Christian living.

Recall the prayer of the leper in today's Gospel: "If you will to do so, you can cure me." What magnificent theology. What magnificent faith. What magnificent confidence in faith!

"If you will to do so, you can cure me." The petitioner was a leper; one ostracized from society, therefore; an outcast. Lest we miss the significance of this circumstance, we are reminded of the frightening Mosaic precept about lepers in today's First Reading. We are in effect brought back in mind to an early period of civilization, when medicine was primitive, and when a disease like leprosy so struck terror into men that it caused permanent exile from society.

Jesus answered: "I do will it. Be cured." Jesus makes us clean. With Jesus in our midst, no one need remain impure, in exile. All men are saved, as Paul reminds us again in today's segment from his First Letter to Corinth.

Even a great sinner like Augustine could be purified. Augustine prayed the leper's prayer—"Lord, if you will to do so, you can cure me"—and became a saint. As a youth he embraced the world and its impurities, which all but enslaved him. Jesus helped him turn his embrace to all that is pure, to Godliness and eternal life.

St. Margaret of Cortona is another case in point. For almost a decade she lived with a man outside wedlock. Returning home one day, she was led by his hunting dog to his mangled corpse; he had been murdered and cast into a pit. Overcome with a sense of revulsion for her diseased state of soul, she knelt in the footsteps of the leper of today's Gospel. We now venerate her as one of the most brilliant lights of the Franciscan tradition.

St. Paul in today's Second Reading, reminds us that unless we take Christ for our model in this world and follow him, we are not living. A life not oriented toward him is only a process of deterioration, a spiritual leprosy, really, that eventually leads to our destruction.

Christ's path is the only one that leads to health and eternal life. All we need do to find this way is to pray, as the leper prayed, for the health that Jesus alone can give.

Over the centuries, Christ awaits us still, with the words: "I do will it. Be cured."

SEVENTH SUNDAY
IN ORDINARY TIME (B)

Baptismal Faith, Commitment, and Witness

Isaiah 43:18-19, 21-22, 24-25; Second Corinthians 1:18-22; Mark 2:1-12.

> *Aim: (1) to explain how faith is needed for baptism especially with reference to infant baptism; (2) to stress that baptism calls for faith, commitment and witness.*

Today's beautiful Gospel, from Mark, is one of the classic Biblical witnesses to the validity of infant baptism.

Why was the paralyzed man forgiven by Jesus? The Gospel clearly states (the original Greek is very explicit here as well as in St. Luke's account of the same incident) that the paralytic was cured precisely because of his friends' faith, because of *their* faith: the faith manifested by the crippled man's friends who literally tore the roof off the house wherein Jesus was preaching and lowered the poor unfortunate to our Lord's feet. Today's Gospel reads, "When Jesus saw *their* faith, he said to the paralyzed man . . ."

Thus Scripture sets forth the doctrine of salvation through "the faith of the community." This is what happens in infant baptism. Although there is a general rule that Christ's saving action is impeded without antecedent personal faith, occasionally the faith of others, of the community, can be an environment for salvation.

In the case of infant baptism, the believing Christian community, the Church, represented by the baptizing priest, the parents, the godparents, the witnesses, as well as by the parish and the Church, "supplies" in a sense the required dispositions of faith in behalf of the infant.

Take a closer look at this mystery of salvation through the faith of the community—in a broader context than infant baptism. Take this question: Is it possible that *we* can inspire and sustain others in faith and thereby occasion their being forgiven and cured by Jesus? Can we be stretcher bearers for the sick of soul?

Take the case of St. Monica. For years she prayed for her son Augustine's conversion, but thought her hopes all dashed when he booked passage to Milan, then a city of vice. But in Milan Augustine became fascinated by the masterful sermons of Ambrose, and now we venerate all three as saints: Monica, Augustine, Ambrose. Owing to the faith of Monica and Ambrose, Augustine the great Doctor of the Church emerged.

Like the stretcher bearers of today's Gospel, Monica literally succeeded in placing her morally crippled son at the Savior's feet. Seeing her faith, and the faith of Ambrose, Christ responded with his healing powers.

Now as yesterday—recall Isaiah in today's First Reading—God wants to blot out man's iniquities. Today, too, God wants man to say "Amen," or "Yes," to his wonderful promises of forgiveness—as today's Second Reading reminds.

For this, faith is essential. And today so many men, in desperate need of God's pardon, are as crippled—spiritually—as the paralyzed man of today's Gospel.

They literally need to experience the faith of others who by faith will bring them to the feet of the loving, healing Savior.

EIGHTH SUNDAY
IN ORDINARY TIME (B)

Title: Christian Marriage and Sexuality

Hosea 2:16-17, 21-22; Second Corinthians 3:1-6; Mark 2:18-22

Aim: (1) to explain the uniquely sacred nature of Christian marriage and the holiness of human sexuality; (2) to cite the immorality of contraception.

Who, of the Old Testament prophets, was the one who divorced his wife for her infidelity but eventually took her back because of his overwhelming love for her despite her sin?

The answer is Hosea, the prophet who gave us today's First Reading. Hosea, responsive to the Spirit's inspiration, drew from the tragedy of his own marriage, a poetic parallel between God's love for his people and the love of a devoted husband for an unfaithful wife, whom he loves nonetheless.

In this marriage-metaphor, God's love for man attains the summit of Old Testament expression. Jesus, the Prophet of Prophets, later used the same metaphor when speaking of himself and the Kingdom of God. In today's Gospel, for example, he refers to himself, during a discussion about fasting, as a bridegroom; we are invited to think of the messianic era as a time of marriage (Mt 22:1-14; 25:1-13). Later, St. Paul, in his Epistle to the Ephesians, was to draw a spectacular direct parallel between Christ on the one hand, and on the other hand, the Church viewed as a bride.

Talking about Christian marriage—writing about marriage (to borrow Paul's thought in today's Second Reading)—requires a mind-set about marriage totally new in the history of the world.

Christian marriage defies description in pre-Christian words or phrases. There is no mode of expression prior to the Christ event that can describe marriage as we know it: not simply as a sacred contract (as the Greeks and Romans of old knew it) but a covenant of man and wife with the living Lord Jesus. So marriage really occasions a sanctuary. The living Lord Jesus commits himself to be with marrieds: to help them, grace them, sustain them.

As Christ is with his Bride the Church always, so Christ remains with the couple united with him in marriage. This means that Christian marriage is a permanent state; it cannot be dissolved by any human authority.

As marriage is graced by God, so of course is human sexuality. Sexuality is obviously good, since it reflects God's creation. Gn 1:27-28, for example, reads that God created male and female and blessed them; Ep 5:22 places this Old Testament revelation into our Christian context.

The Bible as read within the Church also tells us that sexuality is essentially unselfish, since it is oriented toward self-donation in marriage. Used outside of vowed marital commitment in Christ, sexuality is disoriented. Thus we believe that any deliberate, direct use of sex outside of the married state runs counter to our commitment to discipleship in the Lord.

Again, to cite Paul's thinking in today's Second Reading, our way of viewing marriage and sexuality requires a new and fresh way of thinking. Excluded from the Christian's behavior, therefore, will be any actions performed directly to prevent conception—what is termed contraception; excluded too are all forms of direct sterilization for the same reason. The Church's doctrine was spelled out by Pope Paul VI in the encyclical *Humanae Vitae*.

One of the secondary lessons of today's readings, surely, is that Christianity is different; radical, even; so novel, in fact, that even the institution of marriage cannot be described in terms of what preceded Christ's coming. Again, marriage for a Christian cannot be discussed without reference to an entirely new vocabulary.

NINTH SUNDAY
IN ORDINARY TIME (B)

Observance of Sunday

Deuteronomy 5:12-15; Second Corinthians 4:6-11; Mark 2:23-3:6

Aim: to show (1) why Sunday is God's special day; (2) how best to participate at Mass on Sundays.

Today's First Reading, from Dt (from a Greek phrase meaning "second law"), immediately ushers in the theme of today's Bible readings; namely, the significance of the Sabbath, our Sunday.

For the Israelites of old, the Sabbath was a sign of God's covenant. During the Babylonian exile, observance of the Sabbath was recognized as a characteristic of all Israelites—much as going to Sunday Mass is a mark of Catholics today.

To worship God and to rest on the Sabbath was a law in Israel. It is cited as a mandate in both listings of the Ten Commandments, the one found in the Book of Exodus and today's First Reading, from Dt. (The word "Sabbath" comes almost directly from the Hebrew word *sabbat*.)

After the Babylonian Exile, an excessively legalistic, somewhat puritanical interpretation of the Sabbath began to take hold of the Israelites, so much so that in Jesus' time, it was widely viewed not as a festive observance, but rather an ungodly burden. Jesus, in today's Gospel, corrects this erroneous interpretation.

Because the Sabbath was so holy and so clear a mark of the

Israelite, because the Sabbath was revealed to the Chosen People by God, Jesus' declaring himself Lord of the Sabbath was in effect a declaration of his intimacy with the Eternal Father.

In New Testament Revelation, a sign of the covenant is the new Sabbath, or Sunday, the Lord's Day. As Vatican Council II reaffirmed in its *Constitution on the Liturgy*, the first day is the *Lord's Day par excellence* by virtue of an "apostolic tradition," the reason being, that our divine Lord rose from the dead on a Sunday (No. 106).

The identification of Christians with Sunday (and its vigil) is also clear from the earliest history of the Church, the Acts of the Apostles (cf. 20:7). For Jesus' first disciples, Sunday was the Lord's Day.

So it is for us, too. Not primarily because of a Church law, however. This is not fundamentally why we assemble for the Eucharist today. To do so would be to draw upon ourselves the very censure Jesus voiced in today's Gospel. No; we meet for the Eucharist on this, the Lord's Day, in order to encounter the risen Lord Jesus on this "little" Easter, as it were. As Christians we hold Sunday to be holy because it commemorates the day, when God-made-man conquered death and sin and ignorance and disease, re-created this sinful world, and entered into it with his insuperable power to transform it and all that it contains.

Every time we meet for the Eucharist on a Sunday we say in effect with St. Paul in today's Second Reading that our power to survive in this world of darkness and affliction comes from God, and that our suffering with Christ in this age will mean our rising with him on an eternal Sunday.

We *wear Sundays* on our sleeves; sincere Sunday worship is a Catholic's insignia of commitment.

Test ourselves: If Sundays mean little to us, isn't it because Christ the living Lord means little to us?

If, on the other hand, Sundays lead us closer to our Lord; if our days are as nothing without the Sunday Eucharist, then we know really what Jesus said in today's Gospel.

TENTH SUNDAY
IN ORDINARY TIME (B)

Objective Morality

Genesis 3:9-15; Second Corinthians 4:13-5:1; Mark 3:20-35.

Aim: to explain (1) that there is an objective moral law, (2) that evil can never be good, and (3) that extreme situation ethics must be rejected.

Jesus' words today about a house divided are especially familiar to Americans; Abraham Lincoln referred to them in his "house divided" speech.

Read alongside today's First Reading, the story of Satan's intervention in our world and the first sin. The slanderous blasphemous accusation that Jesus worked miracles by the power of Satan, together with Jesus' response "How can Satan expel Satan?" reminds us of the wall between evil and good.

As disciples of Christ, we believe that good is not evil, and evil is not good. This sounds obvious until one recalls that today there are efforts to pretend that good and evil are not always, or necessarily, contradictory; or at least that good can merge into evil, and evil into good, so much so that neither good nor evil is discernible.

Extreme situation ethics or context morality is one contemporary force suggesting this confusion. This refers to the kind of morality that determines the goodness or wrongness of a human act merely or chiefly on the merits of the "situation" in which the act is performed, and without any key reference to God's Word.

Again, evil cannot be good, there is an impenetrable wall between the two. Adultery, which is forbidden by God's law, is evil; it can never be good. Perjury can never be good. Direct abortion is evil; again, direct abortion can never be good. No so-called human "situation" or "context" can magically turn these wrong acts into right acts.

One of the specious arguments used in "context" morality is that there should be no guilt so long as one acts "meaningfully," in an attempt to do the "most loving thing."

The Gospel, on the other hand, reminds us that the "most loving thing" for the Christian is always God's will. Hence anything contrary to God's will—hatred, fornication, blasphemy—cannot possibly be labeled a "most loving thing."

An especially demonic distortion of this whole subject today, moreover, is a tendency by some to call good, evil. Thus marriage can be discounted as dehumanizing; likewise, parenthood; also, reverence for life, even religious worship.

Alexander Solzhenitsyn, the Nobel laureate for literature who acquired his credentials to prophesy in the Gulag Archipelago, said during a BBC interview rebroadcast in this country in March, 1976:

". . .Those people who have lived in the most terrible conditions, on the frontier between life and death . . . all understand that between good and evil there is an irreconcilable contradiction, that it is not one and the same thing—good or evil—that one cannot build one's life without regard to this distinction."

As Catholics we know how true these words are. We cannot build our lives as if good and evil were not contradictory. We know that unless we live by this belief, the eternal dwelling place of which St. Paul speaks in today's Second Reading will not be ours.

As Catholics we know that there is an objective morality, founded on God's unchanging word.

We know that Jesus is the way, the truth, and life; that to live meaningfully we must strive to follow him, who is sure to judge us at death—each one of us.

ELEVENTH SUNDAY
IN ORDINARY TIME (B)

Faith

Ezekiel 17:22-24; Second Corinthians 5:6-10; Mark 4:26-34.

Aim: to explain the virtue of faith as a gift of God which gives us the capacity to know God, God's truth and God's teachings on life and death.

Curiously, both the First Reading and the Gospel today have to do with the mystery of organic growth.

Ezekiel, in the First Reading, foretells the restoration of a messianic king from the royal dynasty of King David. But his prophecy is structured on the image of a tree planted by God, a tree which, though planted by a single tender shoot, will become so gigantic that it will harbor beneath its boughs all winged creation. In the Gospel, Jesus delivers the well known parable of the tiny mustard seed which, once planted, can develop into a giant shrub "with branches big enough for the birds of the sky" to dwell in.

One way of interpreting these two readings is viewing them in terms of the Church, our historic Roman Church, which though planted by God in a tiny land within the hearts of a few disciples, has become the venerable, ageless, perennial catholic oak in whose shade all peoples find the fullness of God's truth and goodness.

However, if we read today's Gospel and First Reading alongside today's Second Reading, from Paul, we can perceive them as relating also to the theme of each Christian's dynamic growth in faith through Christ. For a few moments today, we concentrate on this second interpretation, arising from Paul's Words today: "We *continue* to be confident . . . *We walk by faith*."

Faith, after all, is a gift from God planted in our hearts through Christ our Lord at baptism. Like the mustard seed, it can grow into a flourishing plant. What is required is that we *continue* to nourish it, safeguard it, treasure it. In fact, our faith—your faith, my faith—can become so sturdy and large an oak that others can find confidence, security, even salvation, within the shade.

How is growth in faith realized? The answer is by uniting ourselves ever more closely to the divine Gardener who gave us the parable of the mustard seed: Jesus of Nazareth. Growth in faith is growth through Jesus: "to please him," as St. Paul says today.

The observance of God's law is an obvious requirement, therefore. So is the imitation of Christ, who came to show us the perfect way, truth and life. Growth in faith means relying upon God to help us always keep in mind that God's wisdom essentially transcends the greatest wisdom of this passing world; and that despite a hundred and one difficulties about our being able to understand, we know for certain that God's word is unassailable and indestructible.

Taking a theme from the Gospel and First Reading today, we could think of faith in terms of spiritual ecology. We could think of our acts of faith as trees planted in an increasingly scarred world, where forests are disappearing and the beauty of God's creation is being made over by the alleged, but empty, genius of human technology. And just as many concerned activists today demonstrate against technologies which pollute our earthly environment, we could, through a strong personal faith, demonstrate against the pollution of minds by ideas which deny the Gospel, its mandate to repent and believe the Good News, and its revelations about life and death.

TWELFTH SUNDAY
IN ORDINARY TIME (B)

Faith

Job 38:1, 8-11; Second Corinthians 5:14-17; Mark 4:35-41.

Aim: to explain (1) the human factors that led us to faith, (2) how people lose faith, (3) the value of our faith.

"Who can this be that the winds and the sea obey him?" Jesus' disciples, almost swamped by a bad squall on Genesareth, asked this faith-question in today's Gospel.

Job, in today's First Reading, was also almost inundated by storming waves of darkness. From the tempest God addressed Job; God's word controlled the rising waters.

One theme that sounds clearly from today's liturgy, therefore, is that Christ is our only sure way, truth, and life in this storm-troubled world. Life for us has no better purpose than embracing him in faith. Just to be in Christ, Paul says in today's Second Reading, makes us totally new men, absolutely immune from all earthly intimidation.

Our embracing Christ as the keystone of our lives is linked to many complex factors and experiences, of course. Most of us were fortunate enough to have deeply believing parents, who nourished and safeguarded our faith. Too, we were raised in a Catholic environment in which so many emotional and intellectual forces have been helpful: beautiful liturgies, helpful sermons, confessions, which give great peace, the help of good priests and religious; and the renewed intensity that Chrismas, Holy Week and Easter invariably occasion.

Fundamentally, though, we believe because God has given us a grace which we have accepted with love, and which we have tried to sustain and to nourish. We know full well that this gift can be lost; that unless we appreciate its beauty, power and richness, and unless we renew this appreciation regularly, we can dispossess ourselves of it.

Sustaining and nourishing one's faith means, for example, that when one assembles for Sunday Mass, he re-intensifies his belief that Christ is really and truly present: in the assembly, in the Bible and the preached word, and, supremely, in the communion. Sustaining and nourishing one's faith means that as one departs from Sunday Mass he is determined anew to implement the principles of Christian living derived from the Mass; namely, the principles leading to the transformation of oneself, one's family, and one's neighborhood, according to the model of Jesus.

At least we know that anyone who works at his faith, retains it. And that one who has problems with faith does so because, ultimately, he has not worked at it.

There is nothing real or lasting that does not reflect the faith premise. Faith lends meaning to every honest corner of life. There is nothing more precious or humanly meaningful for the pilgrimage of life. Without faith, we are like ships without rudders, riding the seas without direction to nowhere.

To live by faith is to possess riches beyond earthly count. Faith's worth now will appear clearly in heaven; faith's foundation is the timelessness of eternal joy with God. And, as C.S. Lewis once remarked, unless a subject is timeless, it's not worth taking time for.

In today's Gospel, the disciples grew anxious in the boat as evening drew on. "Evening" can be a figure of speech for one's latter years. If we work hard at our faith as the years go by, then the evening of our lives will find us steeled in belief. God assist us to this end.

THIRTEENTH SUNDAY IN ORDINARY TIME (B)

Reverence For Life

Wisdom 1:13-15; 2:23-24; Second Corinthians 8:7, 9, 13-15; Mark 5:21-43.

Aim: to explain (1) human life as God's special gift; (2) contemporary threats to human life in our society, especially direct abortion.

God does not rejoice in the destruction of the living. Today's First Reading, from the Book of Wisdom rings out with the word that all life comes from God's hand and is therefore holy. Death results from sin. In today's Gospel we are further reminded that Christ is Victor over death, which Paul, in today's Second Reading, views as an alien intruder.

Our Christian faith insists that human life must be revered, all human life; for human life belongs to God and reflects his creative goodness.

One area in which this principle has special meaning today is that surrounding abortion. Direct abortion is evil; there is no questioning this. As such, it can never constitute a good; can never effect good. On the contrary, evil spawns evil; direct abortion can only occasion further evils, proximate as well as mediate.

This is true wisdom. The problem today is that many have repudiated God's truth for the alleged wisdom of the world. In fact, ours is a world in which evil is made to sound almost respectable, is openly defended by pseudo-sophisticated champions with no credentials to speak at all in the areas of natural ethics or morality, is given verbal cosmetic treatment (e.g., "therapeutic abortion") to render it more attractive.

Direct abortion makes sense only in the kind of world envisioned by existentialist Jean-Paul Sartre when he said, "It is absurd that we have to be born, and it is absurd that we have to die."

Dietrich Bonhoeffer, the Protestant theologian and minister who died in a Nazi prison, wrote: "One is distressed by the failure of reasonable people to perceive either the depths of evil or the depth of the holy."

In Nazi Germany apparently reasonable people failed to perceive the depths of evil which the first hints of anti-Semitism logically and necessarily implied. They did not understand that each time they joined in insulting a Jew on their block they were laying a brick for the cremation ovens of Treblinka or Auschwitz. They could not foresee that each time they applauded an anti-Semitic speech they were already in the process of fueling The Holocaust.

Meanwhile, many others who declined to insult or to applaud, failed to recognize the depth of the religious dimension of reality. Without God there is no reality; all things shatter like thin glass and disappear; all things betray the man who betrays God—to borrow from Francis Thompson's immortal poetic idea.

To reject abortion is to act realistically. To defend abortion is to defend a fiction, an absurdity; to lay a brick for further absurdities.

Moreover, to take a cue from today's Second Reading, our plentiful wisdom regarding reverence for life should be witnessed to openly, for others to share. Death, to any human being, disturbs the Lord of Life, who took a little girl by the hand and said, "Get up." Our prayer today is that more and more might see Jesus, as we do, as the Lord of Life before whom death is an alien intruder.

FOURTEENTH SUNDAY IN ORDINARY TIME (B)

Self Discipline; Fasting and Abstinence

Ezekiel 2:2-5; Second Corinthians 12:7-10; Mark 6:1-6

Aim: to teach (1) self discipline (such as fasting and abstinence) as a valued religious practice; to be carried on in obligatory and also voluntary fashion.

In one sense, all three Bible readings today focus on prophets and prophecy—*and* (in view of today's Gospel) the fact that prophets often go unheeded.

Prophets are persons who speak for God. There is a popular misunderstanding in this regard; "to prophesy" is often meant only as "to foretell." Predicting the future can constitute one aspect of prophecy; of course. But a prophet is really one who speaks for God: one who is sent to speak in God's name.

Prophets frequently disturb the world; the people of Ezekiel's time were not all especially pleased with his message that their sins had occasioned their trouble: their being exiled to Babylon. In today's First Reading, God even refers to the Israelites as a rebellious people, obstinate to prophetic voices.

Paul, who in today's Second Reading reminds us that self-discipline can make us really strong, was himself not always appreciated. In fact, some of his own converts—the Corinthians, to whom he had brought the faith and to whom today's Second Reading is addressed—once abandoned Paul to follow instead a false prophet whose presence and eloquence attracted them.

And when Jesus, the Prophet of Prophets, spoke, there were some who refused to believe *him*: they even asked him for his credentials, as today's Gospel recounts. Christ's message was so different from what some of his listeners wanted to hear.

Part of Christ's message is of course the universal need for self-discipline as a key to salvation: fasting and abstinence, for instance. This is a lesson not particularly liked by an indulgent world; when preached even today it occasions some to turn away and look for other prophets, who preach comfortable living.

This is not to say that in our human weakness, we are not tempted to live as comfortably as we can—by minimizing the thought of fasting or abstinence, say. Paul, in today's Second Reading, admits to his begging God three times to remove a certain affliction from his life. (We don't know what it was: an eye-ailment, perhaps, or maybe a recurring malarial fever.) Jesus' reply to Paul rings out through the centuries to us: "My grace is enough for you, for in weakness power reaches perfection."

Like Paul we too are tempted in our weakness. We tend to ignore certain prophecies: again, the need to fast, the need to abstain from certain foods (such as meat) as the Church invites us to do every Friday, urgently so during the Fridays of Lent. But Christ tells us that our weakness can be corrected by his grace. We have but to want his help—seriously, sincerely—and we *can* respond to the Gospel imperatives of self-discipline.

Not to commit ourselves to some form of self-discipline—to the necessity of fasting, expecially during Lent; and of observing some form of abstinence from food on Fridays, especially during Lent—is to join with the group of dissenters in today's Gospel. It is like saying, in effect, "Where did Jesus get the wisdom to tell us that self-discipline is so necessary?"

Recall that Jesus left Nazareth because the people found him "too much for them;" certain of his prophesies disturbed them too much.

Are we of the same bent? Or do *all* of Jesus' prophecies have meaning for us such as self-discipline?

FIFTEENTH SUNDAY
IN ORDINARY TIME (B)

Predestination And Divine Adoption

Amos 7:12-15; Ephesians 1:3-10; Mark 6:7-13

Aim: to explain (1) the mysteries of our predestination and adoption through Christ; (2) and that Christ is now encountered in his Body, the Church.

Today's Second Reading, from Paul's Letter to Ephesus, is an extraordinary revelation. In it we learn that we have literally been predestined by God to be his adopted sons and daughters in Christ. Before the world began, we are told, God in his love freely willed not only our redemption, but also our adoption as his children.

The magnitude of this mystery staggers the mind when it is seriously pondered.

How can God—the Creator who fashioned the atom and the farthermost galaxies—adopt a human being, a creature, so much so that the creature can properly invoke his or her Creator as "Father"?

To adopt means to receive another into one's own family. By adoption an outsider becomes a full member of a family: the adopted takes the name of the adopter; he even has rights of inheritance.

Further, adoption presumes similarity of nature. An angel cannot adopt a human being; nor a human being, an angel. Different natures preclude valid adoption.

How is it then—to return to the question—that God, who is

divine, can adopt a human being? How can God secure us the right to address him properly as "Father?"

The answer is there, in today's Second Reading, related by St. Paul, relying on the Spirit's guidance. God adopts us by first giving us a share of his own divine life—call it God-life, or grace (because it is gratuitously given). God literally penetrates our human natures, elevates them without altering what is essential to our natural selves, and makes us God-like. Because we are gifted with a share in God's own life, therefore, we are enabled to be adopted in the proper sense.

Amos, the prophet of today's First Reading, was overcome with amazement that God would reach out and choose him, a simple shepherd and farmer, to prophesy in God's name. Yet Amos' elevation in dignity pales before God's choice of each one of us through the mystery of divine adoption in Jesus.

"In Jesus," we say, because it is through Christ, God-made-man, that we enter and remain in God's family. The fullness of divine life is communicated to Jesus, and through Jesus' humanity to all who are now his brethren in the flesh.

Now, in these post-Pentecostal times, the sacred humanity of Jesus is encountered, we believe, in Jesus' Mystical Body, the Church, whose origins we recall in today's beautiful Gospel, from Mark. It is through the Church, principally through its seven sacraments, that we acquire, and grow in, the God-life by which our divine adoption is made possible and sustained.

Our being chosen by God in Christ means, first, our being baptized into his Church, our being healed by his forgiveness, our being nourished at his eucharistic table.

We are now gathered at this table, the table of the Lord through whom we properly address our Father, in the sacrificial banquet of his divine Son, which we call the Mass.

SIXTEENTH SUNDAY IN ORDINARY TIME (B)

Union with Jesus the Shepherd in the Church

Jeremiah 23:1-6; Ephesians 2:13-18; Mark 6:30-34.

Aim: (1) to explain Jesus' mission in terms of leadership and companionship, and (2) to accent that Jesus as Shepherd is now encountered in the Church.

Jeremiah, the sensitive voice of today's First Reading, prophesied in the sixth century before Christ. (Incidentally, Jeremiah is the longest book of the Bible).

The segment of Jeremiah read today is a celebrated passage, depicting God's gathering the lost sheep of Israel and leading them back to pasture. Nebuchadnezzar, the Babylonian King, had entered Jerusalem; thousands of Israelites were taken hostage and deported to Babylon, whose ruins can still be seen in modern day Iraq. Jeremiah foretells that God will ransom his people, that the Babylonian Captivity would end.

God depicted as a shepherd was an intensely meaningful figure for the Israelites of old. To them the figure immediately conveyed two ideas: leadership and companionship. A shepherd is a person of strength who supports others. And he is deeply involved with his charges, cherishing each one of them, ever ready to carry any one of them (cf. Isaiah 40:11).

Through Jeremiah, God predicts a time when he will raise up new shepherds, a time without fear or terror, a time in which "not one shall be lost."

This prediction was perfectly fulfilled in Jesus of Nazareth, whom we see today feeling compassion for the crowds because they were like sheep without a shepherd.

In many New Testament texts, Jesus identifies with the good shepherd of Jeremiah's prophecy. In Mt 15, Jesus is portrayed as the one sent to the lost sheep of Israel; in Lk 12 he is leader of the "little flock" of disciples; in Heb 13, he is called greater than the "prince of shepherds," referring to Moses, who shepherded Israel out of Egypt into the doorway of the Promised Land.

John's Gospel is the supreme expression of Jesus the Good Shepherd. Therein we see the Savior as the gate to good pastures, the sole life-giving leader who unites the sheep with himself in a bond of love, sealed with his willingness to give his life for the sheep.

This same Jesus, we now encouter in his Mystical Body, the Church, about which Paul writes so beautifully in Ephesians, from which today's Second Reading is excerpted. It is through the Church, headed now by Peter's successor—the Supreme Pontiff—who was commissioned by Christ to feed his flock, that the leadership and companionship of the Lord is most fully seen and experienced—as the Second Reading today implies.

We have, in this one, holy, apostolic and Catholic Church, to which we adhere, the living presence of Christ the Good Shepherd, actually leading us and living in our midst.

To be separated from Jesus the Good Shepherd? One thinks of the Israelite exiles, who, in Babylon, lamented:

"By the streams of Babylon we sat and wept when we remembered Sion . . ." (Ps 136).

Appreciate the gift of God.

SEVENTEENTH SUNDAY IN ORDINARY TIME (B)

The Mass

Second Kings 4:42-44; Ephesians 4:1-6; John 6:1-5.

Aim: (1) to explain the Mass as a re-presentation of the Last Supper and Calvary; (2) to describe in general the main parts of Mass as: a) Liturgy of the Eucharist, preceded by b) Liturgy of the Word, with the subdivisions of each. (These two parts are interdependent and mutually supportive.)

This week the Sunday Bible readings inaugurate a series of summertime reflections on the Eucharist. Like the multitudes gathered on the grass before Jesus in the Gospel, we are invited to listen to him teaching us about the Bread of Life, and to receive this Bread with renewed awareness of its unique sacramental nature.

Today's First Reading recounts a miracle of feeding wrought through the intercession of Elisha the prophet. It looks forward to the day when Jesus, the Prophet of Prophets, would multiply bread in anticipation of his changing bread into his own Body and Blood to feed us on *our* pilgrimage to eternal life as one people united with him (Second Reading).

All the lessons today, then, bid us reflect upon the Mass, which, in perfect fulfillment of prophecy, began over 19 centuries ago in the Upper Room of Jerusalem, to perpetuate the Sacrifice of the Cross in our midst until Jesus the High Priest and Victim of the New Testament, now risen and ascended to the Father, comes again.

Like the disciples in the Upper Room, we too assemble; first to hear God's living word spoken in our midst (chiefly through the Bible readings and the homily), and to respond to his word in faith (through the various acclamations, prayers, hymns and the Creed); then to participate in the Eucharistic Prayer, through which Christ becomes really present under the appearances of bread and wine; and to receive this Eucharist in communion.

Because of its instructional nature, the first part of Mass we call the Liturgy of the Word. After blessing ourselves and confessing our unworthiness in the penitential rite, we join the priest-celebrant in the Opening Prayer. Then the Word of God is proclaimed; on Sundays, there are three readings—the first usually from the Old Testament.

These Bible readings constitute an integral part of the Mass, for they help us, through the Spirit, to call to mind the countless dimensions of the Christ event: who Jesus was, why he came to save us, how we can unite ourselves to him in thanksgiving and fulfillment. And these readings also serve to prepare us in faith for the second part of the Eucharist, when Jesus' Real Presence is renewed in our midst and given to us as our food.

The Liturgy of the Eucharist, the second part of Mass, reenacts a miracle before which even Jesus' multiplication of bread pales. Through the Eucharistic Prayer, in which the Father is asked to send the Holy Spirit into our midst, and in which the words Jesus said over the bread and cup at the Last Supper are repeated by the celebrant, bread and wine are changed into Jesus' Body and Blood, and then offered to us as food for our souls in obedience to Jesus' own invitation, "Take this and eat it" (Mt 26:26). (The traditional word used by the Church for this miracle is "transsubstantiation.")

"The hand of the Lord feeds us;" thus the Psalmist said long ago in today's Responsorial Psalm. All this is fulfilled in the thanksgiving, memorial sacrificial banquet of the Lord's Supper, for which we are now met, in response to Jesus' own directive, "Do this as a remembrance of me" (Lk 22:19).

EIGHTEENTH SUNDAY IN ORDINARY TIME (B)

The Mass

Exodus 16:2-4, 12-15; Ephesians 4:17, 20-24; John 6:24-35.

Aim: to explain why Catholics attend Mass and how meaningful attendance is secured.

In today's First Reading we are told that the Israelites, having achieved their escape from Egypt through God's intervention, were miraculously fed—sustained in their journey to the Promised Land— by bread from heaven, which they called *manna*.

Jesus, in today's Gospel, identifies with the Old Testament manna; he is the Bread of Life which the manna in the desert prefigured.

To understand this, an entirely new way of thinking must be acquired, as St. Paul reminds us, in today's Second Reading, for faith in general.

We acquire this new way of thinking, and we nourish it, through the Mass, by means of which, through the manna of the New Testament, we are transformed into more Christ-like persons, able and ready to keep up the pilgrimage of this life toward our eternal homeland, and to help others to do the same.

From one viewpoint, today's Bible lessons answer the question as to why Catholics attend Mass.

Catholics meet for the Eucharist because the Mass represents the actualization of the Church in miniature; it is at the altar that the Church's transformation of the world begins. It is at the altar that the Catholic gives his Yes of consent in response to the divine summons to renew the earth, as Archbishop John F. Whealon of Hartford has put it (*The Catholic Transcript*, 27 February 1970).

The word "meet" is extremely important here. The Scripture speaks of the early Christians *gathering* or *assembling* for Mass. (Cf. 1 Cor 11:18, for instance). The Eucharist is a *communal* event; it constitutes the highest actualization of the Church, the redeemed Christian *community*. In it the individual encounters Christ as a member of the redeemed community, the new People of God of the eternal covenant sealed with Jesus' own Blood.

Now since the Sacrifice of the Mass represents the highest possible actualization of the Church, "nowhere is everything which the Church is, and has the mission to announce, more intensely manifested than in the celebration of the Eucharist" (*The Celebration of the Eucharist*, by Karl Rahner and Angelus Hauessling: Herder and Herder, 1967).

Which is to say that it is in the Mass that the work of transforming—changing, renewing, revitalizing, Christianizing the earth—begins.

It is from assembling for the Eucharist, then, that the Christian achieves the strength and the courage to go forth and live the three dimensions of the Church's "life-style:" fellowship, witness and service. It is from assembling for the Eucharist that the Christian derives fresh enthusiasm for announcing the Good News of God's Incarnate Son in the world in which he lives and moves.

Obviously this requires sincere participation on the part of the worshipper. It means that he or she carefully listens to the Bible Readings, responds meaningfully to the various acclamations, joins with his heart in the priestly prayers, especially the great Eucharistic Prayer, sings the hymns as well as he can, and receives Communion with deliberate faith, hope and love.

In this way the Mass *can* transform us.

NINETEENTH SUNDAY IN ORDINARY TIME (B)

The Mass and Spiritual Hunger

First Kings 19:4-8; Ephesians 4:30, 5:2; John 6:41-51.

Aim: (1) to describe the Prefaces and Eucharistic Prayers and to describe how a Catholic participates in these parts of Mass; (2) to accent the Eucharist as necessary food.

Once again, this Sunday, the Scripture readings focus on the Eucharist: the Bread of Life by means of which our deepest hunger—spiritual hunger—is satisfied—the Bread of Life about which Jesus said, in today's Gospel, that those who eat of it shall never hunger again—the Bread of Life prefigured by the miraculous food provided Elijah, in today's First Reading.

This Bread of Life comes to us through the Mass: the thanksgiving, memorial sacrificial banquet of the New Testament by which Christ, Eternal Priest and Victim, mysteriously offers himself as "a gift of pleasing fragrance" to the Father—to borrow St. Paul's phrase in today's Second Reading.

The heart of the Mass is the Eucharistic Prayer or Anaphora, which we also call the Canon. ("Anaphora" is a Greek derivative meaning "offering.") In this Prayer said by the priest and introduced by the preface—which is not simply an introduction, but a thematic proclamation integral to the Canon—the elements of bread and wine are changed into Christ's Body and Blood through a mystery the Church terms "transsubstantiation."

There are presently four standard Eucharistic Prayers in general use by the Western Rite. The first is the old Roman Canon. The second, the briefest (75 terse lines), is based on the third-century Canon of St. Hippolytus, the oldest known fixed Canon, originally written in Greek (when Greek was the language of the Mass even in Rome). Eucharistic Prayer III is an entirely new Canon which stresses the work of the Holy Spirit in the Mass and in the worshipping community. Anaphora IV, finally, is a finely executed verbal painting of the whole of salvation history, accenting the various covenants God has made with mankind.

Through the Eucharistic Prayer, which is a prayer of thanksgiving, the Father is invoked to send forth his Holy Spirit (this is known as "epiclesis," from the Greek for "invocation") that the bread and wine presented might be changed into Jesus' Body and Blood in a memorial reenactment of the Last Supper and the Crucifixion, so that we might receive him in communion.

At the core of the Anaphora, the words which Jesus said over the bread and wine in the Upper Room on Holy Thursday are spoken by the priest in the Lord's name. Following these words, the priest says, "Let us proclaim the mystery of Faith" to which the congregation responds with a formula of belief. At the close of the Eucharistic Prayer, the Priest elevates the Eucharist with a prayer of praise, and the congregation clearly affirms its faith with the Great Amen.

"Let us proclaim the mystery of faith." Surely this means that the Eucharist is the divine, real and effective Sign of all truth, the very sanctuary of all our belief.

Our deepest yearnings, our most severe hungers, can be satisfied here: in the Eucharist. It is here that we come to know infallibly that Jesus, who is Lord, *lives*, and *intervenes* in our lives, and awaits us *now* at the final stage of this transitory life.

Christ *is* risen; Christ will *come* again.

TWENTIETH SUNDAY
IN ORDINARY TIME (B)

The Mass

Proverbs 9:1-6; Ephesians 5:15-20; John 6:51-58

Aim: to describe in general and in detail: (1) the Communion Rite of the Mass; and (2) how a Catholic receives Holy Communion or makes a spiritual Communion.

Today we conclude the summertime series on the Blessed Eucharist with Bible readings that accent Holy Communion.

The Eucharist, which perfectly fulfills the symbol of the manna of the Old Testament, is the food that gives us life forever. Today's First Reading, from the Book of Proverbs, offers a future invitation to a banquet prepared by God. The Responsorial Psalm thanks God for this food; the Second Reading, from Paul to the Ephesians, echoes this note of thanksgiving.

Today's Gospel clearly teaches us that the Eucharist was given to us to receive as food. It is precisely in the act of eating that eucharistic encounter with Jesus is made.

In describing the Eucharist as food, one key difference from ordinary food in this analogy must be accented. Whereas ordinary food, bread for instance, is assimilated into man; the very opposite takes place in Holy Communion. Here, as the Church Fathers never tired of insisting, man is assimilated into the Bread of Life.

To receive communion worthily, it is first necessary of course to be in the state of grace. But the measure of the union God wishes to have with us is reflected in our own dispositions of love for him; the more intense the faith, hope and love we have for Christ, the more perfect our communion with him will be. It is in this area that the answer can often be found as to why we can go to communion frequently, yet not register progress in our Christian lives.

Our disposition at communion will spontaneously overflow into thanksgiving for so incomparable a gift. Do you remember how the disciples gathered up the left-over fragments of the loaves and fishes when Jesus multiplied them? (Mt 14:13-21). Can't this be translated into terms of our need, after banqueting at the Table of the Lord, likewise to collect the fragments—in a mystical sense?

And what about allowing our thanksgiving to flow into the actions of our day, to allow our communion to mean a going forth with Christian joy to live what the Mass can effect: our own transformation and service to others in Christian gladness?

Put it this way. Day after day we leave many areas we have passed in fragments: broken pledges or harsh words, for example. "Gathering up the fragments" can mean that through communion we determine to return to the places we have disturbed and put them together again (by kindness, or concern, or sympathy).

A final word about communion. We can also experience it in a spiritual sense, as for instance, when we make a visit to the Blessed Sacrament or make a Holy Hour before the Blessed Sacrament solemnly enthroned. Then our hearts can be filled with sentiments of thanksgiving for this Bread from Heaven, and with resolutions to purify our dispositions for our next Holy Communion.

One means of reminding ourselves always of the need for faith, hope and love and thanksgiving at communion time, is to respond deliberately and sincerely with the "Amen" we are invited to say to the word, "The Body of Christ."

TWENTY-FIRST SUNDAY
IN ORDINARY TIME (B)

Christian Faith and Current Challenges

Joshua 24:1-2, 15-17, 18; Ephesians 5:21-32; John 6:60-69.

Aim: to explain (1) that Christian faith entails unreserved belief in Jesus as Lord and Savior, and (2) that abandonment of faith cannot be attributed to causes other than abandonment of faith.

Today's First Reading recalls the figure of Joshua, who succeeded Moses. Moses died just before he could lead the Israelites into the Promised Land; Joshua took over Moses' work. Mysteriously the name "Joshua" comes from the same root as "Jesus," in fact, the source of the name "Jesus" is the Hebrew *Yesua*, a late form of *Yosua*, meaning "God—Yahweh—saves." In this sense, Moses represents the Old Testament; he could lead God's People only so far. The completion of the journey, the entrance into the Promised Land, was assigned to Joshua, who symbolizes Jesus, even as to the meaning of his name.

It is in Jesus, therefore, in faith in Jesus, that we achieve the fulfillment of God's promises. The liturgy invites us to think of Jesus, the Son of God Incarnate, when we join in Joshua's prayer in today's First Reading:

"As for me . . . we will serve the Lord . . . Far be it from us to forsake the Lord for the service of other gods."

Faith in Jesus—a committed, loyal, persevering, enthusiastic faith—is crucial today, when a host of new challenges to belief are emerging from all sides, and when so many individuals claim (at least) to have surrendered to these challenges, especially with excuses drawn from current theories in psychology or sociology.

One of these theories is called "separation anxiety;" the assumption by some is that the Church has "changed" so since Vatican II that they have been "separated" from the familiar in ritual, doctrine and discipline.

"Separation anxiety" may sound like an easy explanation, but it really doesn't get to the bottom of the problem; it can't probe the innermost depths of the soul.

Too, sociological surveys may help isolate extrinsic and accidental characteristics of those who doubt or abandon the Church, but they can't relate precisely to that sacred area in which the Spirit alone can enter, in which the individual confronts God in the innermost depths of his personality.

Some people claim, that they "used to be such good Catholics," but now that "everything is changed" they can no longer believe. Faith does not disappear of itself; for it to weaken or vanish, it must be either ignored, wasted or rejected.

Christ gives the light and the capacity to anyone who *wants to believe* in his Church, his principal Sacrament and, hence, his visible presence in this world. Refusal to open one's heart in belief hinders faith, as today's Gospel, from Jesus' Eucharistic sermon, reminds us.

Anyone today with faith in Jesus can retain his faith in Jesus, if only he or she prays (as Peter prayed in today's Gospel):

"Lord, to whom shall we go? You have the words of eternal life. We have come to believe."

Indeed, anyone who lives by these words will unquestionably share in the celebration of the union between Jesus and his Church— a union described, in today's Second Reading, in terms of wedding joy.

A person has problems *with* faith only because he or she has problems *of* faith. He or she who wants to believe, *can* with Jesus' help, continue to believe.

TWENTY-SECOND SUNDAY IN ORDINARY TIME (B)

Traditions, Works, and Actual Grace

Deuteronomy 4:1-2, 6-8; James 1:17-18, 21-22, 27; Mark 7:1-8, 14-15, 21-23.

Aim: to explain (1) that even the holiest Traditions must be kept and observed with love; and (2) that God grants actual graces for such observance.

Traditions are important. Some traditions are more important than others. Take, for instance, God-given or inspired Traditions, such as the moral law, the Ten Commandments, cited in today's First Reading, from the list in Deuteronomy. But even these Traditions are not to be observed simply according to the letter.

"This people pays me lip-service, but their heart is far from me ... Therefore, empty is the reverence they do me . . ." Isaiah's words, reaffirmed by Jesus in today's Gospel reading, compel our strictest attention.

What is true religion? Is it defined simply in terms of external ritual acts? Like genuflecting? Or lighting a devotional candle? Or carrying palms? Is it, rather, obeying the Ten Commandments as laws imposed upon us?

Today's Scripture lessons emphasize that whatever our worship, whatever our observance of the law, all is sterile unless it proceeds from a sincere heart. We are called by God as persons, not robots or automatons. The holiest of Traditions must be kept and observed with the heart.

"Kept and observed," we say. Faith must be accompanied by works; today's Second Reading, from James, reminds us of this. "Act" on God's word, he tells us. "Welcome it" with "its power to save you."

Sometimes we tend to forget that God literally helps us to act in accordance with our sincere belief; to *do* as we affirm. Yet our faith, clearly, is that God is always present to us with what we describe as "actual" graces. These are the supernatural aids given us by God so that we can live by what we profess—the Ten Commandments, for example, or the Sign of the Cross. Thus, if we sincerely believe in the Sign of the Cross which we make with a reverence corresponding to our belief, we will be graced with the help needed to implement this Sign in our lives: by suffering service to others, for example. Or, in the case of lighting a devotional candle: if our faith is sincere, the candle can occasion divine help to illumine others in Christ's light through loving witness to Gospel truth.

We could relate all the foregoing to this Sunday Eucharist. Why are we assembled here today? Surely we have come to worship God in faith, hope and love, so that our worship is fundamentally a matter of the heart. At the same time, however, do we not intend to act upon this worship in which we are now involved? Are we not convinced that just as the bread and wine, symbolizing all creation, are changed into Jesus' Body and Blood, so, in like manner, through our participation in this Mass we can be changed into more Christ-like persons, and thereby spiritually energized to help transform our homes and neighborhoods according to the pattern of Christ our Lord?

"Act on the word"—St. James phrase—is supremely true of this Mass.

TWENTY-THIRD SUNDAY IN ORDINARY TIME (B)

Mortal and Venial Sin

Isaiah 35:4-7; James 2:1-5; Mark 7:31-37.

Aim: to explain (1) the two kinds of actual sin, and (2) the three conditions necessary for a mortal sin.

In one sense, a basic sin against Christianity is *not listening*. For listening to God's Word opens the way to faith. Moreover, faith is practiced by listening to the word.

Listening is a mystery. It is not the same as physically hearing, since it involves the heart as well as the ears and the mind. In fact listening is so deep and complex a mystery that many contemporary philosophers as well as theologians are engaged in an examination of it in the premise that true listening permits personal encounter. In faith, of course, the personal encounter is with the living Lord Jesus in his Church, principally through the sacraments.

Jesus often dwelt on the mystery of listening. In Mk 4:3 he bids us "Listen carefully to this."

Listening to Jesus sets the stage for man's free option: the option to accept Christ and make a commitment in faith, or not to accept and to refuse commitment.

To what are we invited to listen? Specifically? Surely one of Jesus' fundamental messages is a summons to repentance. We have no need of a Savior unless we acknowledge both our sinfulness, and our inability to overcome it without God's help.

In other words, sin and repentance are basic themes we must listen to; unless we listen to them, we cannot frankly acknowledge and deal with them.

Sin is the opposite of Christian love. Sin is a personal offense against God, which means that it is a refusal to accept him and his word.

Sin is called "mortal" (from a Latin word for "death") when it constitutes alienation from God. This happens when an action is in itself seriously wrong, assuming of course that sufficient advertence and freedom of the will are verified. Thus we say that three elements contribute toward mortal sin: serious matter, sufficient advertence and full consent of the will.

Serious matter is known to us from the Bible, from the Church teaching us, and from reason. The Bible, for example, cites actions which exclude from the kingdom of heaven unless they are repented of. Thus St. Paul, in First Corinthians, writes: "Do not be deceived; neither the immoral, nor idolaters, nor homosexuals, nor thieves, nor the greedy, nor drunkards, nor revilers, nor robbers, will inherit the kingdom of God" (6:9-10).

Another area involving serious matter is cited in today's Second Reading: the area of social justice. Discrimination against others, we are reminded, is a form of favoritism that is clearly un-Christian.

Venial sin traditionally refers not so much to a turning away from God, as to a shortcoming, or a misstep. Perhaps the matter is not serious; perhaps free consent was not given; perhaps sufficient advertence was not given.

The fact of sin and Jesus' summons to repentance must be heard if we are to be saved. Today's First Reading enthusiastically looks forward to a Savior, whom we know is Christ the Lord. Again, though, what need have we of a Savior unless we realize that we are in desperate need of being saved? That we are sinners? This is a truth which Satan, the Father of Lies, prefers us not to *hear*.

TWENTY-FOURTH SUNDAY IN ORDINARY TIME (B)

The Sacraments in General

Isaiah 35:4-7; James 2:1-5; Mark 7:31-37.

Aim: (1) to present the seven sacraments as grace-giving signs and actions of Christ at key times in our lives; and (2) to hold up the norm and ideal of sacramental living as our response to the actions of Christ for us.

St. Augustine, the great Doctor of the Church, used to take the opening theme for his Sunday homilies from the Responsorial Psalm. (Once, the story goes, when the lector read or chanted the wrong verse, Augustine had to extemporize.)

Today's Responsorial Psalm reads: "I will walk in the presence of the Lord in the land of the living." This verse—from Psalm 116—was fulfilled in Jesus of Nazareth, the living Lord who is present to us as really as he was in the scene of today's Gospel, when he preached the absolute necessity of assuming his cross and following him. Now, of course, he is present in his Mystical Body, the Church.

In the Church, Christ has left us seven principal means by which we encounter him: the seven sacraments, which are infallible and effective signs of his presence in our lives.

Just as we are born physically, so we are born to eternal life through the Sacrament of Baptism. As this sacrament is conferred upon us, we literally embrace Christ our Savior giving us the new life he ushered in by his death and resurrection.

As we mature in chronological age, so through the Sacrament of Confirmation we are configured more closely to Jesus.

Just as we suffer bodily illness and weakness, so too we are affected by spiritual disorder or disease: sin. Here Jesus meets us in the Sacrament of Penance or Reconciliation, both as a cure and for strength against relapse.

To survive in the body we must sustain ourselves by food and drink; otherwise we perish. The Eucharist is *the* sustaining food for our spirit, so necessary in fact, that without it we could not maintain life. St. John's sixth chapter tells us this plainly.

As serious illness sets in, or as advanced age slows down our physical or mental capacities, we need special helps. For this, the Sacrament of the Anointing of the Sick, or Extreme Unction, was instituted. Here Jesus meets us precisely in our grave illness or advanced age, and helps us immerse our sufferings—and ourselves— in his Passion, death and resurrection.

Finally, the two major states of life are consecrated with Jesus' presence in the Sacraments of Matrimony, by which marriage, family life and the continuance of the human race are sanctified; and Holy Orders, by which the spiritual paternity of Jesus' priesthood is passed on through the centuries.

Every time we receive a sacrament, we encounter the risen Lord who allows us to cry aloud with Isaiah, in today's First Reading: "See, the Lord God is my help; who will prove me wrong?"

Recourse to the sacraments—usually Penance and the Eucharist—is the principal manifestation of faith in practice—to borrow that historically significant phrase from today's Second Reading. This is why we commonly describe those Catholics who often meet Jesus in the Sacrament of Penance and in the Eucharist as "practicing Catholics."

The "good works" of our faith begin with embracing Jesus in the sacraments, supremely in Mass and Holy Communion.

TWENTY-FIFTH SUNDAY IN ORDINARY TIME (B)

The Laity in the Church

Wisdom 2:17-20; James 3:16, 4:3; Mark 9:30-37.

Aim: (1) to show the Church as basically made up of laity, baptized in Christ (2) to emphasize the importance, the dignity—the priesthood—of the laity in the Church.

Today's Second Reading, from the Letter of St. James, almost sounds as if it were composed by a modern day sociologist or psychologist, doesn't it? Take the line, "You envy and you cannot acquire, so you quarrel and fight."

Is it necessary that we grapple with others and fragment community to achieve our goals? No, we are told. Have faith, work for justice and peace; God will grace our efforts. The surest way to acquire justice and peace is by witnessing to and implementing justice and peace.

The task is not easy. As today's First Reading prophesies, evil men usually lie in wait to stop those who try to make the world better: "Let us beset the just one, because he is obnoxious to us; he sets himself against our doings."

Yet to make this world a better place—a little better place—is our Christian Vocation. To this we are summoned by Jesus. Life is a treasure bestowed on each person in a unique way; what matters is how one uses the little life that God has given us. Suffering service in the footsteps of Jesus of Nazareth—the point of today's Gospel— must be the life-style of the Christian.

By and large this describes the role of the laity, of whom the Church is basically constituted. To be a layperson in the Church *is a vocation.* And whatever discussion may be possible regarding degrees of excellence characterizing vocations in themselves, the best vocation for an individual, concretely speaking, will necessarily be that to which he or she has been called by God. Which means, for most, the lay Christian vocation.

By virtue of baptism, the laity are charged with looking for opportunities to announce Christ to a confused or errant world; Vatican II strongly reaffirmed this. (*Degree on the Apostolate of the Laity* of Vatican II, Section 6). This entails witnessing: (1) communication of God's words of life to others; and (2) testimony to these words by acts and general attitudes.

Too, whereas there is an essential difference between the ordained ministerial priesthood and the lay vocation, it is nonetheless valid and meaningful to speak of the priesthood of the laity. For the layperson also participates in Jesus' priesthood, not only by sharing in the Eucharist and the sacraments, not only by joining in prayer and thanksgiving, but also "by the witness of a holy life, and by self-denial and active charity" (*Dogmatic Constitution on the Church* of Vatican II, Section 10).

Today the witness and actions of the laity are especially needed in several problematic areas. One is marriage, and human sexuality in general. Another area is reverence for life, now under attack through abortion and euthanasia. A third is racial or ethnic justice. A fourth is honesty in business. Another is entertainment.

These are some areas in which the laity today not only witness and act effectively, but in which, for the most part, the role of the laity is surpassing. It is a holy function, of a holy vocation.

TWENTY-SIXTH SUNDAY IN ORDINARY TIME (B)

Occasions of Sin and Temptation

Numbers 11:25-29; James 5:1-6; Mark 9:38-43

Aim: (1) to define an occasion of sin and a temptation; (2) to give helpful spiritual guidance concerning each.

At first, today's Bible readings invite reflection on the truth that any person of good will who tries to follow in Jesus' footsteps, graces this world. Jesus says, in the Gospel, "Anyone who is not against us is for us."

One is reminded of a news photograph of Pope John XXIII embracing a Buddhist monk and explaining that we as Christians respect anything that is good or true in religion. One is reminded of Mohandas Gandhi, who kept a picture of Jesus in his room till his dying day; and who, by any assessment, tried to implement the Sermon on the Mount, which he knew.

Surely we've got to learn, all of us, how to discern God's word in the wisdom of persons who strive to speak responsibly in truth; today's First Reading also reminds us of this need.

But there is a specific sentence in the Gospel that also requires frequent pondering on its own, a rather chilling sentence which, while filling out the context of listening to wisdom from every source, cautions us against false prophecy. We mean our Lord's clear warning that anyone who causes scandal, who leads others astray, is thereby separating himself from Christ's love.

This part of the Gospel requires emphasis today, when even the traditional phrase, "occasion of sin," is rarely heard. By it we mean, of course, any person, place or thing that can lead us into evil, whether in thought, desire, or deed. Films can be occasions of sin: films which graphically portray evil as indifferent, say. Likewise, television programs, magazine articles, books; also, certain conversations, *and* certain individuals.

One of the errors we tend to commit when discussing occasions of sin is to cite things such as those we have just detailed, all either pertaining to entertainment, or else largely relating to the virtue of purity. We generally neglect to cite our lifestyle as a possible occasion of sin: the quest for material gain; for example, or for worldly status. Yet life in Christ *can be lost* by immersing oneself in a climate of amoral business practices, or in a mindless ambition for power and wealth in a corporate structure. Today's Second Reading, from James, is a dramatic warning against our enslaving ourselves to wealth for wealth's sake.

One of the most urgent imperatives of every Christian, clearly, is a thorough examination of conscience, frequently during the year, especially before approaching the Sacrament of Penance, regarding the occasions of sin on one's life. We must ask ourselves whether there are things, persons, or places that can effect serious temptations— attractions of our wills—against God's law. Not to do this is to allow ourselves to become unaware of the dangers we are entertaining.

At the same time, we must ask ourselves, at least, whether we are scandals to others, in any way.

God, we know, will not allow that we be tempted beyond the strength he gives us to withstand the enticements of Satan and his evil influences (1 Cor 10:13). But, again, to toy with temptation, especially by dallying with, or entering into, situations which we know from experience are clearly occasions of sin for us, is to presume on his mercy.

TWENTY-SEVENTH SUNDAY IN ORDINARY TIME (B)

Marriage and Divorce

Genesis 2:18-24; Hebrews 2:9-11; Mark 10:2-16

Aim: (1) to explain the sanctity of Christian marriage; (2) to explain the Church's teaching against divorce and remarriage, and to offer pastoral norms for the divorced.

What else are we invited to reflect upon by today's Bible readings if not the sanctity and permanence of marriage? The Gospel, which refers back to today's First Reading, is so clear on the subject.

Marriage, we believe, is not merely the consecration of man to a woman, and of a woman to a man. It is also a true consecration of the union itself of a bride and a groom, by which union, the couple enter into *a special covenant* with the living Lord, Jesus.

For a Christian, therefore, marriage is not defined simply in terms of a legal contract between husband and wife. Nor is it just a sacred contract; the pagan Romans knew that marriage is a sacred contract. No; for a Christian, marriage is a covenant with Christ, a permanent agreement involving promises made by Christ to grace and protect those united in him. This is why an act of worship is required for Christian marriage; wedding vows constitute an act of worship. The engaged couple, regardless of how deep their love may be, cannot inherit the privileges of the Sacrament of Matrimony until they have solemnly ratified their mutual love in a sacrifice of worship; until, in other words, they have (as we say) exchanged their lifelong vows within Jesus' mystical Body, the Church. For, again, Christian marriage involves not only the offering of a bride and groom's mystery to one another, but the oblation of their total mystery together as part of a dynamic covenant with the risen and reigning Lord Jesus, the same Jesus who, as today's Second Reading reminds us, is not hesitant to call us brothers and sisters since he has assumed our humanity.

Because Christian marriage involves not only the union of a man and woman, but also the union of the couple with the living Lord Jesus, marriage is a lifelong institution, requiring of the spouses the fidelity with which Jesus commits himself to their union. The Church has always firmly taught that a sacramental marriage between Christians, on which there has been true matrimonial consent and consummation, is absolutely indissoluble, save by the death of one of the spouses. Our faith in this regard is clearly expressed in the form of matrimonial consent in the wedding ceremony. For example, the groom says:

"I . . . take you . . . to be my wife. I promise to be true to you in good times and in bad, in sickness and in health. I will love you and honor you *all the days of my life.*"

Divorce and remarriage, therefore, is inconsonant with Gospel truth; as Catholics we must reject it.

A society such as ours, where divorce and remarriage is nonchalantly accepted without critical examination, provides a climate for confusion. Sincere concern for those who have suffered divorce should characterize the Catholic community. And, as the *National Catechetical Directory for Catholics of the United States* admonishes: "Divorced persons and their children should be welcomed by the parish community and made to feel truly a part of parish life. Catechesis on the Church's teaching concerning the consequences of remarriage after divorce is not only necessary but will be supportive for the divorced" (No. 131).

As Catholics, our regard for marriage flows from its surpassing dignity: the union of the spouses with Christ our Lord.

TWENTY-EIGHTH SUNDAY IN ORDINARY TIME (B)

Celibacy, Vowed Chastity and Marriage

Wisdom 7:7-11; Hebrews 4:12-13; Mark 10:17-30.

Aim: (1) to present the Gospel and Traditional Catholic teaching on celibacy, vowed chastity and marriage as an example of the wisdom of God's word, essentially transcending the highest wisdom of men.

"God's word," today's Second Reading reminds us, "is living and effective, sharper than any two-edged sword."

This means that the Bible as read within the Church—the Scriptures and tradition—not only represents perfection and fullness of truth, but is also dynamic, incomparably challenging, and efficacious. of faith.

How unsophisticated it is to suppose that *ultimate* wisdom can more readily or more thoroughly be discovered elsewhere.

The Ten Commandments listed in today's Gospel, constitute a rather obvious example of God's wisdom, which in whole or in part, is either questioned, rejected, or just ignored by the world.

Take, however, the closing portion of today's Gospel (long form); the portion in which Jesus tells us that anyone who gives up home and parents and children for his sake will be rewarded a hundredfold. This is one of many Biblical texts focusing on Jesus' call to the life of celibacy or vowed commitment to chastity for his sake. It is a vocation which diocesan priests assume by virtue of their ordination, and which religious priests, sisters, monks and brothers embrace by vow.

Priestly celibacy or vowed chastity is understandable only in the light of the faith that God's wisdom transcends ours. Jesus, remember, revealed celibacy or vowed chastity as a charism. In Mt 19:11-12, we read that anyone who opts for this state of life for the sake of the Kingdom of God *can* possess it.

"The choice of celibacy," wrote Pope Paul VI, "does not connote ignorance, or despising of the sexual instinct and affectivity. That would certainly do damage to the physical and psychological balance. On the contrary, it demands clear understanding, careful self-control, and a wise sublimation of the psychological life on a higher plane. In this way, celibacy sets the whole man on a higher level and makes an effective contribution to his perfection" (*Sacerdotalis Caelibatus*).

To assume celibacy, then, is to rely on the Gospel.

"Rely on the Gospel"—there's the key. Once again, priestly celibacy or vowed chastity cannot be adequately comprehended save through faith.

Another example of divine wisdom's surpassing that of the world is marriage. How can we be so certain—absolutely certain—that marriage is permanent and God-graced, and will always remain so?

The answer is that we know because we have a Revelation. God's word, which transcends essentially the feeble efforts of mortals perfectly to understand, tells us unequivocally that when a man and a woman exchange marital vows in Christ they enter into a permanent, holy union that will endure. And that, for a Christian, no conjugal living is graced by God unless it is entered into by means of a covenant with Christ—by vows taken within the body of the living Lord, Jesus (Cf. Mk 10:6-9; Ep 5:32).

To accept all this requires faith, of course. But once faith is experienced, doubts disappear, and a degree of certainty which the world cannot possibly offer is acquired.

Faith is the priceless gem of which today's First Reading speaks: no earthly riches can compare.

TWENTY-NINTH SUNDAY IN ORDINARY TIME (B)

Suffering Service for a Better World

Isaiah 53:10-11; Hebrews 4:14-16; Mark 10:35-45.

Aim: to explain that a Christian is called to help make a better world by following Jesus in the path of suffering service.

Jesus is the Suffering Servant par excellence; this is so clear from today's Bible readings—all three of them: the Old Testament prophecy of the Second Isaiah, the Epistle to the Hebrews; Mark's Gospel. So that we who are called to discipleship must orient our lives toward suffering service in the footsteps of the Master.

Such is the ultimate answer to man's ancient search for life's meaning.

One question life asks of us all—daily, even hourly—is the unselfish giving of ourselves for others. As Dr. Viktor E. Frankl, the Viennese psychiatrist who suffered in a Nazi concentration camp, has emphasized, we would all do better if instead of *demanding* from life, we were to *give* to life (*Man's Search For Meaning*, 1959).

One thinks of mothers of three small children, or of five or of six; women who sacrifice youth and beauty, and sometimes health, in loving service to new generations: mothers who ask not what life can give to *them*, but what they can give *to life*. One thinks too of fathers who work long hours, sometimes at two or more jobs, to support their families, and help their children get started in this difficult world; they too know the meaning of suffering service, and well. This is Christ's way.

One also thinks of the teacher who spends a whole lifetime simply helping youngsters to read, or to spell, or to do arithmetic; or of the social worker who gives up her own time to help a teenager find himself, or to relate to others; or of the nurse who arrives early at the hospital, and rarely leaves without caring for some patient on her own time, whether the patient or her supervisor is appreciative or not.

There are large, more dramatic examples of suffering service, of course: great missionaries and Christian witnesses. But these are the exceptions. Most suffering service in the footsteps of Jesus mirrors Jesus' own circumstances: he was known only in his own country; he never ran for public office; he never wrote a book or held high secular position; and he was falsely accused and crucified.

Moreover, it is in suffering service that the Christian finds personal fulfillment; Jesus told us that anyone who gives up his life for the sake of the Lord finds it. We must believe, with all our hearts, that God has called us to shed abroad, by means of our suffering service, by means of our being "persons for others," the radiant light of his glory for a better world.

Again, it is not what we can wrest from life that matters; rather it is what we can give to life.

Anyone who wishes to be first as disciple, Jesus says today, must serve the rest, must in fact defer to others' needs. Think of St. Francis de Sales, or the Cure of Ars, or Mother Elizabeth Seton. Think of Father Damien of Molokai, who literally offered his life for the sake of the abandoned lepers of Hawaii—thereby choosing a "living death" for Christ's sake. When his body was returned to Belgium, a king and a cardinal led the procession to reverence it, and American novelist Robert Louis Stevenson wrote one of the world's most celebrated open letters in Damien's praise, a classic that pales, however, before Jesus' own approval for anyone who commits himself to him in suffering service.

THIRTIETH SUNDAY IN ORDINARY TIME (B)

Holy Orders

Jeremiah 31:7-9; Hebrews 5:1-6; Mark 10:46-52

Aim: To explain (1) the various ministries which a young man receives on the way to priesthood; and (2) the special importance of ordained priests for the Church.

Today's Second Reading, from the monumental Letter to the Hebrews, reminds us of Jesus' High Priesthood. With a human as well as a divine nature, Jesus stands between us and the Father, and with his one eternal sacrifice makes atonement—"at-one-ment"—for us with God. The text closes with a section of Psalm 110:4, that celebrated reference to the Order of Melchizedek, a mysterious figure in the Old Testament who offered a sacrifice of bread and wine (Gn 14). This is a text traditionally interpreted in terms of the New Testament priesthood; namely, the Sacrament of Holy Orders.

In Catholic belief, Holy Orders is the sacrament by which ministers of Christ's grace and word are set apart and sent by the Church to mankind according to the Lord's own will. "Ministry" reflects the Greek *diakonia*, commonly translated as "service," and understood as encompassing various offices and functions within the Church. All true ministerial service must mirror Christ's own mission of healing, forgiving, illumining, reconciling, and liberating from sin or its effects—as seen in today's Gospel, and as prophesied in today's First Reading, from the highly attuned Jeremiah.

Holy Orders pertains to ministry within the Church, in its strictest sense. "Orders" implies ranks or grades; in the Sacrament of Holy Orders there are three: bishop, priest or presbyter, and deacon. These are described as the *ordained* ministries.

The ordained ministry, we hold in faith, is essentially distinct from the common priesthood of the faithful; Vatican II reaffirmed this (*Dogmatic Constitution on the Church*, No. 10); moreover, it entails a permanent character by which the ordained is sealed forever in a special configuration to Christ the High Priest (*Ibid.*, 21). This permanent character is a reminder that Christ has irrevocably associated his Church with himself for the world's salvation; the ordained minister is a sign that God's gift will not be taken back.

Bishops, we believe, are successors of the College of the Apostles in teaching authority and pastoral service; hence they possess the fullness of Orders and are able to ordain other bishops, priests or deacons. Priests or presbyters serve as assistants to the bishops, primarily in the same principal roles of preaching God's word, presiding at the Eucharist, reconciling sinners and in general, celebrating the sacraments and shepherding the faithful. Deacons are set apart for the ministry of the word (they too can preach); of the altar (they assist at the Eucharist, can baptize solemnly, witness marriages and confer certain Church blessings); and of charity. (The diaconate can be assumed as a major step toward priesthood, or it can be a permanent state in itself.)

There are also official nonordained ministries within the Church, that of lector, for example (installed to read the Scriptures in church), or acolyte (commissioned to serve at Mass). Extraordinary Ministers of the Eucharist also share in the nonordained ministry: likewise, some cathechists.

In varying ways, bishops, priests and deacons are those through whom Christ is made present in human history by word and sacrament until the Lord comes again. The reality of the New Testament priesthood is, ultimately, the reality of Jesus' ministry—a ministry so beautifully described again in today's Gospel.

THIRTY-FIRST SUNDAY IN ORDINARY TIME (B)

Precepts of the Church

Deuteronomy 6:2-6; Hebrews 7:23-38; Mark 12:28-34.

Aim: to explain the Church's regulations on Easter Duty: (1) the minimum of communion and Penance at least once a year; (2) the norm of frequent communion and regular Penance.

In today's Gospel, Jesus refers back to today's First Reading, the great Old Testament prayer known as the "Schema," which our Jewish brethren know as well as we do the Our Father. "Hear, O Israel" it begins; "The Lord is our God, the Lord alone!" In Hebrew it reads, phonetically: "*Sh'ma Yisrael. Adonai Elohaynu Adonai Echod.*"

"The Lord is our God." Through Christian Revelation we know that this Lord, this *our* Lord and God, revealed himself in human nature, Jesus of Nazareth, who became our eternal High Priest, and in whom we see and embrace God. Today's Second Reading accents this Revelation.

The principal moments at which this Revelation is accomplished in our lives occur through the sacraments, supremely so in the Eucharist, in which Jesus—the same Jesus of Nazareth who once walked our earth and died on a cross for us—literally comes to embrace us as the risen Lord.

Isn't this why we hold the Eucharist as the most precious God-gift in our lives? Isn't this why we approach the Eucharist as frequently as we can: weekly, as a rule, more often if we can? There is a Church precept, we know, reminding us to receive Communion at least during the Easter time; i.e., from the period beginning with the First Sunday of Lent through to and including Trinity Sunday. But this precept is simply meant as a crutch for those who require regulations as a means toward mature growth. Christianity is not a system of regulations; rather it is a way of life, a desire to embrace and live in and by the living Lord Jesus. Pope Pius X, in his famed 1905 decree on frequent communion, entitled "The Holy Synod of Trent," reaffirmed the Church's perennial doctrine when he wrote:

"Frequent and daily Communion, as a thing most earnestly desired by Christ our Lord and by the Catholic Church, should be open to all the faithful . . . so that no one who is in the state of grace, and who approaches the holy table with a right and devout intention, can lawfully be hindered therefrom.

"A right intention consists in this: that he who approaches the holy table should do so, not out of routine or vainglory or human respect, but for the purpose of pleasing God, of being more closely united with him by charity, and of seeking this divine remedy for his weaknesses and defects."

The reference to the "state of grace," we all understand. It means absence of mortal sin.

Confession, like Communion, should be frequent in one's life, for it constitutes an encounter with the living Lord Jesus. Again, there is a Church precept requiring Confession at least annually during the Easter season. But this is also a crutch for those who need norms. Sacramental confession is always required as an ordinary means of forgiveness from mortal sin. But it is the Church's clear teaching that frequent sacramental confession should be encouraged. The Catholic who approaches Penance monthly, or even weekly, literally encounters the Lord Jesus as compassionate Judge and Healer in a mystery so awesome that the very thought of it should bring us to our knees.

"The Lord is our God, the Lord alone."

We say this—Jesus is Lord—especially when we sincerely approach him in sacramental Penance and the Eucharist.

THIRTY-SECOND SUNDAY
IN ORDINARY TIME (B)

Generosity of Spirit

First Kings 17:10-16; Hebrews 9:24-28; Mark 12:38-44.

Aim: to explain that God wants not things, *but* persons, *who generously give of their hearts.*

Generosity is a virtue brought sharply into focus by today's Bible readings.

In the First Reading, we meet a widow—the very word meant a total dependent in ancient times—ready to share her last few morsels of food with the man of God, Elijah. For her generosity of spirit, she is rewarded many times over; her family is graced through her.

In the Gospel we see another widow. Again, she was impoverished—a situation perhaps many today can relate to realistically, given the situation of the diminishing dollar in social security checks and annuities. Her contribution to the Temple treasury was minimal in the eyes of men, at least when contrasted from the sizable donations made by wealthy contributors.

To understand what was happening in each of these stories, it is necessary to ask the question: What, actually, was each of these widows contributing? Wasn't it that each of these widows was giving not simply a *thing* (e.g., food, money), but rather *her very self?* In both cases, it is generosity of spirit that is rewarded, surely not the small material gift cited. God wants not *things*, but *hearts*. Generosity of spirit testifies to a loving, offered heart.

Today's Second Reading, a passage from the scholarly Letter to the Hebrews explaining the Hebrew Day of Atonement—Yom Kippur—touches upon this truth. Jesus' willing sacrifice as the eternal High Priest is described by the author of Hebrews in another place against the backdrop of Psalm 39: "Sacrifice and offering you did not desire, but a body you have prepared for me; Holocausts and sin offerings you took no delight in. Then I said, . . . 'I have come to do your will, O God'. . ."

Again, God wants hearts—persons—not objects. The countless lambs and goats and oxen sacrificed in Old Testament times were simply symbols for offerings of the heart.

To view all this from another perspective, God loves pure motives. Religion is primarily not a matter of what we do, but *why* we do it. Pure motives take precedence in our worship of God, both in himself (here, at Mass, for instance) or as he is seen in others (the so-called social Gospel).

To translate this into concrete terms, it is beneficial from time to time to challenge our motives for religious commitment. We should ask ourselves, for example, why we are here today at Mass. Is it primarily because of an established routine of life? Is it simply because we "feel bad," as we say, when we don't get to Mass on Sunday? Is it merely that? Is it chiefly because we adhere to a tradition rooted in our ancestry or ethnic background or family habits? *Why* are we here? *Why* do we participate?

Similar questions can be asked about every area tangent to our faith: why we find marriage within the Church so crucial; why we see to it that our infants are baptized and our children receive First Communion and Confirmation; why we call a priest when someone we know is dangerously ill; why we contribute to this parish and the missions; and so on.

To all these questions there is only one fundamentally valid and enduring answer; namely, a loving heart. In the simplest of terms, we love our faith for we love our God, and there is nothing that takes precedence. As one of our greatest English Catholic poets, Coventry Patmore, expressed it while dying, "I loved my God best." God grant that we may live out our lives so well that we will spontaneously say the same at our dying moment.

THIRTY-THIRD SUNDAY IN ORDINARY TIME (B)

Judgment, Purgatory and Hell

Daniel 12:1-3; Hebrews 10:11-14, 18; Mark 13:24-32.

Aim: (1) to explain the doctrine of Purgatory, and (2) to explain the possibility of hell against the doctrine of the two judgments.

Today's Gospel, from Mk, alludes to today's First Reading, from the Old Testament Book of Daniel, written in the second century B.C. Together they form the familiar prophecy of the Son of Man coming in judgment at the end of time. By virtue of Jesus' priesthood, acquired through his humanity, through which he offered his perfect sacrifice for us on the cross (as today's Second Reading reminds), Jesus will first judge us.

This affords us an opportunity to reflect on the doctrine of the two judgments: the General Judgment and the Particular Judgment, as well as the consequences of these judgments, especially purgatory, and the real possibility of hell.

We profess the General Judgment every time we say in the Creed at Sunday Mass "He (Christ) will come again in glory to judge the living and the dead." Since this General Judgment constitutes the consummation of creation, with which all history concludes, it is also called the Last Judgment. This General Judgment is explicitly found in the Bible. Today's Gospel is one instance. Another is Mt 25:31-46.

The Particular Judgment is the one which occurs after death. It is contained implicitly in the Bible; in, for example, the story of Lazarus and the rich man (Lk 16:19-31).

The Particular judgment either opens up the assurance of heaven, or it closes the door thereto. Prior to entrance into heaven, the possibility of purgatory is discussed by the Church.

Purgatory *is* a doctrine, one which is solemnly taught by the Church. What this doctrine entails has been set forth in three General Councils: Lyons (1274), Florence (1431-45), and Trent (1545-63).

Lyons affirmed, for example: "But (as regards) those who have died in a state of charity, truly repentant (for their sins) but before they have brought forth fruit worthy of repentance: their souls are purified after death by cleansing pains." This is to be understood in the sense that at least the punishment due to forgiven sins is fulfilled by means of the mysterious purgatorial experience.

The Old Testament text customarily cited as referring to Purgatory is Second Maccabees 12:43-46. Some New Testament texts are Mt 5:25 ff.; Lk 12:58 ff.; 1 Cor 3:15.

In Mt 12:32, Jesus speaks of a certain sin "which will not be forgiven either in this world or in the next." Surely the reference here is to that kind of sin—i.e., conscious withdrawal from the range of God's grace—which would so predispose a person (by his own free, deliberate choice, of course) that he would in effect repudiate the possibility of renovation in God.

Doubtless our understanding of purgatory will progress as our theology of death develops. From reading St. Paul to the Corinthians (the celebrated 15th chapter) and the Book of Revelation (Chapter 21, beginning with "Then I saw a new heaven and a new earth"), it is clear that death for a Christian is not really a departure, but an arrival at a destination; a renovation, not a deterioration. Purgation is but one aspect of this renewal, only a prelude to it.

Another possibility—we must face it—consequent upon the Particular Judgment is hell. Hell means of course eternal separation from God, man's only meaningful goal. It is a doctrine that tells us in a stark, unmistakable manner, that permanent alienation from God is possible.

Judgment; heaven and purgatory: or hell: this is our faith.

SOLEMNITY OF CHRIST THE KING (B)

The Two Kingdoms

Daniel 7:13-14; Revelation 1:5-8; John 18:33-37.

Aim: to explain (1) the Kingdom of Christ and of the Father, and (2) that the coming of the Kingdom can be hastened.

Jesus' Second Coming to claim his Kingdom, that he might turn it over to his Father, is at the heart of today's Bible Readings. The First Reading projects a vision which we traditionally interpret as referring to Christ; the Second Reading provides an explicit glimpse of Jesus, the Alpha and Omega, coming amid the clouds; and the Gospel records Jesus' claim to Kingship before Pontius Pilate.

That Jesus is a king, indeed "King of Kings" as he is called in the Book of Revelation (19:16), is a familiar doctrine to most Catholics. But there is one aspect of this doctrine not widely known or appreciated; namely that the full, effective exercise of the Lord's Second Coming will not be perfectly fulfilled until Jesus hands over the Kingdom to his heavenly Father.

On that day, St. Paul tells us in 1 Cor, God will be "all in all" (15:28). That day was described by the Church Fathers as the "eighth Sabbath," because it will inaugurate an entirely new era.

For the first time, and for all eternity, everyone who has voluntarily subjected himself to Christ will literally think, will, and act in the full awareness that God is in him and for him. For the first time and for all eternity man will rest from his laboring by himself and thus—in Father Yves Congar's phrase—"receive everything from God, with thanksgiving."

One way to view this doctrine is to say that Jesus, as the Suffering Servant of Yahweh, foretold by the Second Isaiah, *organized the Kingdom* which is now in existence. But the Father alone can set the date *for its consummation*, when, as St. Paul tells us, Christ delivers over the Kingdom to God the Father after destroying "every sovereignty and every authority and power" (1 Cor 15:24).

"The reign of God," explains Father Congar in his *Jesus Christ* (Herder and Herder, 1966), "involves two phases. In a first earthly, phase, its realization is achieved . . . 'in the Lord,' but in the Lord precisely as he came to us, namely, *in forma servi* (i.e., as a servant) . . . In the final phase, the reign must be that of the Lord *in forma Dei (i.e., as God)."*

Having subdued all things (e.g., illness, ignorance, death, the powers of evil, sin) to himself, Jesus will then hand over the Kingdom to his Father, so that God might begin to be everything to everyone.

Another dimension of this doctrine is that all who have sincerely enlisted in Jesus' realm, will, beginning with the "eighth Sabbath," be associated with the Lord. This is clear from such texts as Rv 3:21 and Ep 2:6.

No wonder therefore that the primitive Christian community exclaimed *Marana tha* (Come, Lord Jesus!). (Read 1 Cor 22, and Rv. 22:17, 20).

The Scriptures also tell us that God's final response to *Marana tha* can be hastened by intensification of Christian witness during this first phase of the Kingdom, so that the doctrine of Christ's reign is not merely theoretical.

Today we renew our enlistment, and, of course, our loving commitment, to Jesus, Lord of Lords and King of Kings, forever and ever. Amen.

CYCLE C

FIRST SUNDAY
OF ADVENT (C)

Preparing For a Holy Christmas

Jeremiah 33:14-16; 3:12-4:2; Luke 21:25-28, 34-36.

*Aim: (1) to show this as a special time for reflection, (2)
to encourage Advent thoughts of life and death, of the
importance of Christ and Christmas.*

Today's Gospel gives us a sense of *deja vu* (a strange sense of
having heard it before, though it is being read for the first time this
week). It is, in fact an echo of last Sunday's prophecy of Jesus' coming
to this world as Lord and King at the end of time. But it is a bit more
detailed. (Today's evangelist, Luke, was an artist at heart, hence liked
to detail.)

Like last Sunday's Gospel, this prophecy is directly related to the
destruction of Jerusalem by the Roman legions, in 70 A.D. And it
also pertains to the end of the world, when the Son of Man is sure to
come in judgment. So that we are invited to think about the future:
my future, and such thoughts as *my* death and *my* judgment.

There is a third way, however, of approaching today's Bible
readings. In them we are given infallible norms for living in the divine
favor against the day when—in Jesus' words—the appointed time for
our judgment in God's presence will come. In a sense, we are being
told, in today's Bible readings, not only to remain vigilant, but we are
given some helps for maintaining vigilance, especially in the context

of the darkness that so frequently surrounds us—a darkness emerging from so many things: financial troubles, illnesses, family difficulties, depressions and anxieties of all kinds, physical debilities, loneliness, rejection or abandonment by friends, bereavements—all those things that contribute to this world so disordered by sin.

First, we should never fall into the error of thinking that the world around us is only darkness. Stand up in the midst of trial, Jesus tells us, for "our ransom is near at hand." As Jeremiah, in today's First Reading, reminded the disconsolate Israelites in the midst of tragedy that God will come to save them, so we are reminded that even in the midst of the blackest night there is always light. And it is a light meant for us—for you and for me.

If we happen to live in a time of tension, or violence, or earthquake or turmoil, as we all certainly do (these are not peaceful times for nations or the Church), we have it on God's own word that we, and not our grandparents, say, were purposely chosen—for this our age. God trusted us to be alive now. He trusted us not to fail him. The second-century Christians used to say: "For the sake of us Christians, this era exists. We have a mission, therefore, to help witness to light in the midst of darkness, of solution—God's pledge—in the midst of apparent chaos.

A second norm for vigilance evident in today's Bible readings is prayer. "Pray constantly" to remain secure in the Faith regardless of the pressure; so Jesus reminds us. Christ will strengthen our hearts; yes; St. Paul reaffirms this in today's Second Reading. But he assumes that we follow the Lord's instuctions, among which is the need to pray.

Again, our stance must be optimistic. We must learn to see some light even in the darkest situation. We can do this in faith. As Christians we can be sure that total darkness is never upon us; there is always some light.

Secondly, we must pray. In the ultimate analysis, prayer is what matters: sincere prayer.

Advent, then, is a time to focus our minds and hearts, on optimism and on prayer. In practice, the latter comes before the former. Prayer serves optimism.

The world's greatest optimists were the saints. Pessimism and prayer don't go together.

SECOND SUNDAY
OF ADVENT (C)

Repent of Your Sins

Baruch 5:1-9; Philippians 1:4-6, 8-11; Luke 3:1-6.

Aim: (1) show how easily we deceive ourselves into thinking we are sinless and forget our sinful condition; (2) to present Christ as our Redeemer who makes possible forgiveness and reconciliation.

Those majestically stirring, almost heraldic phrases introducing today's Gospel: "In the fifteenth year of the rule of Tiberius Ceasar, when Pontius Pilate was procurator of Judea, Herod tetrarch of Galilee," and so on—rhythmically build up messianic suspense. They can almost be read as a drum roll. Yet, curiously, it is not the Messiah at all to whom this powerful introduction leads. Rather, the heraldry is for the Messiah's precursor, St. John the Baptizer. Prerequisite to Christ's coming, therefore, is an adequate preparation. We must meet John before Christ.

John the Baptizer's mission was of course to "make ready," to "clear a path" for God's corporal intervention in mankind's daily affairs. So too, the mission of the prophet Baruch, (200 B.C.), who foresees the Day of the Lord in today's First Reading. Some of the very expressions used by Baruch are echoes of Isaiah's earlier projections—those references, for example, to "age-old gorges" being "filled to level ground," and mountains being "made low."

So today we focus on the mystery of preparation. It *is* a mystery, a supremely personal one. Which is to say that it is a concept that can only be understood by, and appreciated by, *me*. To recognize Christ, *I alone* am competent and, of course, responsible.

Preparation, in John the Baptizer's message, means conversion and penance. Both are eminently personalist notions. Strictly, one can correct only oneself; doing penance is one of those acts that cannot be delegated to others. No one can repent of my sins other than I myself.

Why is it, moreover, that it is often so difficult to do what we know we must do? Why is it that we find ourselves so like Hamlet, procrastinators always, willing to think about conversion and betterment, but tomorrow—*domani*, as the Italians say; *manana*, in the Spanish.

Why is it, for example, that every Advent we find ourselves praying something like, "Lord, make me a less prejudicial person—but not yet." Or, "Make me a more charitable person, or less selfish person," but not yet.

St. Augustine, the great Doctor of the Church, dwelt considerably on his inability to realize self-conversion: Some of the paragraphs on this subject from his *Confessions* are especially meaningful because they are universal in application:

"You showed me on all sides that what you say was true, and by the truth I was convinced. I had nothing at all to answer but those dull and dreary words: 'Soon; Soon;' or 'presently:' or 'Leave me alone but a little while.' But my 'presently, presently,' came to no present, and my 'little while' lasted long.

"What words did I not use against myself! With scourges of condemnation I lashed my soul, to force it to follow me in my effort to go after you. Yet it drew back . . . It feared—to have that disease of habit healed whereby it was wasting to death . . ."

Advent is a time, then, to compel ourselves into acknowledgement of our inadequacies—but *now*. Not tomorrow. To repent of our sins *now*. To resolve to go to confession now, before Christmas is upon us.

As we wait during this Advent time, recall that God also awaits us. And though he waits for us with a holy patience, though he searches us out as we try to hide from him, though he tries to draw us into the open, there to see him for all his loving mercy; though he waits for us, it is nonetheless a terrible thing to play the procrastinator before him—Creator, Judge, Lord of Lords and King of Kings.

THIRD SUNDAY
OF ADVENT (C)

The Meaning of Christian Joy

Zephaniah 3:14-18; Philippians 4:4-7; Luke 3:10-18.

Aim: (1) to explain Christian joy as being dead to self and sin, and alive to God; (2) to encourage such a dying to sin and living joyfully in Christ.

Rejoice because the Lord is near: this is an overriding theme of today's Bible readings. Christmas joy is joy in and with Christ; St. Paul tells us this clearly in today's Second Reading, from his great "epistle of Joy," Philippians. Hence another reminder, today's liturgy is, that Christmas is not a secular feast, that Christmas for a believer simply cannot be celebrated like just another holiday in the secular calendar. In fact, the more we desire for ourselves this Christmas, the more we shall be tempted to view Christmas in an isolated, selfish light; and the less a cause for true celebration Christmas will be.

We are all somewhat aware of the phrase, "Christmas neurosis." It is alleged by some—often a psychologist, writing in a Sunday tabloid around this time of year—that the Christmas season (indeed, any holiday season, such as Thanksgiving) is a potential period for widespread depression.

For example, a sense of loneliness seems especially intense among some people at this time of the year: the single working girl, for example, alone in her apartment in New York City, away from her family in the Midwest; or the college freshman who cannot afford to go home for the holidays and must spend Christmas in a far away college dormitory.

Certain guilt feelings can flare up during this time of year, too. The example of the woman who, as the psychologists say, has secret doubts about her ability to fulfil an adult female role, is depressed by the thought of having to be at her mother-in-law's for Christmas dinner, there to endure a secondary role and extravagant remarks about her mother-in-law's table.

Financial anxieties can also be fired particularly at this time of the year. Some fathers, pressed by the thought of post-Christmas bills for gifts given, tend to be depressed by the very thought of this holiday season.

Finally, there is the general experience, at this time of the year, of extraordinary emotional involvement. Consequently, there are emotional let-downs, small depressions, as it were.

All these traumas, surely, are somehow associated with personal problems or disorders; one can hardly attribute them to the Advent season. The roots of depressions are *personal*; depression at Christmas—or on any other holy day—cannot possibly result from the day. Yet isn't it true that there can be a link between these traumas and our not viewing Christmas by the only light in which it makes sense; namely, the light of faith? Isn't it also true that Christmas celebrated in faith can yield an inner peace, indeed a joy, that helps lift us from our sadness or loneliness or anxiety to the certainty that the Lord *does provide* and that the Lord will continue to *provide for me*?

How can we acquire a true perspective at Christmas? What can we do? How can we arrive at the knowledge and the feeling that Christmas means peace and security and freedom from fear in the certainty that the Lord provides? How, in the face of self-conflict, guilt feelings, loneliness, the need to pay bills, family worries—all the other ills that seem so visible at this time of the year?

Prayer is the key; sincere prayer that, as all today's Bible readings emphasize, we may know that the Lord our God is in our midst, to renew us with his love, to give us gladness of heart.

Paul, in today's Second Reading, puts it plainly: stop thinking about oneself; start thinking about Christ, in whom alone we find ourselves. Rely solely on God, *present our needs* to him—just do this. No need for lengthy agonizing over details as to how to solve our problems. These only increase anxiety. No; Paul says, dismiss anxiety from our minds; simply present ourselves before the Lord. He is our peace.

Thinking about ourselves is difficult not to do, of course; it requires discipline. One potent means, St. John the Baptizer cites, in today's Gospel; namely, start thinking about others, about people with greater problems—perhaps greater anxieties—than we have.

This is a crucial message. The most beautiful Christmases we can spend, the most memorable, will always be those marked with efforts to forget about ourselves and to reach out to make others happy.

The peace of Christ at Christmas can help us surmount our natural human depressions.

FOURTH SUNDAY OF ADVENT (C)

Poverty in the Christ Life

Micah 5:1-4; Hebrews 10:5-10; Luke 1:39-45.

Aim: (1) to show poverty as the heritage of Mary and Joseph in Bethlehem and Nazareth; as the lifestyle of Jesus; (2) to encourage similar simplicity and poverty in ourselves.

Today's Gospel reminds us, through that beautiful account of Mary's visiting her cousin Elizabeth, that all Christians, like Mary, are signs—or should be signs—of Jesus' Presence in the world. Today's Second Reading teaches that one way we can be useful signs of Christ—Christ-bearers, like Mary—is to give of ourselves to others. And today's First Reading reminds us that we shall have more and more to give others as we come to realize that our greatest riches are the spiritual favors bestowed by God.

The overall message is so relevant, isn't it? Surely these are thoughts that should be foremost in our minds as Christmas draws close. Not whether we will get that stereo cassette we want, or that new skiing jacket, or whatever. No.

Christmas isn't a holiday invented by department stores as an opportunity for exchanging material gifts.

Christmas is at its roots a Christian feast; the name means Christ's Mass, the Mass celebrating the birth of Jesus, who is God, into the world: Jesus, the King of Kings and Lord of Lords forever and ever, yet who was born into poverty, of a poor mother, who grew up in poverty and died in poverty.

Even the town of Jesus' birth, Bethlehem, was insignificant in the eyes of his own nation. The prophet Micah, referring to it in today's First Reading, describes it as "too small" for special mention among the tribes of Judea, where Mary visited Elizabeth, in today's Gospel.

And consider the stable, the manger in which the Eternal Word of God, conceived of the Virgin Mary, chose to be born among us; it remains forever a dramatic sign of the poverty which our Savior chose to embrace. Christ was not born in a regal place decorated with marble and illuminated by silver candles, but rather in a cave, a manger. And the first men invited to render him homage were shepherds: hard-working, ordinary, sincere, penniless men in the eyes of the world.

God's love of poverty—his benediction of the poor, those who literally have no one but God to rely upon—was a principal reason why our Lord was born in Bethlehem, in a cave, in a manger; poverty is a principal reason, too, why shepherds were chosen to be his first courtiers.

Poverty means the spirit of dispossession; the spiritual attitude by means of which one is free of the *need* for worldly goods, material wealth—even if one happens, by circumstance, to be affluent. It is that soul-stance by means of which one recognizes the real worth of man: a child of God destined one day to be with him forever in a home where large bank accounts and ranch houses in suburbia and new automobiles have no permanent meaning. In the Gospel, Jesus warns us to provide ourselves with wallets that cannot wear out in time, with bank accounts that will endure foverer (Lk 12:32-34).

The figures of Mary and Joseph, this Advent time, prepare us for this lesson of poverty, perfected in Jesus, born in Bethlehem's manger. We are reminded by the Bible, therefore, that poverty—the spirit of dispossession—is a positive value especially worth acquiring. It is a sober, if not a bit disquieting reminder, to those of us who are tempted to view Christmas as a cornucopia of material things.

The truth is that it's the other way around. The less we desire of material things for Christmas, the more precious this season will necessarily be—if we believe.

God is born into hearts immersed in the spirit of poverty.

FIRST SUNDAY OF LENT (C)

Be Converted From Sin and the World

Deuteronomy 26:4-10; Romans 10:8-13; Luke 4:1-13.

Aim: to explain conversion or metanoia *as: (1) a turning away from sin; (2) a turning to Gospel living; (3) a continuing process that is shown by our different attitude and lifestyle, and our being and acting the person God wants us to be.*

The word for "conversion" from sin to God in the original Greek New Testament is *metanoia*. Curiously, it's now being widely used as an English word, especially among youths. *Metanoia* signifies a radical change of heart, the kind of change that entails a single-purpose plan from the moment conversion is decided, and the kind that is affirmed, or confessed, unreservedly, for the rest of one's years.

Christian discipleship demands no less: a clear, irrevocable and firmly made mind-set; an attitude as simple yet definitive as Jesus' words to the devil in today's Gospel: "You shall do homage to the Lord your God; him alone shall you adore."

One element common to all three Bible lessons today is an unreserved affirmation of faith. The First Reading is a confession of faith in thanksgiving for the Exodus, God's greatest single intervention in behalf of the Israelites of old. The Second Reading recalls the key confession of Christianity, from which the historic creeds took growth; namely that Jesus, who died, is now the risen and living Lord. And in the Gospel, our Lord replies to Satan's wiles with a threefold confession, one which sets the theme for his ministry of inaugurating his Kingdom, and which he will reaffirm later before Pilate's judgment seat (1 Tm 6:13).

The Lord in whom we are saved (to borrow from today's Second Reading) calls us in the freedom of love to follow him into the desert for his words and his embrace. No spectacular miracles, no compulsion, no worldly persuasion. Only an invitation of the heart to change our lives in a loving and penitential confession of faith in him and his merciful forgiveness.

Such a confession obviously means a new lifestyle. A lifestyle that reflects a personal relationship with the living Lord, sustained by prayer, by the Eucharist and frequent confession, by the bearing of crosses, imposed or assumed, for Christ's sake. A lifestyle that will grow, not weaken, as we mature, and that we will manifest to others. A lifestyle that will be perceived by others as kindness, honesty, hope, prudence, courage, piety and, of course, confidence that Christ *does live*, and *awaits* us now with his eternal embrace. A lifestyle that will make this Lent not just a series of days on the calendar, but a sacred retreat in which our singlemindness of purpose will become stronger and more dynamic.

The Russian novelist and philosopher Dostoevsky once remarked that in the three questions addressed by Satan to Jesus in the desert, are foretold all the temptations against Christianity in the history of the world (*The Brothers Karamazov*). Each question demands a clear and firm, "Begone, Satan," the kind of response that can only come from one who has steeled himself against temptation by turning irrevocably to God from the innermost depths of his soul: a *metanoia*.

SECOND SUNDAY OF LENT (C)

The Scandal of the Cross

Genesis 15:5-12, 17-18; Philippians 3:17, 4:1; Luke 9:28-36

Aim: (1) to explain the cross in Jesus' life and in the early Church; (2) to explain the cross in our lives; (3) to encourage carrying our cross.

Abraham, "our Father in faith" (as the Roman Canon, the first Eucharistic Prayer, calls him) is presented to us in today's First Reading; he is the first great model of the pilgrim of faith. As God called Abraham, he has also called us to a new land—given us a new citizenship, to borrow Paul's beautiful idea in today's Second Reading. Meanwhile, we must proceed in this difficult vale of tears, below the summit of the mountain of the Transfiguration (today's Gospel scene), where our homeland really lies.

Incidentally, that First Reading requires some explanation. It's about God's making a covenant—a pact—with Abraham. One ceremony by which ancient covenants were ratified was by the covenanters passing through the midst of the parts of slain animals. By this rite, those who entered into the pacts said, in effect, that they would rather be torn in two than violate their part of the agreement. Note though: in this case, only God, and not Abraham passed through the halfed animals. This is to show us that God acted spontaneously, of his own free will.

But back to the main theme: our Abraham-like pilgrimage here below, to the Mount of the Transfiguration.

Raphael, in his painting of the Transfiguration, depicts an agonized boy surrounded by people in chaos below the mountain. The Gospels tell us that when Jesus descended the mountain, he suddenly met this youth (cf. Lk 9:37 ff.). From the summit of the mountain, where all was peace and tranquillity and light, Jesus led his disciples to Abraham's world of pilgrimage, a world of darkness, confusion, and anxiety. And he immediately ministered to this youth, by curing him.

Jesus leads us today, too, down from the mountain into this difficult world. Here we are called upon to bear the burdens of an imperfect world tainted by sin, by following the Savior in his continuing work—through his Body, the Church—of healing, comforting, encouraging, inspiring, peacemaking, so that others may *at least know about* the summit of the mountain where peace and fulfillment await us forever.

Like Peter and the Apostles we would like to remain at the mountain's top; the best moments we have spent in prayer, especially here at the Eucharist, are difficult to leave. The Mass and prayer energize us to make the ascent, of course. But we must keep in mind that the climb to the mountain's peak is only possible through the cross of service, the cross which humbles us so thoroughly that it can be called a scandal; the cross that really makes us servants for others in Jesus' footsteps to the point of our being perceived as fools in the eyes of those who do not know Christ.

Being "persons for others" in Jesus' footsteps, regardless of the ridicule or humiliation or pain, is the sure way back to the mountain where Jesus' glory can be experienced forever.

When the early Christians signed themselves with the cross, they meant all this—even to the point of martyrdom, which awaited them almost every day. Whenever we sign ourselves, some of our reflections in today's liturgy should come to mind.

THIRD SUNDAY OF LENT (C)

The Need to be Reconciled with God

Exodus 3:1-8, 13-15; First Corinthians 10:1-6, 10-12; Luke 13:1-9.

Aim: to encourage (1) repentance for our sins and (2) timely and regular use of the Sacrament of Reconciliation.

Today's First Reading is from the Old Testament Book of Exodus, the story of Israel's flight from Egypt under Moses, beginning around the year 1290 B.C. The passage just read provides us with an insight into Moses' vocation. In it we find, for the first time, God's proper name, revealed to Moses by God, present in the burning bush. We usually pronounce the name *Yahweh*, a Hebrew verb that means "I am who am," and which contains within itself a wealth of mystery.

Note that God's name is a verb. Someone has said that "God is a *verb*." A verb connotes activity. God defines himself, therefore, as an act: not a Being simply for himself, but a Being who is outgoing *for us*. To Moses' question, "What is his name?" God answers, in effect: I am the One whom you will recognize by my mighty deeds in your behalf: by my guiding you from Egypt into the Promised Land and into a new covenant.

God's final and perfect reply to Moses' question is *Jesus Christ*. In Jesus we see the supreme fulfillment of God's acting in our behalf. For Jesus went to the cross for us that we might be fully reconciled to God. What is necessary, of course, is that we repent our sins and accept Christ as our Lord and Savior.

When we hear Jesus in today's Gospel, from Luke, warning us not to postpone our renewal or conversion—since the hour can be later than we think—we hear God voicing this warning. Jesus is God. This Jesus has been sent to us by the Father to be our Savior, to lead us into a promised land by acquiring our freedom from sin, our liberation from the powers of evil; and to live with us forever.

We who know these things have a serious obligation to live by them, as Paul vigorously lectures the Corinthians in today's Second Reading. Paul reminds them, *and us*, to study the Exodus carefully again, and lo learn from it.

Like the Israelites, we must acknowledge our plight; namely, that we are sinners in need of God's mighty act of reconciliation. Paul says that anyone who thinks himself sinless should watch out.

So we prepare for another good sacramental confession this Lent. And we prepare now, readying ourselves not to let another week go by without immersing ourselves anew in the mystery of the supreme mighty work of God in history: Jesus' Cross and Resurrection, by which we are reconciled to God as his children, gifted with an eternal homeland.

On Ash Wednesday, when we began this Lenten season, the Second Reading at Mass read: "*Now* is the acceptable time! *Now* is the day of salvation!" (2 Cor 6:2). Will we make use of this unique time of grace to renew our contribution through a carefully prepared and made Lenten confession? If so, the third and final visit of the divine Gardener—to recall today's Gospel—may occur *this very Lent.*

Do we believe today's Gospel, which tells us with infallible wisdom, that this Lenten confession may be our last? Do we believe today's Second Reading, which also tells us that anyone who thinks he is standing upright should watch out lest he fall? It is always later than we suspect.

FOURTH SUNDAY IN LENT (C)

How a Catholic Receives Forgiveness of Sins

Joshua 5:9, 10-12; Second Corinthians 5:17-21; Luke 15:1-3, 11-32.

Aim: (1) to explain the various ways of obtaining forgiveness and (2) the Sacrament of Reconciliation as the ordinary way; (3) to encourage use of this Sacrament now and regularly.

Today's Gospel (the story of the Prodigal Son) is a perennial favorite. "Prodigal" means "wasteful;" a prodigal person is an extravagant spendthrift, one who scandalously wastes money. In the Gospel, we read about a son who in effect rejects father and home, demands his inheritance, takes up on his own, and dissipates his funds on loose-living, partying, drinking. Then came a depression, and he found himself without resources; and, as usually happens in the case of people who try to purchase friendship, without friends. As soon as it appears he was without resources, they abandoned him.

Jesus recounted this story to his followers because he wanted to give us a dramatic example of how much God cares for us, of how ready God always remains to embrace us again, no matter how *far away* we have strayed, no matter *how long* we have been away from him, and even if we have *wasted* his graces. He is always waiting to take us back into his own household.

Which is to say that in God, regardless of the circumstances, a homecoming is always a real possibility.

Consider the history of the Old Testament Israelites, a history recalled in today's First Reading. God had intervened to free them from slavery in Egypt. Yet they wandered from him; worshipped false gods, even. One would think that God might give up on them. On the contrary, he had made them a promise that he would give them a new land, and make their lives all new, as St. Paul recalls in today's Second Reading; despite their aberrations, God would not abandon his people.

And God does not abandon us today. Despite our repeated wanderings, he gives us a second chance. And a third; and a fourth. Though we are prodigal children—sons and daughters who refuse to communicate with God (by prayer, say), who even ignore or repudiate our divine inheritance, our opportunities of grace given us—he nonetheless stands ready to welcome us to a joyous homecoming the moment we rush back to him, beg his forgiveness, and reclaim our inheritance.

What is necessary, of course, is an act of contrition on our part. We must acknowledge our errant ways, reject them, and propose to amend our life, satisfying for the wrong we have done. We describe this stance as an act of contrition, which can assume many forms, but always includes a sign of contrition and willingness to make amends for love of God. At the first opportunity, we bear this contrition to the Sacrament of Reconciliation, where, by means of priestly absolution, we have certain assurance of God's welcoming our return.

Where serious sin is at issue, sacramental confession is mandatory by virtue of divine precept. This means that in the case of mortal sin the ordinary means of the prodigal son's receiving God's welcome is in the Sacrament of Penance.

God is ever ready to take away and forget our past. As prodigals all, we must believe that where he is concerned, it is always possible to go home again.

This Lenten season is a right time to grow in an appreciation of this beautiful and comforting truth.

FIFTH SUNDAY OF LENT (C)

The Kinds of Sin

Isaiah 43:16-21; Philippians 3:8-14; John 8:1-11.

Aim: to teach the distinctions between (1) original sin and actual sin; (2) mortal and venial sin; (3) to encourage avoidance of actual sin.

Today's Gospel, from St. John's account, is the beautiful story of the woman caught in adultery. Individuals who deemed themselves sinless made her stand in the midst of a crowd, where they accused her. Jesus' reply, we all know by heart; it's one of the most comforting sentences of our faith: "Let the man among you who has no sin be the first to cast a stone at her." Her accusers all crept away, and she was left alone with Jesus.

Jesus did not condone her sin; he told her to sin no more. But his heart did go out in mercy to her; he forgave her. (Incidentally, where was her partner to the adultery? Where was he? Why didn't he come forward for confession, and for forgiveness?).

One lesson that stands out today is the reality of sin. Sin is not a myth, but an ugly reality. Adultery is the specific sin cited today. The same holds true of perjury or abortion or blasphemy or fornication or serious injustice; sin is an ugly reality.

The primordial sin, which we call original sin, is a condition of alienation from God inherited from Adam by virtue of our human nature. Original sin is not an actual sin committed by each one personally, but, as Pope Paul VI explained in his *Credo of the People of God* (30 June 1978), it is "human nature so fallen, stripped of the grace that clothed it, injured in its own natural powers and subjected to the dominion of death, that it is transmitted to all men. . ."

Actual sin is the kind of sin for which we are personally responsible—for example, the sin of adultery which the woman in the Gospel committed. Sin means a turning away from God, an offense against him. If it involves a serious matter, and is committed with full consent of the will and sufficient awareness, it is lethal to God's life in us; hence, called mortal. Where an offense does not violate essential values in the divine plan, or when it lacks the perfection of human action because it is done without sufficient awareness or freedom, it is called venial. Venial sin means a turning aside from God, though without at that time intending to repudiate one's fundamental orientation Godward. It is obviously a sidetracking that can set the stage for dangerous misdirection.

As sin is real, so confession is for realists. The fresh beginning promised to the sinner in today's First Reading follows upon sincere confession of sin. The justice of Christ which can be our joy, as the Second Reading affirms, is only for the realist: the one who admits his sinfulness and his need for divine forgiveness.

Jesus once said—upon overhearing a slurring remark made to his disciples by the Pharisees—"People who are in good health do not need a doctor; sick people do . . . I have come to call, not the self-righteous, but the sinners" (Mt 9:12, 13).

Is it even possible for a Catholic to understand the meaning of these words and at the same time not possess a deep love for the Sacrament of Penance? Love for the sacrament by means of which our sins are literally taken away by the living Lord Jesus, who, now glorified at the Father's right hand, still mediates for us?

PASSION (Palm) SUNDAY (C)

The Sufferings of Jesus Christ

Isaiah 50:4-7; Philippians 2:2-11; Luke 22:14-23:56.

Aim: (1) to explain the sufferings of Jesus; (2) to show them as endured to encourage and help us.

As always, on Palm Sunday, the First Reading was from the Second Isaiah's celebrated Servant of the Lord hymns; specifically, the third, which projects a mysterious, innocent figure under attack. This prophetic figure was of course Jesus, who, as St. Paul reminds us in today's magnificent Second Reading, is exalted as Lord because he took upon himself suffering and death.

The suffering and death assumed by Jesus is epitomized in his Passion and crucifixion, about which we read today, from St. Luke's account. While on Palm Sunday the Church bids us recall Christ's glorious entry into Jerusalem, celebrated with palm fronds, it also invites us to keep in mind that Jesus entered the sacred city to fulfill the Servant of the Lord prophecy all the way to death on the cross.

Each of the four Gospel Passion accounts has its own characteristics. St. Luke's—today's—is clearly the tale of a martyr who freely surrenders his life for others while deliberately affirming his concern and compassion for them.

For example, when Jesus, having been condemned to carry his cross to execution, met a group of women weeping for *him*, he immediately turned the situation of his suffering around manifesting sympathy for *them*: "Daughters of Jerusalem, do not weep for me.

Weep for yourselves and your children . . ." (23:28). Later, while hanging from the Cross, Jesus prayed for his executioners (and us): "Father, forgive them . . ." (23:33). Moreover, in the very midst of his torment, he reached out with forgiveness to one of the thieves crucified next to him, and promised him eternal life. "This day you will be with me in paradise" (24:43).

Luke's Passion narrative also captures, by implication, some of the other ways in which our suffering Savior was ready to pardon his persecutors even as they inflicted injury upon him. Thus, in the Garden scene, when the Apostles chose to sleep while our Lord prayed in a bloody sweat, Luke does not overly dwell on their callous indolence; rather, he passes over it, even as Jesus did. And the incident of Judas' kiss—the horrendous kiss of betrayal—is glossed over quickly, so as not to be emphasized. Luke also omits the detail that the Apostles took flight when Jesus was arrested—again, as a subtle sign that Christ does not wish to remember acts of betrayal against him so long as they are repented.

There's the key point: "so long as our sins are repented." The sufferings inflicted upon Jesus for our sake, he does not hold against us so long as we acknowledge them in repentance. Peter, who betrayed him three times in his crucial hour, was later chosen to lead the Apostles, to be the first Pope. But Peter wept for his sin; later, too, he protested his love for the risen Lord three distinct times, in symbolic reparation for his threefold denial.

Recalling Jesus' sufferings and death is not simply meant as a historical rehearsal of sympathy for so innocent a victim's being slain. Recalling his Passion and death is intended to draw us to repentance; and, of course, to humble thanksgiving for our having been saved through his most Precious Blood.

EASTER VIGIL (C)

The Resurrection of Jesus: Reason for our Joy

Genesis 1:1-2:2; 22:1-18; Exodus 14:15-15:1; Isaiah 54:5-14; 55:1-11; Baruch 3:9-15; Ezekiel 36:16-28; Romans 6:3-11; Luke 24:1-12.

> *Aim: (1) to list some major worries of people today and (2) to show how Christ's Resurrection gives meaning and joy in answering these worries.*

Jesus, risen from the tomb of Good Friday *lives*; this is the heart of the Resurrection feast. Christ is in our midst; he walks with us in this vale of tears; he intervenes in our lives; he awaits us now with his eternal embrace.

Like him we are destined to rise in the flesh; St. Paul stresses this in today's Second Reading. The new light of this Easter Candle we blessed earlier in this liturgy is symbolic of a light that can never be extinguished: the light of Christ which guides us through the grey and often twisted paths of this world, the light of Christ which brightens even the darkest recesses of life's journey here below. All the Old Testament prophecies we listened to this evening—prophecies pledging God's intervention in behalf of our freedom and our future welfare—were fulfilled when Christ conquered the tomb.

Because of Christ's Resurrection, peace and joy are secured for everyone who believes. Since Jesus lives, he provides. His parables about the lilies of the field or the birds of the air are not merely optimistic poetry; they express reality. The Lord who lives provides for those who follow him. He has put off death itself as easily as he discarded the wrappings in which he was buried—as St. Luke tells us in today's Gospel.

"Death itself," we say, for according to one theory popular today, all our fears or anxieties are ultimately reducible to fear of death. At least it is a principal anxiety against which men and women fortress their lives in a vain attempt to safeguard their youth or attractiveness or strength or name or accomplishments. Thus, some strive for wealth; others, for status; others for power, political, economic, social, still others, for applause. From another view, some worry excessively over finances, or promotions, or acquiring prestige; or they are overly anxious about the aging process or the prospect of illness.

People who are anxious over nothing but the values of this world, and who burn out their energies solely with it in mind, are not really alive. Bishop Ottokar Prohaszka, the great Hungarian preacher who died in 1927, once compared such people to the "living dead" of Henrick Ibsen's play, *When the Dead Awaken* (1899). "Dead and alive," Bishop Prohaszka wrote, are those people who exhaust their mental and physical energies in wild passions, only to discover (at life's close, frequently) that they have not really been living all along, but were in fact dead. Such are the artists, he explained, who view the beautiful merely as models and not as values whereby they can enrich their own lives and the lives of others. Such, too, are those who have wasted their brief years in an insane scramble for higher and higher status, or for earthly possessions. Or those who have reduced the world to a labyrinth with no exit, a confusing, meaningless maze of merely horizontal, spatio-temporal corridors and doors that lead nowhere. Or those who simply exist in the assumption that it is absurd to live and absurd to die.

As Christians we are not dead but alive, alive with Christ's refreshing life. In him life has meaning, and to live is a joy. Anxieties and worries, haunting as they may be, can be set aside, as surely as the shroud in which the risen Jesus was once bound, was discarded.

SECOND SUNDAY OF EASTER (C)

The Forgiveness of Sins

Acts 5:12-16; Revelation 1:9-11, 12-13, 17-19; John 20:19-31.

Aim: to examine (1) the power to forgive sins, given by Jesus to his Church and his priests; (2) how we must confess our sins to benefit from this power.

The liberating power with which the risen Lord Jesus invested his Church—freedom from unclean spirits, as today's First Reading recalls—is epitomized in his words to the Apostles in today's Gospel: "If you forgive men's sins, they are forgiven them; if you hold them bound, they are held bound." The slavery of sin is really the basic and worst slavery; all other evils in this world stem from sin.

That Christ gave his Apostles and their successors the power to forgive sins in his name is obvious from the Gospel. "And their successors," we say, because Jesus prefaced his empowering words with the phrase, "As the Father has sent me, so I send you." He meant to confer the power to absolve in the context of his own mission, which, he himself said, was to save not the self-righteous, but sinners. And since this mission will remain operative as long as sinners exist, the power to implement his mission of pardon and peace will exist as long as men exist, for all men are sinners.

Actually the power Christ gave was twofold: to forgive *and* to hold bound. The Apostles and their successors—the ministers of the

Church ordained to exercise this power: bishops and priests—must make a judgment as to whether *to forgive* sin or to *hold it bound*. For this judgment, a case must be presented: what we call confession.

The Church cannot eliminate the need for confession of sin because it was revealed as a positive value by Christ. The Church has solemnly witnessed to this truth; for example, at the Council of Trent. Thus, the new *Rite of Penance* stipulates:

"Individual, integral confession and absolution remain the only ordinary way for the faithful to reconcile themselves with God and the Church, unless physical or moral impossibility excuses from this kind of confession" (*Rite of Penance*, No. 31).

Confession is not simply a dialogue between priest and penitent. Rather, it is a sincere, truthful and integral acknowledgement of the number (or frequency) and kind of all serious sins. Too, one's confession must be contrite; it must reflect sorrow for sin, detestation of sin, and a firm resolution to avoid sin. Finally, confession must include at least a will to satisfy for sin (sometimes restitution is required, as in cases of calumny or theft).

The absolution given by the priest in confession is not simply a prayer that God will grant forgiveness. Rather, it is a statement to the effect that God *has reconciled* the penitent; it is a real absolution from sin by the power of Christ speaking and acting in and through his Church, by his priest.

In the Sacrament of Penance—the Sacrament of Reconciliation—we encounter the risen Lord literally repeating the words of today's Second Reading:

"There is nothing to fear . . . I was dead but now I live—forever and ever. I hold the keys of death and the nether world . . ."

There *is* nothing to fear as long as in our sinfulness we confess to Jesus with Thomas' phrase in our heart: "My Lord and my God."

THIRD SUNDAY
OF EASTER (C)

The Primacy of Peter

Acts 5:27-32, 40:41; Revelation 5:11-14; John 21:1-19.

Aim: to explain from Scripture: (1) the basis for the Papacy and (2) the basis for the Pope's teaching authority.

Before the Resurrection, Jesus, in response to Simon the Apostle's confession of faith in him, changed his name to "Rock"—"Peter"—and pledged that he would build his Church on this Rock, to whom he would confer the keys of the kingdom of heaven (Mt 16:17 ff.).

In today's Gospel we see the risen Lord exact another act of faith and love from Peter: a threefold confession, this time, mirroring Peter's threefold denial of Christ during his Passion. And in response to Peter's clear affirmations, Jesus said, "Feed my lambs . . . Feed my sheep."

Thus Christ, the Eternal Shepherd, inaugurated his Church upon his vicar, Peter, the rock foundation and keeper of the keys. Peter, in other words, was given primacy over the other Apostles; we call this the doctrine of the Petrine Primacy or Papal Primacy. (Today, in ecumenical dialogue, it is also described as the Petrine Function.) Since Peter was Bishop of Rome when he died a martyr there (on the place where St. Peter's Basilica now stands), the Church holds that the Bishop of Rome, the Roman Pontiff, is the successor of Peter in those offices that belonged properly to him as first head of the Church—first Pope.

St. Paul testifies to Peter's unique, supreme pastoral authority (Cf. Gal 1:18, 1 Cor 15:3-7). For one thing Paul usually lists Peter first among the Apostles. And Luke, in the Acts of the Apostles, singles out Peter with the significant phrase, "Peter with the Eleven" (2:14).

Throughout the centuries, including the first few critical centuries, four truths about Peter and his successors are evident.

The first is that the Roman Pontiff is the chief bishop, primate, and leader of the entire Church of Christ on earth.

The second truth is that the Pope possesses episcopal jurisdiction over all the Church's members. This means that the Papacy is at the summit. Whereas all bishops are in a sense comparable in jurisdiction because each presides over his own diocese, the Pope presides over the faithful everywhere.

The third is that to be a member of the Catholic Church one must be in communion with the Roman Pontiff. The Church has visible unity.

The fourth truth is that God will see to it that the Roman Pontiff does not commit the Church to error in a matter of faith.

Participating in Peter's Primacy, as our present Holy Father does, is of course a graced privilege. But it is also a service of martyrdom, as today's Gospel prophesies with reference to Peter's death. After all, today's Second Reading stresses that Christ became victorious by first becoming a victim. And today's First Reading recalls that the moment Peter and the Apostles began to witness for Christ they were opposed and subjected to ill-treatment.

Peter himself, so gloriously privileged, was crucified as Christ had been. Again, Peter's Primacy demanded martyrdom. Today we should not only thank God for so worthy a successor in Peter's Chair, but pray that God will continue to strengthen him in his suffering service to the world.

FOURTH SUNDAY
OF EASTER (C)

How Priestly and Religious Vocations are Developed

Acts 13:14, 43-52; Revelation 7:9, 14-17; John 10:27-30.

Aim: (1) to explain what an ordained ministerial or religious vocation is; and (2) to encourage many more of the parish to say "Yes" to such vocations.

The theme of Jesus the Good Shepherd, clearly sounded in today's Gospel, is also hinted at in the other two readings: Luke's account, in Acts, of the decision by Paul and Barnabas to evangelize the Gentile nations; and the Apostle's apocalyptic scene of the Eternal Lamb who will shepherd a huge crowd of people from every nation, race, tribe and language (Rev).

Back in Old Testament times, God urged his people forward as a shepherd guides his sheep; Ps 95:7 witnesses to this, as does Ps 80:2. The Prophet Ezekiel details God's shepherd-like qualities; Ezekiel foretold that eventually there would be but one shepherd, under whom God's people would not only increase, but who would be the convergence point of union with others (24:23 ff.).

Jesus, God made man, fulfilled the Old Testament prophecies of God's shepherding his people. Nowhere does this fulfillment come to light more eloquently than in St. John's Gospel, from which today's reading is taken.

In the Gospel we hear Jesus identifying with the Father. As the Son of God incarnate, he literally invites us into the inner life of God. He does this precisely because he is the Gate of the Eternal Sheepfold. The Sheep—the persons—who listen to his voice, we are told, will be known by him, will follow him, and will be given eternal life by him.

Belief in Jesus, therefore, faith in Jesus as the Son of God Incarnate, is the basic essential stance of the Christian—a name first used at Antioch, the scene of today's First Reading.

To preach this truth belongs to the ordained minister. By God's own design, the multitude which no one can count, described in today's Second Reading, is gathered through ordained ministers: bishops, priests, deacons.

By God's design too, the work of adding to the Church is continued and quickened by committed Christians in vows: by nuns, monks, Sisters, Brothers. Through these, too, as well as through dedicated lay apostles, Jesus' pastoral care is maintained.

How priests or Sisters or Brothers are chosen by God is a mystery, of course, since no one is worthy. Though God chooses, through his Church, there are factors of a vocation toward which we can contribute.

One is prayer. We must pray for vocations, since, as Jesus himself told us, prayer is the ultimate essential (Lk 10:2, 3).

Another is creating an environment for ministerial or religious vocations. In a home where priests, deacons, and religious are respected, children are drawn to respect for those who exercise these vocations. The same holds true of solid Christian values: in a home where worldly values—material gain, selfishness, secularistic attitudes—are rejected, spiritual values, especially those relating to the privilege of collaborating with Christ in ministry or vows—are likely to be appreciated.

Humanly speaking, therefore, God's invitation to his special service can begin within the pastoral unit of the home.

FIFTH SUNDAY
OF EASTER (C)

The Meaning and Importance of the Catholic Church

Acts 14:21-27; Revelation 21:1-5; John 13:31-33, 34-35.

Aim: to show (1) the meaning of the (Roman) Catholic Church; and (2) the importance of being a practicing and witnessing Catholic.

Today's First Reading looks in at St. Paul and St. Barnabas during Paul's First Missionary Journey. It depicts a scene of zealous, non-stop activity in the effort to build up the Church—the foundation of the new Jerusalem seen by John in a vision in today's Second Reading. In fact, Paul had just been stoned for preaching the Gospel and healing at Lystra in Asia Minor. Left for dead, Paul rebounded quickly, and with Barnabas set out for Derbe, then back to Lystra, then to Iconium, to Perge, then back to the sea and home to Antioch.

The scene is not supposed to be lost on us whose faith has been nourished by preachers like Paul and Barnabas, pioneering new frontiers, building churches, and sustaining faith—through and following the recent *aggiornamento* until the present hour.

It's a beautiful scene, of course. Paul and Barnabas, hurriedly rushing from one town to another, eventually to Europe even, where most of our own ancestors received the Gospel, first preached there—

in Europe—to a group of charismatic women praying at a river back in northern Greece.

What impelled such activity? What impelled such response: churches established all over the Middle East, then in Greece and Rome itself? Churches everywhere; numbering hundreds and hundreds of nameless disciples committed, willing and—yes—ready to lay down their lives for the Way of Christ?

A fundamental answer is found in today's Gospel, from Jesus' Last Supper homily to his Apostles in the Upper Room; Jesus' own and entirely new mandate, the eleventh Commandment: "Love others as I have loved you."

Paul was later to say in one of his epistles—when challenged about his apparently limitless energy—"the love of Christ impels us" (2 Cor 5:14).

How did Christ love us? The answer is that he went to the Cross for us in order to save us and live with us forever. From the Cross, his Church was born; the meeting in the Upper Room of Holy Thursday became a gathering of all peoples of all times; its center, Rome, where Peter, Jesus' Vicar on earth died for the faith.

We as Catholics believe that our Church—our historic Roman Church founded on Peter and the Apostles by Jesus—is Christ's principal sacrament in this world, that it acts and speaks for Christ, that in it we find the fullness of grace and truth.

In this our Church we see a glorious link across the ages between ourselves and that zealous, bustling band of disciples recorded in today's First Reading, a band bound together with Christ's love.

Pope John Paul II, speaking in Mexico in 1979, reminded us that to love Christ means to love the Church. Citing the Church Father, St. Cyprian, he said: "She (the Church) must be called upon, respected and served, for 'one cannot have God for his father, if he does not have the Church for his mother,' . . . one cannot love Christ without loving the Church which Christ loves . . ."

SIXTH SUNDAY
OF EASTER (C)

What we Know about Heaven

Acts 15:1-2, 22-29; Revelation 21:10-14, 22-23; John 14:23-29.

Aim: (1) to explain the Church's teaching on heaven;
(2) to encourage prayers to the saints in heaven.

Today's Second Reading, from the Book of Revelation, also known as the Apocalypse (the last book of the Bible), provides us with a resplendent vision of the celestial Jerusalem—heaven, in other words. There we see the Church glorified, the Church founded upon the Twelve Apostles, the same Apostles who are depicted busy in council in today's First Reading, from Acts. Note the contrast, however: the Church depicted in Acts is the Church we know so well, making progress only with agony in this vale of tears, as it is confronted with new situations and new problems to solve in the light of God's Word.

Today's Gospel is taken from Jesus' farewell address to his disciples; risen from the grave, he must return to the Father to his—and our—eternal homeland, heaven.

Heaven (our English word reflects an Old English word designating the sky) is, we believe, a state or place of fulfillment, perfect fulfillment, in that we will see and possess God, for whom we were created. St. Augustine, in a celebrated statement, explained that we were made for God and hence are necessarily restless until we rest in him.

In heaven we will no longer view God dimly, as in a mirror. There we shall see God. Theologian Frank Sheed, in his *Death into Life: A Conversation*, once noted three especially dramatic uses in the New Testament of the verb "to see" in the context of heaven. First, our Lord spoke of the "angels who *see* the face" of his Father continuously (Mt 18:10). Thus, their seeing God is a fundamental part of their very existence, just as breathing is of our existence here. Too, the First Epistle of John tells us that in heaven we shall see God "as he is" (3:2). Lastly, St. Paul writes, in 1 Cor, that although we see God as in a mirror dimly now, tomorrow we shall see him "face to face."

In heaven seeing means more than mere physical vision, the kind for which eyes serve as earthly instruments. Seeing in heaven will be like knowing; it means seeing with our intellects. In this life, our knowledge of God is conditioned by the ideas of God we have. In heaven, we shall be graced to see God directly, as he is. There, we will no longer require the senses, such as physical sight; there we will no longer need earthly ideas. This is why our beholding God, our knowing God, in heaven, is called in Tradition the Beatific *Vision*.

Whether heaven is a place or a state can be discussed at great length. But the discussion is academic. What matters is that heaven is where Christ is. As St. Paul wrote in Philippians, heaven means to go home and be with Christ forever (1:23).

No wonder that the Apostles sorrowed so over Jesus' farewell, today's Gospel. They too longed to be with him forever—which, again, is what heaven means. For, as Christianity's supreme poet, Dante Alighieri, wrote, in our Faith's greatest poem, *The Divine Comedy*, when he saw the Beatific Vision: "And in His will is our peace."

Heaven, we believe, is everlasting fulfillment in God. Today, we know those who have preceded us in the Faith are enjoying this fulfillment. We venerate them as saints—Peter and Paul, our parish patron, _____, the Americans: Frances Cabrini, Elizabeth Seton, John Neumann, Isaac Jogues and the North American Martyrs. We know that we can invoke these saints for help, and, accordingly, do so today.

SEVENTH SUNDAY
OF EASTER (C)

The One Church of Christ

Acts 1:12-14; First Peter 4:13-16; John 17:1-11.

*Aim: to explain (1) the one Catholic Church of Christ
under the successor of St. Peter, and (2) ecumenism as
a priority today of the Lord's Church.*

Today's magnificent Gospel, excerpted from Jesus' Last Supper
sermon to his Apostles, is the Lord's own prayer for Church unity—
and for what we call ecumenism, meaning the quest for unity in
Christ.

By Christ's own desire, all those who call upon his name should be
one in him. This is to say that there is only one Church of Christ. Our
faith is, clearly and unreservedly, that the fullness of grace and truth
resides in our Church, founded upon Peter and the Apostles; and
whose center is Rome and the successor of Peter, our present Holy
Father. Thus, our own historic Roman Catholic Church is uniquely
Christ's own Church, to which Jesus will return—as today's Second
Reading states.

Pope John Paul II, speaking to the assembled bishops of Latin
America at Puebla, Mexico, on February 28, 1979, recalled that our
Church was founded by Jesus our Lord as a "fellowship of life, love
and truth"—concepts reaffirmed during Vatican Council II,
especially in the *Dogmatic Constitution on the Church*, Section 9.

Moreover, the Church is the body, the primordial sacrament, of the Lord Jesus, in whom the whole fullness of the deity dwells (*Ibid.*, sec. 7).

On the one hand, the Pope reminded, the Church is born of our response in faith to the Lord Jesus Christ. This is to say that the Church is "the assembly of those who in faith look to Jesus as the cause of salvation and the sorce of unity and peace" (*Ibid.*, sec. 9). On the other hand, we are born of the Church. We are generated by her through baptism, nourished by the Eucharist and God's word. Citing theologian Henri de Lubac, the Holy Father said: "We are her (the Church's) children. With just pride we call her our mother, repeating a title coming down the centuries from the earliest times."

The love we have for our Church mirrors the love we have for Christ, for the Church is Christ's Mystical Body. "Love Christ, love the Church," is an ancient adage. Many men and women, beginning with St. Stephen, whose martyrdom is described in today's First Reading, have exemplified this adage by surrendering their lives.

Love for our Church is the reason why we pursue ecumenism— the quest for Christian unity. The Church cannot move forward ecumenically unless it steadfastly continues to insist upon the unicity—oneness—of Christ's Church, and the role of Peter and his successor—the Pope—in integrating all Christianity within one visible body.

Today we remind ourselves that whereas a fragmented Christianity is not Christ's will, neither can his Church ever be a religious "conglomerate" of churches.

How all Christianity can be one under Peter seems difficult of solution to us as human beings. But unity is Christ's will. So long as we work and pray that his will be accomplished, he will show us the way to unity. To this end, we respect the consciences of all believers, and join with them in this great task of our age, especially through prayer, dialogue and common witness where possible.

TRINITY SUNDAY (C)

The Creed: A Summary of Our Beliefs

Proverbs 8:22-31; Romans 5:1-5; John 16:12-15.

*Aim: to (1) explain the Creed (Apostles' and Nicene);
and (2) to encourage an attentive proclamation of the
Creed in union with the worldwide Catholic Church.*

This year on Trinity Sunday the Gospel and the First Reading focus on the wisdom which our faith provides; while the Second Reading reminds us that this wisdom is an anchor-like support assuring us hope in our confused world.

The wisdom we acquire through God's Word can be summarized in the early creedal statement, "Jesus is Lord" (1 Cor 12:3; Rm 10:9; Ph 2:11; Col 2:6, etc.). This affirmation presupposes three others: (1) God exists; (2) God rewards and punishes; (3) in God there are three Persons: Father, Son and Holy Spirit.

"Jesus is Lord." We call this a creedal statement, or, simply, a creed. "Creed" derives from the Latin verb *credere*, meaning "to believe." A creed, therefore, is a summary of basic tenets of belief.

Two of the most ancient elaborations of "Jesus is Lord" are the Nicene Creed, which we say at Mass on Sundays; and the Apostles' Creed. Church creeds such as these—there are others, some liturgical, some doctrinal, some catechetical—are precious statements. Hammered out painstakingly and with precision, they will perdure to the end of time.

Each word in a Creed is important; it belongs there for a good reason. In the Nicene Creed, for instance, we profess belief in the resurrection of the flesh; thus we say, "We look for the resurrection of the dead." In the Apostles' Creed, we say the same thing in another way; namely, "I believe in . . . the resurrection of the body." These sentences confess explicitly and exactly the bodily resurrection, a doctrine essential to our entire faith-affirmation.

Even the reference to Pontius Pilate is highly significant; our faith is that Jesus suffered and died under this Roman procurator. The phrase "under Pontius Pilate" inserts Jesus' Redemption within our very history; it affirms Jesus' Passion and death as *historical*, not simply poetic.

Creeds, as we said above, provide sure anchors in the confused religious climate of the world, and thus give us hope. For example, when challenges are voiced with respect to, say, Jesus' divine nature, or to his historical character, we have but to refer back to our precious creeds, such as the Nicene or Apostles' Creeds, to bolster our stance.

Whenever we recite a Creed sincerely and meaningfully, as we pray we might do again today, we are really saying, in effect: "This is the faith of our fathers; by this we all stand, thus we all believe."

These very words were shouted aloud in unison by all present on October 22, 451 at Chalcedon, in Asia Minor, when our Nicene Creed was first formulated.

Learn and review often the great historic Creeds, like the Nicene and Apostles' Creeds; they say *what* we believe, *precisely* what we believe; and they say it *best*. They are precious treasures, whose wealth increases as life lengthens—if one really believes.

CORPUS CHRISTI (C)

How a Catholic Receives the Lord

Genesis 14:18-20; First Corinthians 11:23-26; Luke 9:11-17.

Aim: to explain (1) how to receive Communion; (2) when to receive; (3) when not to receive Holy Communion.

Today is *Corpus Christi*; the Latin phrase means "the Body of Christ." It is a liturgical opportunity for us to meditate upon and thank Christ for his gift of himself in the Blessed Eucharist.

Today's First Reading, the story of Melchizedek, a mysterious figure who offered bread and wine in the presence of Abraham, is read by Catholics as dimly prophesying the institution of the Eucharist. Today's Second Reading, from St. Paul, is the oldest written Biblical account of the first Mass at the Last Supper; St. Paul's First Epistle to Corinth was written before the Gospels. Today's Gospel is from Luke's description of one of Jesus' multiplications of loaves and fishes, a sign which proximately looked forward to the Last Supper and the Eucharist.

In the Gospel, note that the time was sunset, and that the crowds who came to hear Jesus were fatigued and hungry. In response, our Lord prepared places for them in his presence, where he fed them. Here we are reminded that the Eucharist is a place for rest and for banqueting in the taxing pilgrimage of earthly life. Here, in the Eucharist, we are comforted and strengthened by God's word, as against the wearying confusions, crises, and falsehoods of this life;

and we are privileged to dine on the Bread of Life which alone satisfies our most profound hunger, a spiritual hunger for truth and goodness.

Surely this means that the Eucharist demands thanksgiving. Isn't this why, after we have received our divine Lord in Communion, we spend a few moments at least "gathering up the fragments" as the Apostles did, lest we fail to appreciate so great a gift as the Eucharist?

Of course our thanksgiving for communion really begins before we have received. Isn't this why we say at least some prayers of preparation, fold our hands in prayer when coming up the aisle and returning from the communion station? Isn't this also why we make some sign of reverence—a genuflection or the Sign of the Cross—just before we receive? And why we cross our hands, if we receive on the hand, raising them high, throne-like, to accept the Eucharist?

Reverence while receiving communion is a means not only of expressing our appreciation in faith, hope and love for the Eucharist, but also of renewing and intensifying our thanks. For even though we may approach the communion table in the state of grace, which means we are not conscious of any unconfessed mortal sin (to receive the Eucharist in a state of serious sin, we know, renders us guilty of sinning against the Body and Blood of Christ): the intensity of our encounter with Christ depends upon our interior dispositions of faith, hope, love and appreciation. (This helps explain why frequent communion may not lead to increased union with Christ.)

Today's Gospel notes that the crowd fed by Jesus ate "until they had enough." Christ wills our union with him to be complete. Any imperfections in this union are always on our part. Again, reverence before and after Communion, prayerful preparation, and a sincere thanksgiving are all required.

At any rate, today's meditation on the Eucharist should be taken as a warning never to allow our reception of communion to become so routine that no preparation, no thanksgiving, and no reverence are felt or expressed.

SECOND SUNDAY IN ORDINARY TIME (C)

The Baptism of Jesus and Our Baptism

Isaiah 62:1-5; First Corinthians 12:4-11; John 2:1-10.

Aim: (1) to explain what happened when we were baptized (specifically, a new birth to eternal life, replete with extraordinary powers of soul, and joy); (2) to present our baptism as a commitment for life to live in Christ and in grace.

In today's first Bible reading, from the Second Isaiah, we read that God will give his people an entirely new name, for he delights in his people. In the Second Reading, an especially mysterious passage from St. Paul's Letter to the Corinthians, we read that God will give his people such gifts as the power to express knowledge and prophecy. And in the Gospel, that very happy word-picture of Jesus' saving his host the embarrassment of running short of wine just when the wedding reception was going on well, God gives us, in Jesus, the first public sign of his real intervention in our lives, a sign of joy.

Jesus' first intervention in *our* lives—in your life and mine—also occurred at a celebration: the celebration of our baptism. At Cana of Galilee, he changed water into wine. Through his cross and resurrection, he changed ordinary water into far more than wine; he changed ordinary water into waters that give life eternally, the saving waters of baptism.

At baptism we were given a name. In today's First Reading, a new name is promised to all who are chosen by the Lord. In our Christian tradition, a name signifies the fresh life which the new birth of baptism initiates. We know that the Church is desirous that this name be that reflecting our Faith—a saint's name, preferably.

The new name given us at baptism is also a sign of the identity which this first encounter with the living Lord Jesus bestows upon us. From the moment of our baptism we know the answers to questions such as "Who am I?" and "What is my purpose in life?" Reborn in Jesus, we know that we are God's adopted sons and daughters, destined for fulfillment in him forever. Baptism, therefore, is the ultimate source of joy in our lives. Because of our baptism and the identity it gives us as God's children, we know for certain that God is saying to us (as today's First Reading puts it) not "Forsaken" or "Desolate," but rather, "my Delight," and "espoused."

Because of our baptism, too, we know that a host of other gifts is showered upon us, the greatest of which entail faith, hope and love, as today's Second Reading emphasizes. We know, infallibly, that Jesus does send his Spirit to us, even simply to help us understand, when everything around us seems not understandable at all in sheer human terms.

Of course Christ's encounter with us in our baptism must be ratified on our part. Baptism means commitment to discipleship. Just as soon as an adult is baptized or just as soon as a youth baptized in infancy arrives at a capacity for mature judgment, personal response to Christ is required. Pope Paul VI once said that to be a Christian, one must determine to be one.

Which is to say that our baptism must be given a chance to flower, and to take effect. The Christian who thinks he can have a new name by virtue of baptism but has no intention of acting on the commitment that this new name entails, is like the man who wouldn't wear a wedding garment in the Gospel parable.

That wedding garment brings us back to Cana, and Jesus' miracle there, the story of today's Gospel. The Gospel says that changing water into wine was the first sign Jesus worked there.

Baptism is the first sign worked by the living Lord Jesus in our lives. It can be followed by many more—but only if we keep commitment.

Again, to be a Christian, one must work at it. Our new name, bestowed in baptism; our identity as God's children, given us in our baptism: both demand that we respond, personally, to Christ's intervention in our lives.

THIRD SUNDAY
IN ORDINARY TIME (C)

The Purpose of Life

Nehemiah 8:2-4, 5-6, 8-10; First Corinthians 12:12-30; Luke 1:1-14.

Aim: to show life's purpose as (1) to know God; (2) to love God; (3) to serve God in this world, and to be happy with God for eternity. To encourage living by this purpose (especially through God's word and his presence).

Today's first Bible reading takes us back to the fifth century B.C. During most of the preceding century, the tiny Jewish nation had been exiled in Babylon, modern day Iraq. In the year 538 B.C., King Cyrus of Persia, who had conquered Babylon, began to permit some Jews to return to the Holy Land. Two of the great heroes of faith who helped restore religion and government during the post-exilic period were Ezra, a priest, and Nehemiah, a layman who had been a servant of the Persian king—a royal cupbearer—during his exile in Babylon.

Today's First Reading looks in on Nehemiah's providing that the word of God be proclaimed to the Israelites, many of whom were ignorant of it. When the people were assembled, Ezra proclaimed the Law of God and renewed the covenant by which they were joined to God.

(The proclamation, incidentally, took two days to finish—which is rather long in terms of today's sermons. And it was read from a wooden platform, which, it appears, is the first reference in the Old Testament to the origins of the pulpit.)

The reading of the Law concluded with a great celebration.

Today's Gospel marks a fulfillment of that first proclamation. When Jesus closed the scroll of Isaiah in the synagogue of Nazareth that historic day—the episode recorded in today's Gospel—he was saying, in effect, "God is with you in me, forever. God will not abandon you. I have come to rebuild a new Jerusalem, to help the exiled, the poor and the hungry, to give you wisdom, and to scatter the powers of evil troubling you. Rejoice, therefore; your salvation is at hand."

We, too—you and I—were once exiled, through sin. In Jesus we have found salvation, so certain and so irrevocable, that no evil can ever permanently harm us as long as we remain in him through faith, hope and love. Our discovering this also occurred through hearing God's word; and having heard it, we, too, celebrate, as we do at this very Eucharist. Being a member of Christ's body—to borrow from the figure Paul uses in today's Second Reading—is cause for rejoicing throughout life. We know experientially the full meaning of Ezra's words to the returned exiles in today's First Reading; namely: "Do not be saddened this day, for rejoicing in the Lord must be your strength!"

Life is a joy—not an absurdity, much less a sorrow—when we live it according to God's discovered word, and in his presence. To live to know, to love and to serve God in this world in order to be happy with him in the next, is to celebrate life.

There is nothing that gives real and lasting meaning to human existence other than faith in the God who created us and who has destined us to be with him forever. And this meaning assures peace and happiness. To know that we possess absolute certainty in God's word; to know that we are united to God in Jesus, our Lord; to know that all of God's most lavish gifts pledged to those who accept him are destined for us who keep faith in Jesus: this is what life, a full and rich life, is about.

God grant that we may never lose sight of this principle.

Why can't our lives constitute a continuous chant of the thoughts expressed in today's Responsorial Psalm:

"The Law of the Lord is perfect, refreshing the soul. . .

"The precepts of the Lord are right, rejoicing the heart. . .

"The command of the Lord is clear, enlightening the eye. . .

"Let the words of my mouth and the thought of my heart find favor before you,

O Lord, my rock and redeemer."

FOURTH SUNDAY
IN ORDINARY TIME (C)

Marriage

Jeremiah 1:4-5, 17-19; First Corinthians 12:31-13:13; Luke 4:21-30.

Aim: (1) to accent humble, careful preparation for marriage; (2) to tell how and where a Catholic should get married; (3) to tell of the problems of an unhappy marriage; (4) to explain belief and tribunal practices concerning invalid marriages.

St. Paul, in today's Second Reading, explains that in the Church there are many different works that must be done, and there are many gifts or capabilities—call them charisms—for doing these works. One of many ways to approach this passage is by reminding ourselves that Christians are called to different states of life, one of which is the married state, which reflects God's highest gift, that of love.

As Christians we believe that marriage is not merely a contract between a man and a woman, not even simply a *sacred* contract between a couple, but is, in fact, a covenant made with the living Lord Jesus. "It takes three to get married," is not just a poetic saying, therefore, but a valid theological statement. By virtue of the covenant with which Christ makes a couple one with him, marrieds are ensured divine love, enlightenment and guidance. Those married in Christ, in other words, are pledged by Christ all the gifts or capabilities—charisms—necessary for their marriage. "Married in Christ" means of course married in accordance with the laws of the Church, which is Christ's Mystical Body.

A Christian does not rush into marriage, therefore, simply for emotional reasons or convenience or compulsion. He or she views it as a sacred commitment, a lifelong commitment, requiring deliberation of mind and soul, a commitment that must be prepared for by prayer and intense sacramental encounter, especially through the Holy Eucharist and Penance.

Self-searching is required not only about one's ability to take a prospective spouse, but also as to whether one is ready to ask the living Lord Jesus to commit himself to enter the marriage; since, again, a Christian marriage necessarily involves Christ in a covenantal relationship.

If marriage is a covenant with the living Christ, then it goes without saying that Christ is at the very beginning of marriage, as God was at the prophet Jeremiah's very beginning in today's First Reading. And what God begins, God will bring to perfection, so long as he is followed.

In marriage, God is embraced primarily through matrimonial love, which is essentially sacrificial love. Look at that definition of love in today's Second Reading; each one of the adjectives by which Paul describes love refers to a person outside oneself, the wife or husband in marriage. Love, Paul says, is kind; one is kind *to someone else*: to one's spouse, in marriage. Love, he also says, is not jealous, or rude, or impatient; true love is sincere and does not brood over injuries or celebrate what is wrong.

How many marriages would never be in trouble were all these characteristics of true love carefully cultured by spouses, with the help they can expect to receive from the living Christ, who is, again, a living party to their marriage? (We are not speaking here of situations developing because marriages were never really valid marriages owing to various invalidating circumstances, whose authenticity is judged by diocesan matrimonial courts.) We do know and believe that even in the case of a broken marriage, those who persevere in Christ's word and grace will be aided by him; "those who persevere" here means those who in their sorrow and with divine help keep their vow once made "until death do us part."

'We know that Christ's word about marriage will draw general indignation from a world that claims to know more. Jesus' being driven from the synagogue, in today's Gospel, prophesied this situation.

FIFTH SUNDAY
IN ORDINARY TIME (C)

Our Relationship to the Pope

Isaiah 6:1-2, 3-8; First Corinthians 15:1-11; Luke 5:1-11.

Aim: to explain (1) teaching authority or magisterium in the Catholic Church; and (2) the way a Catholic follows the Church's teaching authority.

In today's First Reading, the prophet Isaiah describes the circumstances of his mission: he was personally deputed to speak for God by God himself. The year was 742 B.C.; the deputation occurred in the Temple of Jerusalem. It is recorded that the prophet recognized his inadequacy, yet cleansed in speech, he proceeds to accept his mission to prophesy.

In today's Second Reading, St. Paul alludes to his mission to prophesy, a mission received by him not in the Temple of Jerusalem, but within the Church of Christ.

The beginnings of New Testament mission, the beginnings of ordination to preach within the Church, are recalled in today's Gospel, the story of Jesus' preaching from Peter's boat, and our Lord's predicting that Peter and his companions would one day be fishers of men.

The Church is a sign of Christ in the world. As such, the Church must speak for Christ; it is inconceivable that our divine Lord would have made the Church his principal sacrament among men yet denied it the capacity to prophesy in his name.

For the Church to be Christ's voice in this world, it obviously must speak with the assurance that it cannot err in teaching God's original message, or anything pertaining to faith or morals to which it irrevocably commits itself. This is what we mean when we speak about the Church's infallibility, clearly attested to in the Bible (Jn 1:14 and 14:6; 1 Jn 5:20; Jn 14:17; Mt 28:19 ff.; Rm 1:16; 2 Cor 6:17; Gal 1:7; 1 Tm 3:15.)

Papal infallibility is in a sense one way of focusing the Church's infallibility; the Holy Father is infallible only insofar as he speaks for, and in the name of, Christ's Church.

Thus an ecumenical council is infallible when it solemnly enunciates a doctrine under the conditions for infallibility cited above (e.g., a matter of faith and morals). Moreover, Vatican II witnesses to the belief that when the bishops throughout the world, without meeting in an ecumenical council, but nonetheless maintaining their union with the Pope and each other, are in unanimity in their authoritative doctrine regarding faith or morals and propose this doctrine definitively, they "infallibly proclaim the teaching of Christ" (*The Dogmatic Constitution on the Church*, Sec. 25).

Also embraced within the larger concept of the Church's infallibility are "all those things . . . to be believed by divine and Catholic faith which are contained in the written or transmitted word of God and are set forth as divinely revealed (and) as to be believed by the Church's solemn decision, or by the ordinary and universal magisterium (i.e., the Church's ordinary teaching authority)."

The authentic voice of the Church in matters of faith and doctrine is heard in the voice of the bishops led by Peter; namely, the Bishop of Rome. Dissident voices do not constitute the voice of the Church. Again, the charism of truth was left to the Church, whose voice is heard in the pope and the bishops, and priests and deacons ordained to preach with the Church's authority.

Today we recommit ourselves to respect and honor the voice of the Church—the voice of the Holy Father and the bishops—in the faith that the Church can and does prophesy in Christ's name.

SIXTH SUNDAY
IN ORDINARY TIME (C)

Social Justice and Peace

Jeremiah 17:5-8; First Corinthians 15:12, 16-20; Luke 6:17, 20-26.

Aim: (1) to explain why a Catholic should be concerned about social justice and peace; (2) to describe selfish apathy as un-Christian.

Luke's account of the Beatitudes is at the heart of today's Gospel. The evangelist enumerates four; to each he offers an antithesis, or a corresponding "Woe." Thus, Jesus blesses the poor, but expresses alarm for the future of the rich; graces the hungry, but has severe reservations about the plight of the well fed.

Curiously, Luke depicts Jesus speaking these four beatitudes not on a mountain, but on a busy plain; moreover, Jesus preaches directly to the disciples, though the crowds are in the background. Could it be that Jesus meant that his words here are likely to be grasped and kept only by the committed follower? As for the location of the sermon—the plain, not the mountain—doesn't it symbolize admirably the motif of Jesus' warning; namely, the imperative of social justice? Isn't it true that words about poverty and hunger and grief and rejection can best be understood by one who has walked the plain places of this world: the factories and hospitals and the many other everyday places of ordinary men and women with calloused hands and tired hearts, who must stand in line almost each day, and who are largely ignored by those with plenty or with status?

The main theme of today's Gospel may not be sociological, but this theme is unquestionably sounded. As followers of Christ, we *are* our brothers' keepers in the sense that we must not close our hearts to those who need us. Disciples of Jesus, the Suffering Servant, who came to serve, not to be served, we must be persons for others. By such service we can help bring peace to a world fragmented by people who are in debt or hungry or depressed or rejected. As members of Jesus' Church we must consciously involve ourselves in Christ's own ministry of healing, reconciling, binding up wounds, wiping away the tears of loneliness and alienation.

In other words, by virtue of our destiny to participate in the mystery of the risen Lord, about which St. Paul speaks so eloquently in today's Second Reading, we have an obligation to search for Gospel means by which those who are now suffering in the world from servitude or oppression of any kind might be freed. No one put this in more concrete Biblical-economic terms than St. John when he wrote:

"He who has the goods of this world and sees his brother in need and closes his heart to him, how does the love of God abide in him?" (1 Jn 3:17).

Possibly the most ignored basic economic doctrine of our Faith is the principle that personal superfluous wealth simply cannot be justly retained in the face of poverty. About superfluous income, St. Ambrose wrote long ago:

"You are not making a gift of what is yours to the poor man, but you are giving him back what is his. You have been appropriating things that are meant to be for the common use of everyone. The earth belongs to everyone, not to the rich."

Social justice and the peace it ensures is not simply a precept for precept's sake. On the contrary, a Christian's responsibility to be a peacemaker through social justice is revealed to us as a positive value. We enrich ourselves by caring for others.

The man or woman who selfishly ignores neighbor ends up like the shriveled bush in today's First Reading.

SEVENTH SUNDAY
IN ORDINARY TIME (C)

Social Justice and Peace

*First Samuel 26:2, 7-9, 12-13, 22-23; First Corinthians 15:45-49;
Luke 6:27-38.*

*Aim: to present the Church's teaching on major
current issues: disarmament, nuclear war, world
poverty, racism.*

Today's First Reading, from First Samuel, presents us with a
story of King David's nobility of soul: his refusal to resort to
violence—to take a spear, literally—against his enemy, against one
who had wronged him. Forgiveness of one's enemies and reconciliation are two themes sounded, therefore. They are echoed in today's
Gospel, from Jesus' Sermon on the Mount, which requires a non-
earthly, spiritual way of living, as St. Paul reminds us in today's
Second Reading. This means, of course, that Christians should be
known as peacemakers.

One can read today's Bible lessons against the backdrop of the
world at large, and by this reading call to mind again the doctrines
enunciated by our Church regarding war and disarmament, together
with the causes of international conflict.

Pope Paul VI, speaking before the United Nations Organization
in New York City in October, 1965, deeply impressed the world with
the words, "Never again war, never again war." This is of course our
hope as followers of Christ. It is an urgent hope today, when recourse

to total warfare—acts of war directed to the indiscriminate destruction of entire cities or vast areas with their people—is readily available to all major powers. As the Fathers of Vatican Council II put it:

"The hazards peculiar to modern warfare consist in the fact that they expose those possessing recently developed weapons to the risk of perpetrating crimes like these and, by an inexorable chain of events, of urging men to even worse atrocity" (*Church in the Modern World*, no. 80).

To lessen the temptation to launch warfare today the Church has repeatedly proposed general disarmament. Vatican Council II labeled the arms race as "one of the greatest curses on the human race" (*Ibid.*, no. 81). And Paul VI, in his UN address, pleaded: "If you want to be brothers, let the arms fall from your hands. A person cannot love with offensive weapons in his hands."

Disarmament, our Church teaches, also frees nations to attack many of the conditions that occasion war: economic misery, hunger, the lack of education, racial or national discrimination, political repression, disregard for human life, unemployment and injustices in general.

The edifice of civilization, Pope Paul argued, has to be built on spiritual principles, for these are the only foundations capable of supporting it always and everywhere. Such principles are found in the Bible; in today's Gospel especially, the Sermon on the Mount.

The building of this edifice is the work and the responsibility of individuals, millions of individuals, each with a conscience, which is, in a real sense, God's voice speaking to the innermost core of the person. International peace begins in the home and the neighborhood; it is launched by each person who really believes in the truth of today's Bible lessons.

Before the UN building in New York City, there is a world famous sculpture based on Isaiah 2:4, the text projecting an era in which God's people would be so committed to peacemaking that they would be able to convert their swords of war into plows for the earth, their battle lances into pruning hooks for trees.

This hope is still a possibility, with God's assistance. But it begins, again, at home, within the heart of each faithful disciple of Jesus: in one's home, neighborhood and town.

EIGHTH SUNDAY
IN ORDINARY TIME (C)

Conduct as a Christian

Sirach 27:4-7; First Corinthians 15:54-58; Luke 6:39-45.

Aim: to describe how externals manifest and help belief (with specific reference to making visits to the Blessed Sacrament, praying, preparing for Mass, even genuflecting).

One message we can detect in today's Bible Readings, especially the opening text from Sirach and the Gospel, is that sincere religion will manifest itself externally, in our actions and words; whereas lack of interior commitment can be perceived in the way one acts or speaks. A man's speech, Sirach cautions us, betrays his mind. And in the Gospel Jesus reminds us that good fruit comes only from a good tree; figs are not taken from thornbushes.

In the first instance, these lessons prompt us to reflect on hypocrisy, which, incidentally, is the only sin that in the Gospels directly drew Jesus' wrath. As Christians who attend the Sunday Eucharist, for example, and who glory in the name Catholic, we must put a guard on our inner dispositions lest we become only pretenders: disciples on the outside, but vacillators within. Being a Christian is, after all, a matter of the heart; we must *be* what we are.

One of the surest betrayals of duplicity, surely, occurs in speech, as both Sirach and the Gospel specify. Thus a Christian in name who misuses God's holy name in ordinary conversation, or whose vocabulary is characterized by a lack of charity for others, or whose common expressions include a host of racially or ethnically offensive phrases, is reminded to examine his conscience and make certain resolutions.

There is another way to read today's Bible texts. One could take them as reminders that we should perform in accordance with our belief in the premise that our external conduct can speak as loudly as words. And one can interpret this even with respect to our conduct here in church: the exterior reverence with which we pray, or genuflect before the Tabernacle of Reservation, or prepare for Mass, or receive communion. Even an occasional visit made to the Blessed Sacrament on a weekday afternoon can speak eloquently of our interior faith and, God only knows, help others in need of spiritual support.

This last point we should never forget. Our conduct *can* support others who are in trouble. On the contrary, our conduct can occasion the decline of others in faith, and, consequently contribute to a general spiritual malaise.

A committed Catholic, Pope Paul VI said in an address during a general audience on May 28, 1975, "has a duty to bear witness and this duty liberates him from timidity and opportunism. It suggests the proper behavior and the right words at the right moment; these arise from an inner wellspring of which perhaps he was not even aware before the moment of testing. . ."

The Holy Father added that we must all live our Christian lives courageously in private and in public. Otherwise, we can "become ciphers in the world of the spirit and perhaps share the responsibility for the general decadence."

Our conduct must always support others—even the way we genuflect with faith. After all, as St. Paul reminds us in today's Second Reading, we are Easter People, destined to rise with Christ:

"Be steadfast and persevering . . . *fully* engaged in the work of the Lord. You know that your toil is not in vain when it is done for the Lord."

Each person, today's Gospel warns, "speaks from his heart's abundance."

NINTH SUNDAY
IN ORDINARY TIME (C)

Non-Christian Religions

First Kings 8:41-43; Galatians 1:1-2, 6-10; Luke 7:1-10.

Aim: to teach the attitude which we should show toward religious groups which do not accept Christ: the Jews, the Moslems, the Eastern religions.

Today's First Reading, from King Solomon's prayer at the dedication of the first Temple, prophesies a pilgrimage of all people, Gentiles as well as Jews, to God's sanctuary. Jesus, in today's Gospel, relates our Savior's compassion for a Godly Roman soldier, a non-Jew, therefore; a miracle is worked in his behalf. What more suitable a topic for today's homily, therefore, than God's reaching out to those who in good faith do not enjoy full visible union with the Church of Christ: those who do not accept baptism, especially our brothers and sisters who are Jewish or Moslems, or those who embrace Buddhism or other Eastern religions?

Our Catholic faith tells us clearly that Jesus came to save all men and women.

In the First Letter to Timothy we read: "For he (God) wants all men to be saved and come to the knowledge of truth" (2:4). When Christ commissioned his Apostles, he said: "Go . . . and make disciples of all nations . . ." (Mt 28:10 ff.). And the night before our Lord ascended the cross of Calvary he stressed the universal scope of his mission when he declared, over the cup of wine, that his Blood was being shed "for all men." (These words are liturgically rendered in the Eucharistic Prayer of Mass.)

Are we to believe then that even those who are not visibly part of Jesus' true Church, to which he invites all men to belong, can be saved?

Vatican Council II addressed itself to this subject in contemporary terms. Those who have not yet received the Gospel, it declared, are nonetheless related to the People of God. In the first place here, of course, are our Jewish brethren, to whom the covenants and the promises were given and from whom Christ was born. The Jewish people, our faith tells us, are dear to God, for he does not repudiate his gifts or designations.

God's plan of salvation also extends to Moslems, who also invoke Abraham and adore the one, merciful God. Likewise, it extends to Hindus, who accent the quest for truth and ascetical practices of deep meditation and flight Godward. And to Buddhists, who in many ways acknowledge the radical insufficiency of this changing world and strive for a state of freedom from material things and spiritual enlightment. And, finally, to those of all religions which "strive variously to answer the restless searchings of the human heart by proposing 'ways' which consist of teachings, rules of life, and sacred ceremonies" (*Declaration on the Relationship of the Church to Non-Christian Religions* no. 2).

As Catholics we reject nothing that is true or holy in these religions. We look with sincere respect upon any norms of conduct which reflect the light that is God. We dedicate ourselves to dialogue and to collaborate with the followers of other religions.

In every case, moreover, persons of other faiths must be honored as persons. For a Catholic, anti-Semitism is a sin; so too, rejection or ridicule of those who follow Islam, or Buddhism, or Hinduism, or other comparable religions they have embraced in a search for goodness and truth.

As Catholics, moreover, we confess, that while we have the fullness of truth and grace in Christ's Church, we know that many outside Christianity can teach us lessons about our failings in commitment.

Today's thoughts should at least remind us of the dignity which we, as followers of Jesus, must strive to maintain—as St. Paul warns in today's Second Reading.

TENTH SUNDAY IN ORDINARY TIME (C)

Christian Burial and Reverence for Dead

First Kings 17:17-24; Galatians 1:11-19; Luke 7:11-17.

Aim: to describe (1) how we bury our dead, visit graves and have Masses said for our dead; (2) our reasons for Catholic cemeteries.

In today's First Reading, Elijah, who prophesied in the ninth century B.C., prayed that God would restore the life of the son of a widow; and God heard Elijah's prayer. In today's Gospel, Jesus, the Prophet of Prophets because he is God, restores to life another widow's son, at Naim.

What more instructive a lesson can be crystallized from these readings that the truth that faith in God's presence when death intervenes, can render death ineffective? Surely both these Bible readings point to the future resurrection in Christ of all who embrace him as Lord.

One way we could approach this subject is by reference to our Church's funeral liturgy, which is, after all, our means of ensuring that Christ is with the person who has died in the eyes of the world; and with us, who mourn for our loss in the death of a relative or friend.

Thus, the ceremonies of the Mass of Christian Burial emphasize God's mercy and the certainty of bodily resurrection for those who have been faithful. And they encourage consoling hope among the living who must one day also follow the deceased before God's tribunal.

The Bible readings alone can transform the sorrow of death into peace of heart for the mourners. In text after text—there are many options for the Gospels as well as the other Scripture lessons—we are reminded that God is a God of the living, that Christ has conquered death (which results from sin), that death need not be feared, that all who believe in Christ will have eternal life, that in Jesus' resurrection all will surely rise in the flesh. Death for a Christian, after all, does not mean an end, but a beginning.

Even our rite of burial reflects the certainty of resurrection in Christ, that our lives will be restored as surely as those of the widows' sons in today's Bible readings—but more so, since resurrection is to a new and better and never-ending life. Thus, we usually bury our dead in consecrated ground. The graves which hold our dead, we know, cannot hold them forever. As Jesus' grave was opened by the power of the resurrection, so every burial place for the Christian believer is but temporary. For a Christian, cemeteries are not forever. We have Christ's own word that whoever believes in him will never die (Jn 11:26).

Every Christian funeral liturgy, therefore, is an occasion for Jesus to enter into our lives again, as really as he entered the life of the widow's son; over the centuries Jesus says, in effect, again: "I bid you to get up."

No wonder that St. Paul was so fiery in writing about the glad tidings of the faith; today's Second Reading, from Galatians is a classic example. The reality of life in Jesus after earthly death *is* overwhelmingly wonderful news.

ELEVENTH SUNDAY IN ORDINARY TIME (C)

Saints For Our Times

Second Samuel 12:7-10, 13; Galatians 2:16, 19-21; Luke 7:36-8:3.

Aim: to tell about (1) saints in general; (2) patron saints; (3) helpful saints for our times.

Luke, whose Gospel is known as the Women's Gospel, today gives us a list of some of the women who followed Jesus and his Apostles. One, he tells us, was Mary Magdalene, who, for one reason in particular, is a model of a saint for all seasons. She was a person of faith who gave Christ priority over everything in her life, for pure love of him. Had she written down the basic motivations of her life, she would have written, in large letters, precisely what Paul wrote down in today's Second Reading:

". . . I have been crucified with Christ, and the life I live now is not my own; Christ is living in me. I still live my human life, but it is a life of faith in the Son of God, who loved me and gave himself for me."

To give Christ priority over everything—to become a saint—begins with an acknowledgement of one's sinfulness; with a contrite confession such as David voiced in today's First Reading: "I have sinned against the Lord."

This means knowing oneself, and well. All the saints knew their weaknesses and sinfulness: Francis and Patrick and Stanislaus and Bernard and Jean Vianney and Elizabeth Seton. Augustine, in his great classic, *The Confessions*, wrote about his early 30's: "The Enemy held my will . . . for from a perverse will was created wicked desire or lust, and the serving this lust became a custom . . . I begged for chastity, but not yet . . . for I was afraid lest you (God) hear me too soon, and heal me of the disease which I had rather wished to have satisfied than extinguished."

God's grace is too powerful for the sinner who sincerely wants pardon and peace. Augustine the libertine became Augustine the Doctor of the Church, one of the most illustrious of all God's instruments in this vale of tears. One who sincerely wants to love God can be loved by him overwhelmingly.

Look at the Magdalene again. She went in search of Jesus and once having found him, remained to accompany him: to listen to his words, to experience his goodness, which is Goodness Personified. She gave Christ the first place in her life; everything else came afterward.

St. Elizabeth Seton, the first American-born saint, is a comparable example; likewise, the other Elizabeth who also shows us how beautiful married life in Christ can be: St. Elizabeth of Hungary. Both these women knew that once one places Christ and his word first, then nothing can ever happen to destroy one's peace or happiness.

The Magdalene, as I noted, found Christ and remained in his company. Her quest finished, she did not retreat.

Augustine, who wasted his youth and early manhood, was later to utter a prayer that should haunt anyone who has found Christ but does not take full advantage of the discovery. Augustine wrote:

"Too late have I loved you . . . too late have I loved."

The saints teach us that the Good News is appreciated always when it is later than we think.

TWELFTH SUNDAY
IN ORDINARY TIME (C)

Catholic Devotions and Sacramentals
as Means of Intensifying Commitment
and Suffering Service

Zechariah 12:10-11; Galatians 3:26-29; Luke 9:18-24.

Aim: (1) to stress anew the interior dimension of discipleship and the need for suffering service; (2) briefly to show how Catholic devotions and sacramentals can be means to interior religion.

Zechariah, the prophet of today's First Reading, was one of the 12 minor prophets of the Old Testament. (The minor prophets wrote the shorter books; those who wrote the three longer books, Isaiah, Jeremiah and Ezekiel, are called the major prophets.)

Today's text foresees a mysterious Prince of Peace who would be "thrust through," as with a lance, for God's people. This phrase was applied in St. John's Gospel to Jesus' being pierced on Calvary. It's a phrase that brings back memories, for many of us, of a prayer we learned in childhood: the Prayer to Jesus Crucified.

Do we still say this prayer after Communion, as we once did, even occasionally, during the few minutes of postcommunion silence? And what about all those other beautiful devotions we once learned: the Way of the Cross, especially in Lent; the Rosary, every day; the Act of Contrition prior to retiring every evening, the various approved litanies: to the Sacred Heart of Jesus, to the Blessed Virgin Mary?

And, while we're on the subject, what about our use of sacramentals: those signs resembling the sacraments by which the Church helps us to dispose ourselves to receive the full effects of the sacraments, and to render holy certain occasions in life? Do we, for instance, still bless ourselves with holy water as a sign of our baptism commitment as we enter Church to participate in Mass as God's priestly people?

Private devotions and sacramentals *are* important to us; they are helpful to us who believe. But they orient as means toward the essentials of faith: interior commitment and suffering service in the footsteps of Jesus of Nazareth.

In today's Gospel, Jesus tells us plainly that willing acceptance of his Cross each day to follow him is essential to the life of a Christian. But note: today's Gospel opens with a reference to Jesus' praying in seclusion. To fulfill our missions as disciples, personal prayer is necessary. Sacramentals are signs that the Church is praying with us; traditional Catholic devotions are prayers especially blessed by the Church.

Misunderstanding the place of devotions and sacramentals can occasion some spiritual dangers. Not to keep in mind that, for example, the Way of the Cross is not an end in itself, but a means toward deeper interior commitmnet and taking up the Cross of Jesus in our lives, can confuse us as to priorities.

There is a highly relevant admonition here for some contemporaries. To follow Jesus doesn't simply mean to identify with a charismatic group, or an evangelical commune, or even to dress in sackcloth as a penitential sign and join the so-called "Jesus Revolution." No; Christianity is first defined by interior faith, as St. Paul insists in today's Second Reading.

Unless one changes *from within*, one's discipleship is not authentic. True disciples are those who elect to take up Jesus' Cross daily—In parenthood, in witness, in vows, in suffering service to humanity—in order to make this world a little better place. Our devotions and our sacramentals serve this purpose.

THIRTEENTH SUNDAY IN ORDINARY TIME (C)

Christian Commitment

First Kings 19:16-21; Galatians 5:1, 13-18; Luke 9:51-62.

Aim: (1) to explain commitment and some of its aspects, such as freedom and perseverance; (2) to explain how interior commitment is strengthened and manifested in Eucharistic worship, including attendance at Mass on Holy Days of Obligation.

Today's Bible readings probe certain dimensions of Christian discipleship.

The first principle we must learn about discipleship in Christ is that it must be offered freely.

Today's curious Old Testament reading, the story of how Elisha became the great prophet Elijah's successor, makes this clear. Elisha asked for a few minutes to go back home, for a formal farewell to his parents. Elijah answered that he had no intention of preventing him; that, in effect, Elisha's becoming a disciple has to flow from his own free will. Elijah refused to hold Elisha to Elisha's promise to follow the older man.

Today's Second Reading, from St. Paul's Letter to the Galatians, clarifies this principle; that the key to Christ's discipleship is the heart. Otherwise—if we don't follow freely—we stand the possibility of turning into the kind of person mentioned, sadly, by Jesus in today's

Gospel: a person with hands on the plow, but eyes turned backward to the glittering lights of the world—not quite secure in our commitment to Jesus.

This leads to the second principle taught in today's Bible readings: the importance of perseverance, of refusing to go back on our word to Christ once it has been freely given.

Thirdly, our discipleship—today's Gospel says this plainly—is going to cost us something. Jesus didn't have a home to call his own. Dietrich Bonhoeffer, the Protestant theologian who died in a Nazi concentration camp during World War II, used to write and talk about "the cost of discipleship." The phrase is so full of meaning, There is nothing about being a follower of Jesus that doesn't require effort. Discipleship demands self—giving sacrifice; it can be costly.

Sometimes we forget that Sunday worship is not only a sign of our commitmnent to follow Jesus, but that it also serves to confirm this commitment. As we assemble week after week to listen to God's word, and to participate in the sacrificial, memorial thanksgiving banquet of the Lord, we can literally enter into an ever-depending communion with the Savior we serve, and thereby are enabled to keep our eyes freely fixed on him. In a sense, dedication to the Sunday Eucharist helps us be strong enough to ignore the enticing idols and false ideas of the world.

The same holds true of the Eucharist on the Holy Day of Precepts: the Assumption and Immaculate Conception of our blessed Lady, All Saints' Day, the Ascension of Our Lord, the Solemnity of Mary, the Mother of the Lord on January 1, and of course Christmas. Eucharistic participation on these days aids our free commitment to discipleship.

But of these latter days—we usually call them Holy Days of Obligation—it can almost be said that *they are as much signs* of our free commitment, as they are aids toward it. In other words, Catholics who refuse even to be tempted to view the Holy Days of Obligation as second in priority, tend to be those who fulfill to the hilt the principles of discipleship cited in today's Bible readings: namely, that following Christ must be free, irrevocable, and costly.

Not that religion is defined simply in terms of worship at the altar. Today's Second Reading reaffirms that Jesus' disciples must be persons for others. But, again, the source of, strength for, and evidence of, one's being a person for others is eucharistic.

FOURTEENTH SUNDAY IN ORDINARY TIME (C)

The Gospel and Superstition

Isaiah 66:10-14; Galatians 6:14-18; Luke 10:1-12, 17-20 (long form)

Aim: to explain that the Gospel frees us from superstitions, and the fears and anxieties they occasion.

Today's Gospel targets a form of ignorance that is being exploited today by films, books, television and charlatans; namely, superstition, diabolical superstition.

Superstition is not a novelty. Some of the ancient pagans thought that devils can mechanically control men, body and soul; and that diabolical curses can turn good people into mindless robots.

Despite the modern world's claims to sophistication, certain of the old superstitions are still current. For example, some otherwise intelligent people believe in a cursed race, or that devils can permanently take over men's lives. Others pass their years under the influence of fortune-tellers, or in the light of crystal balls, or with eyes absolutely fixed on star-charts.

Think too of enlightened people who live in constant fear of evil spirits, or people who panic under the terror of a God falsely viewed as a punishing judge. Think of the paperbacks or films in recent years that record utter horrors people imagine about diabolical possession.

Superstitions. Confusing, paralyzing, insane superstitions.

Jesus' Good News—the Gospel—frees us from all this. Today's First Reading, from the Old Testament prophet Isaiah, reminds us that God desires to fill our hearts with peace and joy, not anxiety or terror. This message is what he commissioned his disciples (today's Gospel) to preach. "I watched Satan fall from the sky like lightning," Christ says. Through the message of Jesus' Cross (today's Second Reading, from Paul to the Galatians), no one, nothing, can permanently or really harm us. Some of the early Christians wore the sign of the cross on their foreheads to show they knew that the power of evil could never affect them as long as they kept faith.

The Good News, in today's context, is God's guarantee that as long as we repent and call upon the name of Jesus in faith, hope and love, we need fear nothing. The Gospel tells us infallibly—there is no possibility of a mistake—that God loves us, that God helps us, that the only way evil can take real or permanent possession of our souls is by our freely wanting evil; that God is a good, loving Father, not a vengeful taskmaster.

Believe this. Live by it. Appreciate it.

So many people in the world today—2000 years, almost, after Jesus' disciples first were sent out to announce the Good News—are searching for a key to happiness and peace, for contentment, for freedom from fear.

Today's Bible readings invite us to think that God often sees us as confused, weak, but sincere pilgrims with a tendency to fear, even panic at times. He loves us for our searching, and he wills to give us peace.

Don't be afraid. Discard superstition. Believe in the peace and joy of the Gospel. To use the phrasings of today's First Reading, when we understand all this, then our hearts will rejoice. The only way that evil can take us is by our freely opting for evil—sin, in other words.

FIFTEENTH SUNDAY
IN ORDINARY TIME (C)

The Virtue of Love

Deuteronomy 30:10-14; Colossians 1:15-20; Luke 10:25-37.

Aim: (1) to explain this virtue as self-forgetfulness and dedication to others; (2) to show its importance and its infrequency in modern society.

Today's first Bible lesson, from the Old Testament Book of Deuteronomy (the word means "second law") bids us observe God's instruction—his doctrine, his law—within our hearts always.

Jesus, in today's Gospel, sums up God's instruction in the twofold law of love: love of God in himself, and love of God in neighbor.

St. Paul, in today's Second Reading, from his Letter to Colossae—a small town in southwest Asia Minor—provides an added insight as to how we can find God in our neighbor; namely, that all persons are united in principle with Jesus, and Jesus is God.

As God comes to us in a manifestation of love, so we can approach God only through love. We must love God as Jesus loved. But since in Jesus God has joined himself to mankind, love of God cannot be separated from love of our fellow men. In Christ God has made man—all men—his brothers and sisters.

"It might even be said," writes theologian Yves Congar, "that, in a certain sense, we cannot fully realize the love of God except in the love of neighbor . . ." (*Jesus Christ*: Herder and Herder, 1966).

In the Sermon on the Mount, Jesus cited the evangelical imperatives pertaining to God only after he had set forth those pertaining to neighbor. Read Mt 5:21-48; then Mt 6:1-18. The former verses include familiar injunctions against calling other people fools, against daring to perform an act of worship with hatred for another human person in one's heart, against adultery, against vendetta, against willful prejudice. The latter define obligations directly relating to God, such as adoration and prayer.

The priority expressed in these two sets of verses is not simply happenstance. For the same order occurs no less than ten times in the Gospel. And this priority is nowhere more dramatically emphasized than in those Christian imperatives which govern forgiveness. Read, for instance, Mt 6:12, which is part of the Our Father: "And forgive us our debts, as we forgive those who are in debt to us."

In sum, therefore: If in Jesus the Father has united himself to all mankind, then our way back to the Father is in and through mankind. One can even say that an infallible sign as to whether we love God is if we have love for men—all men.

Concretely, love of neighbor means sincerely being persons for others. Today's parable of the Good Samaritan invites us to involve ourselves, insofar as we can, in the plight of others, for love of them in Christ.

"For love of them in Christ." Christian involvement entails right motivation. We don't express kindness merely because it's a law. Rather, we are persons for others because we believe that, as today's Second Reading states, loving others means loving Christ, God.

Why is it, we ask, that purified love for others in Christ's name seems so infrequent today? The answer has to do directly with *me*.

SIXTEENTH SUNDAY IN ORDINARY TIME (C)

Prayer

Genesis 18:1-10; Colossians 1:24-28; Luke 10:38-42.

Aim: (1) to describe and define prayer; (2) to show its importance for living a life in Christ.

Today's Gospel depicts one of the most homey scenes in the New Testament. When Jesus arrives at the Bethany home of Martha and Mary, Martha keeps scurrying around, busying herself with various household tasks. Like the woman today, I suppose, who has the four burners on the electric range going all at the same time, the frozen peas and carrots on one burner; the potatoes on another; the kettle boiling away madly on a third; and the bubbling gravy on the fourth. Meanwhile, she's basting the turkey in the oven, reaching out for a potholder with one hand and the salt in another; worried about whether the candles are lit on the table, and wondering if she can open the can of cranberries while she shouts out instructions to her confused daughters as to where to put the butter knives and that they shouldn't forget to fill the water glasses.

Here is a scene of hospitality involving a lot of work. Or at least it would be hospitality if the good woman doesn't literally wear herself out so in the kitchen that she arrives at the dinner table too exhausted to carry on an intelligent conversation, but can only sit there like a statue, smiling whenever someone speaks directly to her, and collapsing the moment the last guest has left.

One point on which civilized people agree is that true hospitality requires not so much giving one's guests food and drink, but the generous giving of one's soul. Good conversation is as important around a dinner table as is good food.

The same rules apply, though more so, to our according hospitality to Christ. Communion of spirit is more important than externals of reverence. And communion of spirit is effected through prayer.

Prayer means talking with God. Back in the seventh century, St. John Climacus described prayer as "a conversation between our conscious personality and God." In a sense prayer is "talking with God," "asking God for his help."

More precisely, prayer means opening our hearts to Christ who in turn prays with us and for us through the Holy Spirit, who impels us to address God as "Father" (Rm 8:15; 26-27).

When we pray, therefore, we are living in Christ; we are in fact experiencing "the mystery of Christ" in us—to borrow St. Paul's phrase in today's Second Reading. We are graced for the hospitality we accord to the Lord even more wondrously than Abraham was favored for his graciousness to the three guests cited in today's First Reading.

Again, though, it is not the external word that constitutes prayer, any more than Martha's etiquette could of itself bring about union with Christ. Rather it is the uplifting of the mind and heart, the interior dedication of the will.

As hospitality means chiefly an open-hearted embrace of soul, and not busyness over externals, so prayer must be the core from which all Christian activity achieves meaning and force.

Sometimes it occurs to us—or at least it should—that we've begun to lose a sense of the presence of God in our lives. We aren't always as aware of his reality as we should be. Prayer—true prayer—can help restore this sense.

SEVENTEENTH SUNDAY IN ORDINARY TIME (C)

Prayer

Genesis 18:20-32; Colossians 2:12-14; Luke 11:1-13.

Aim: (1) to explain why some Christians give up praying; (2) to encourage all to perseverance in prayer; (3) to emphasize the need for sincerity and humility in prayer.

The subject of today's Bible readings—all three—is prayer: what prayer is, what it does, how it is said.

In the First Reading, from Genesis, we see Abraham, our Father in faith, literally persuading God to save two entire cities—two especially notorious cities whose names are synonyms for evildoing—simply by prayer. In the Second Reading, from St. Paul's letter to the Colossians, we see what faith in Christ can accomplish; hence, prayer in his name has to be effective. And in the Gospel, we read one of the two Biblical versions of Jesus' own prayer (today's is from Luke; the other is from Matthew), which we call the Lord's Prayer or the Our Father—*the* perfect prayer, not only because Jesus himself composed it, but also because by it our Lord instructed us as to what every good prayer should represent.

It is easier to talk about prayer than to practice it. But it is important to talk about it, thereby to understand its nature. It should involve praise, thanksgiving as well as petitions for guidance.

Prayer means talking with God; it is the loving conversation that we, God's adopted children, carry on with our heavenly Father in Jesus' name.

Which brings us to a first point about prayer. To pray, we've got to be aware that we're trying to talk with God. *Prayer is meant to restore within us a conscious contact with God.* We pray, therefore, in the realization that we are talking with God. Shakespeare wrote, in *Hamlet*, "Words without thoughts never to heaven go."

Jesus gave us three especially helpful parables on prayer. One is today's Gospel; the story about the man who keeps knocking until someone answers the door. His knocking symbolizes persistence. The lesson is that we must keep at prayer. Perseverance is necessary; we must not give up on prayer, ever.

A second parable Jesus gave us is that about the Pharisee and the Publican. The proud Pharisee's prayer went unanswered. As for the publican, who admitted his sinfulness, who stood in back of church, in the darkness: his prayer was heard. Why? Because he was asking God from the depths of his nothingness, not demanding that God listen to him. This means that we don't *demand* favors from God. We *ask* him with humility.

A third parable Jesus gave us about prayer is the one about the birds of the air and the lilies of the fields. In it Jesus told us to be confident that *he will provide* in answer to our praying. For if birds and lilies are so marvelously sustained by nature, how much more will we be cared for by the Creator of nature?

Four points about prayer could be set forth, then: (1) we must be conscious of the holy action we are performing; (2) we must keep at prayer, not give up; (3) we must remain humble in God's sight; (4) we must be confident that he will answer us.

Sometimes people stop praying. They say that their prayers are not being heard. What they mean is that God has not granted them the specifics for which they have prayed.

Prayers are always heard. They are heard by the loving God who cares for us, so much so that he will not bring us to disaster when we, with our limited vision and small minds, do not quite understand all the aspects of our prayer.

Which brings up a final point. We can never possibly pray for the wrong thing, so long as our every prayer is made in accordance with God's will for us. This is of course one doctrine found in the Our Father. Don't we say, "*Your will* be done on earth as it is in heaven?"

EIGHTEENTH SUNDAY IN ORDINARY TIME (C)

The Emptiness of A Godless Existence

Qoheleth 1:2; 2:21-23; Colossians 3:1-5, 9-11; Luke 12:13-21.

Aim: to show that life without reference to God, our final goal, is meaningless.

Today's First Reading is from the Old Testament Book of Qoheleth, or Ecclesiastes, written around 300 B.C. Today's text contains a well-known phrase: "Vanity of vanities! All things are vanity."

The point of today's First Reading is that this world, viewed merely in itself and by itself, amounts to an empty vision.

One can accept either of two different views of the world. Either we are just here today and gone tomorrow—like the sea or the grass or annual life; or we are here today for a purpose that will only be fulfilled in final union with the Creator: a purpose which the Baltimore Catechism described as "to know, love and serve God in this world, and to be happy with him forever in the next."

Take the first world-view. Say that there is no God, no after-life, no judgment, no heaven or hell, no resurrection. Say that we live and die here, and that nothing of this life endures, except symbolically. Well, if this is true, then everything is permissible. If there is no punishment in an afterlife for perjury, or stealing, or murder, or selfishness, or violence, or meanness, or impurity, or hatred, or racial discrimination, or blasphemy, then why go through the struggle of trying to be honest, or faithful in marriage, or respectful to others, or reverent toward God, or kind, or nonviolent? To what end?

Without belief in God, in the immortality of the person, and in judgement by God, everything is permitted.

Self-satisfaction would be the prevailing law, then, right? Hedonism is what we call this: the doctrine that pleasure is the chief goal of life. The "eat, drink and be merry, for tomorrow we shall die" attitude.

Our world-view as Catholics is the very opposite. We stake our lives on the premise of judgment and an after-life, as well as the belief that this life has meaning only if it is directed toward God.

So today's Bible readings remind us that most things in this world are vain—automobiles, bank accounts, status, ranch houses, beauty, fur coats, jewels—unless they are subjected to the one great goal: to be God-oriented forever.

What advantage, Jesus asks us, is it to have all the money in the world if we can't take it with us beyond death? Grow wealthy only in the sight of God, Jesus warns us. Seek the things that are above, Paul reminds us. Put to death whatever takes us *from* God: any evil, any tendency to lie or be dishonest or prejudiced or impure. All else is vanity.

Those who believe and act on the principle of "eat, drink and be merry, for tomorrow we shall die," tragically, *will* die—and forever.

Make something of our lives, we are told. Have a goal. Give life meaning by living it with Christ, by being a disciple of Christ, by following Christ who alone can, and will, lead us to the Truth, Who surely awaits us at the end of our life's quest.

NINETEENTH SUNDAY IN ORDINARY TIME (C)

Prayer and Faith

Wisdom 18:6-9; Hebrews 11:1-2, 8-19; Luke 12:32-48.

Aim: to give practical advice on developing a strong prayer life in the context of a strong faith; to stress the basic necessity of daily private prayer.

Confident faith in God is one truth which today's Bible readings emphasize. Christian faith means belief that Jesus *lives*, that Jesus *intervenes* in our lives, that Jesus *provides* for us, that Jesus personally *awaits* us now to embrace and reward us for a trial here courageously undergone.

Faith in a wide sense can be predicated on belief in general: accepting unreservedly though not fully understanding. In many areas of life we literally go on by faith alone. We speak of "scientific faith," for example; we believe that the light will go on the moment we touch the wall switch. We don't understand electricity, nor do we understand light. But we believe in both.

Likewise we put faith in people; in our doctor, for instance. Marriage is also an exercise in faith. How can a man or a woman disclose his or her total mystery to the other without a strong faith that mystery will only serve to increase their mutual love, not weaken or destroy it?

Christian faith is religious faith. It is based not on science, not on other human beings, but on God. It means taking God's word for basic truths we can't understand.

Christian faith means staking our whole lives—our values, our goals, our directions—on the principle that Jesus, who is God, has revealed certain truths to us and that we will embrace those, no matter what. Christian faith means that even though we can't fully understand *how* Christ intervenes in our lives and provides for us, we know absolutely in our hearts *that* he does guide us, that he does provide.

Faith means that we can pray to God in Jesus and develop a strong relationship with him. It means that we can talk with him daily—which, indeed, we should do, given this relationship.

Faith means that in our praying we have the confident assurance of receiving what we hope for, as today's Second Reading, from the eloquent Epistle to the Hebrews, stresses. Faith means that God will vindicate us for our praying, as today's First Reading, from the Book of Wisdom affirms.

Faith and praying really go together. Thus, one cannot pray without faith; hence sincere praying is always and necessarily a sign of faith. At the same time, faith draws us to prayer, for it renders God real to us. In fact, faith constitutes an affirmation of Transcendence.

Further, praying supports and strengthens faith. Those of us who try never to begin the day without an Our Father said well, and who try to end each day with a good Act of Contrition, know how these prayers alone can help keep one in God's presence throughout the day. And, finally, faith confirms one's praying. Anyone who really believes, prays well, and often.

Consider an analogy. In our everyday life, how easy it is to converse with someone we know and love. On the other hand, conversation with someone we do not know, or relate to well, comes only with difficulty. The same occurs with respect to God and our conversation with him, which is what prayer is.

TWENTIETH SUNDAY IN ORDINARY TIME (C)

Priority of Loyalty to Christ

Jeremiah 38:4-6, 8-10; Hebrews 12:1-4; Luke 12:49-53.

Aim: to show that following Christ entails acceptance of his Cross in some form, but that this Cross is one of personal fulfillment, peace and eternal life.

"Fire on the earth . . ." What a mysteriously terrifying phrase in today's Gospel. "I have come to light a fire on the earth. How I wish the blaze were ignited. . ."

It's a difficult statement. It gives us a rare glimpse into the soul of Jesus in terms of his mission: a mission prophesied by Jeremiah of old (today's First Reading), Jeremiah who so closely resembled Jesus, expecially in what he suffered. What we're referring to, of course, is the Cross of Calvary, which was essential to Jesus' mission, as today's Second Reading from the Epistle to the Hebrews, recalls.

"Fire on the earth . . ." Peter must have known what this phrase meant, Peter who was crucified in Rome for the Faith. For him it meant that loyalty to Christ must take precedence over all else. Agnes, the little girl who was beheaded under Diocletian knew, the same lesson. So did Thomas of Canterbury—Becket—who was slain before the altar of his own cathedral; likewise, that other Thomas, at the end of the Tudor reign, and also once England's Chancellor, Thomas More, that man for all seasons. He knew.

"Fire on the earth . . ." Think also of Margaret Clitherow, crushed to death with a boulder, for allegedly harboring a priest at her home under Queen Elizabeth. Or think of the great martyrdom of 1622 in Japan: twenty-five died by fire, including five married couples; 30 by the sword, all on one occasion. The captain of an English Ship who witnessed one of the massacres wrote: "Among them little children five or six years old burned in their mothers' arms, crying out, 'Jesus, receive our souls.' "

"Fire on the earth . . ." Think of the Carmelite nuns—about whom the opera was written—during the Terror of 1794 in Paris; as they mounted the scaffold of the guillotine, they were chanting a psalm to God's glory. Think of the young men who died for Christ at Namugongo, in Uganda about a century ago. "You can burn our bodies, but you cannot harm our souls," one of them cried out from the sacrificial pyre which roared into eternal life.

"Fire on the earth . . ." Fire in the Bible is a sign of judgment. In today's Gospel, Jesus also means that fire will occasion judgment; that, in effect fire will separate and purify those who are meant for his Kingdom. It will work through Jesus' word and his Spirit.

Fire endured for Christ—accepting his Cross—(do we see this?)— will roar into eternal life, as did the fires of Namugongo. The Cross is not an end, but a beginning, and the only key to eternal life.

As one poet has suggested, we can only touch God when we have been consumed by him.

Love God best, and all else falls into place.

TWENTY-FIRST SUNDAY IN ORDINARY TIME (C)

Ecumenism

Isaiah 66:18-21; Hebrews 12:5-7, 11-13; Luke 13:22-30.

Aim: (1) to summarize the meaning of ecumenism; and (2) to accent our part in advancing unity in Christ.

Both the Gospel and the First Reading today sound a majestic theme of a universal homecoming at the end of time: peoples of all nations—"on dromedaries" and "in chariots"—peoples from east and west, taking their places in the eternal celebration of God's glory.

Today is an opportune time, therefore, to ponder ecumenism. "Ecumenism" is a Greek derivative meaning, roughly, "worldwide." Vatican Council II described ecumenism or the ecumenical movement in terms of "those activities and enterprises which, according to various needs of the Church and opportune occasions, are started and organized for the fostering of unity among Christians" (*Decree on Ecumenism*, sec. 4).

As Catholics we believe that Christ came to save all men. This is known as the doctrine of the unversality of salvation. At every Mass, the celebrant recalls this doctrine as he pronounces the words of the Lord over the chalice:

"This is the cup of my blood, the blood of the new and everlasting covenant. It will be shed for you *and for all men* so that sins may be forgiven."

As Catholics we also believe that our historic Roman Catholic Church is Jesus' own, one Church, to which he calls all men. Again, to quote Vatican II:

"For it is through Christ's Catholic Church alone, which is the all-embracing means of salvation, that the fullness of the means of salvation can be obtained" (*Ibid.*, sec. 3).

As Catholics we are learning more and more today—not through debate, but rather through dialogue or conversation—how we can emphasize the positive dimensions of our relationships with non-Roman Christians.

Thus, we and all Christians call upon the name of Jesus as Lord. Too, we all revere the Sacred Scriptures. As for the sacraments, we grant, for example, that wherever Baptism is validly administered, the baptized is truly incorporated into the crucified and glorified Christ, and reborn to participation in divine life; hence, baptism constitutes a bond of unity linking all who experience it.

Ecumenism—the quest for unity in Christ—is God's own will; today's Gospel and First Reading indicate this. And ecumenism *will* work, will progress, *because* it is God's will. Jesus, in whom the whole human race is reconciled with the Father, wills that all men be one in him; thus he prayed at the Last Supper (Jn 17:20 ff.).

How can we join in this task ordained by God? First, by prayer. Secondly, by trying to inform ourselves—by listening to sermons such as this one. Also, by *living* our faith-commitment despite trials and obstacles—as today's Second Reading reminds us to do. Fourthly, by trying to avoid words, phrases, actions and attitudes that can be perceived by our separated brethren as irritants.

There is still one further means of joining in ecumenical endeavor. It is to remember always that God judges according to each person's lights and conscience. And that many a person whom we, in our smallness, might think to be outside God's grace, could teach us a lesson or two in faith, love, witness, even holiness.

TWENTY-SECOND SUNDAY IN ORDINARY TIME (C)

Humility and Pride

Sirach 3:17-18, 20, 28-29; Hebrews 12:18-19, 22-24; Luke 14:1, 7-14.

Aim: (1) to explain pride as the first of the capital sins; (2) to show humility as a fundamental Christian virtue.

All three Bible readings today spotlight the virtue of humility. The Old Testament sage, Sirach, commands humility in today's First Reading. Jesus does the same in the Gospel. And the Second Reading reminds us that all our worth is derivative.

"Humility" comes from the Latin word for "earth" or "ground." The significance is that we all come from the dust of the earth and to dust we shall all return. But it would be an error to over-emphasize our nothingness to the point of self-contempt. Such an attitude could actually lead us to worse sin; for if a person despises himself so utterly that he has no value at all, what is there to prevent him from falling into all kinds of vices in the excuse that life has no purpose for him? The ancient pagans knew about this extreme.

The truth is that although we are all vessels of clay, we are graced clay, vessels destined to flow with God's life.

One of the great Greek philosophers of old used to teach this axiom as basic to truth: "Know yourself." To know oneself is to know one's limitations, intellectually as well as physically; emotionally, also. To know oneself is to realize that all one's knowledge is derivative; that one's ability is not really as considerable as it is usually perceived by others.

Again, however, we cannot forget that we are graced vessels of clay. Shakespeare's words in *Hamlet* are theologically sound:

"What a piece of work is a man! How noble in reason! How infinite in faculty, in form, in moving, how express and admirable! In action he is like an angel—in apprehension how like a god!" (II:2).

For the Christian, humility is not modeled by Uriah Heep in Dickens' *David Copperfield*. For the Christian, humility presupposes that man is among God's masterpieces, that man is special because he was created to know, love, and serve God in this world; and to be happy with him forever.

Despite our nobility in God, can any of us look upon a crucifix and dare call oneself good? Have I, for example, never committed a sin? Have I never betrayed my loyalty or broken my word? Have I offended against kindness?

Sinful pride is the opposite of humility. It is refusal to know oneself as one really is. It is denial of our clay-like make-up. One of the so-called capital or key sins, it blurs our vision for our weaknesses, errors, and unattractiveness. It focuses on self so much so that it separates us from others. It is self-complacency as opposed to fear of the Lord. It is blind hostility to true values. When sinful pride is total, it is diabolical and hence can no longer endure any dependence upon God. Above all, sinful pride contradicts the Way of Jesus, Humility personified; hence, the proud person can only but resent Christ our Savior.

Again, we do not minimize our nobility as human beings created by God and destined for his glory. But any boasting we do is in Christ, who has saved us and favored us. Real humility means being able to go on day after day in the knowledge that despite our weaknesses, errors, unattractiveness and sinfulness, God has chosen us, and that our sincere efforts are, therefore, noble, redeeming, and useful *because of him.*

TWENTY-THIRD SUNDAY IN ORDINARY TIME (C)

The Paradox of Christianity

Wisdom 9:13-18; Philemon 9-10, 12-17; Luke 14:25-33.

Aim: (1) to show that only through our acceptance of Jesus' cross can we achieve fulfillment as his disciples; (2) to accent the need for commitment in discipleship; and (3) to cite the Sunday observance as a sign of, and a help toward, committed discipleship.

Christianity is a paradox, and in many ways.

A paradox is an apparent, though not a real, contradiction. In today's Gospel, for example, Jesus says, "anyone who does not take up his cross and follow me cannot be my disciple." But where does following Jesus lead? To riches? To status? To power? Not at all. To a life of suffering service. Our inclination is to ask by what logic can this be.

We don't comprehend. So, if we're really persons of faith, we turn to other parts of the Bible in an effort to understand; in today's First Reading, for example, from the Book of Wisdom. There we discover the same mysterious non-answer. ". . . What man knows God's counsel, or who can conceive what the Lord intends?" Is it that our minds are simply too small, or too dull to comprehend?

Surely this is part of the answer. God's wisdom makes folly of our so-called wisdom. But, we continue to ask: Whom can Christ hope to recruit to his ranks by such a harsh calling as carrying a cross?

Today's Second Reading, from Philemon (one of the most beautiful New Testament books), helps us progress toward an answer. Here we see Paul, in prison, penniless and cold, no doubt; hungry too, and awaiting judgment. Paul was glad to give up all to follow Jesus.

And here we find the poor runaway slave, Onesimus. In his wanderings, Onesimus remembered that his former master, Philemon, had often spoken about Paul—the same Paul who, he has heard, is now in jail. In his misery, Onesimus the runaway slave visits Paul. Paul preaches Jesus' doctine to him—that of carrying the Cross and following our Lord and Onesimus becomes a believer. He is so much a believer in fact that he doesn't even care any more whether in the eyes of the world he is a slave or not, because he now knows the Good News that he is free in Christ. He has no fears about returning to his master, because he now knows that Jesus is at his side.

So, do we see what taking up one's cross and following Jesus does to us? It makes us free. It makes us aware that nothing can harm us in this world; it removes our fears. It gives us strength to stand up in the midst of the evils of this world—slavery to materialism, secularism, the profit motive, technological excess, and so on.

Jesus' Cross—this *is* a paradox—does not crush us; rather, it *frees* us, as it freed Onesimus. And it gives us the heart to help other people become free.

Our being gathered here for Mass today, Sunday, the Day of the Lord's Resurrection, is a sign that we believe this. Every time we assemble for the Sunday Eucharist, we are saying, in effect, that we are committed to the Gospel, especially to Jesus' invitation to assume his Cross. The very way we observe Sundays—by refraining from what could be called "servile" works (arduous works once performed regularly by the nonfree), or by our refusal to do ordinary shopping on Sunday, attests to our belief.

Sunday, the day when we are reminded that Jesus' *Cross* must be accepted, is also the day when we think most about our *freedom.* Christianity *is a paradox indeed.*

TWENTY-FOURTH SUNDAY
IN ORDINARY TIME (C)

Pardon and Hope

Exodus 32:7-11, 13-14; First Timothy 1:12-17; Luke 15:1-32.

Aim: (1) to set forth the doctrine of Christ's willingness and readiness to pardon us for our wrongdoings in the context of the virtue of hope.

"So the Lord relented . . ." What a comforting conclusion to the story of sin recorded in today's First Reading, from Exodus.

The Israelites, singularly chosen by God in Abraham, led out of the slavery of Egypt through his prophet Moses, sustained by divine Providence in the desert, now begin to worship a golden calf—the base of an idol—which they had fashioned at the very moment God was renewing his covenant with them atop Mount Sinai.

Yet, we read: "So the Lord relented . . ."

The same theme of divine pardon is carried through in today's Second Reading, from the beautiful First Letter to Timothy. There we are reminded that like Paul, we in our arrogance, in our unbelief, in our many sins, nonetheless can find forgiveness in Jesus. Moreover, we learn that Jesus came into the world precisely to save sinners—to save us, to put it bluntly.

The same theme is there again, in today's Gospel, which is a brief triology about God's wanting to forgive us. First, there is the parable of the Good Shepherd searching out the lone stray; then, of the woman who loses a coin and finds it (Luke was always careful to add stories which would interest women—one reason why his Gospel is known as "The Women's Gospel"); and thirdly, of the Prodigal Son who is received back by his father without prejudice, despite his sins.

Thus all the readings today remind us that not only does God forgive sins forever, but he welcomes sinners and wants to forgive—if only we sincerely want to return to him in contrition and resolution.

Surely this is one of the most attractive aspects of our Christian Faith. To be forgiven sins we have committed: sins of unkindness, of hatred, of irreverence, of dishonesty; secret sins as well as public sins; sins which have injured others, even. And not only to be forgiven, but to know for certain that we have been forgiven; to be free of all doubts about the matter.

Our faith, then, is a religion of hope. Hope sustains us who are now experiencing the tension between the "already" and the "not yet." By faith we embrace not only what God reveals to us about himself, but also what God pledges in our behalf. Hope allows us to look forward confidently to the fulfillment of these promises.

In a larger sense, hope reminds us that even given our weaknesses, or our tendency to fail, the loving, merciful Savior stands even now at the final goal destined for us and beckons us forward with his grace. Hope means that we are not alone facing a future of uncertainty, but that the living Lord who wills that not one of us be lost is at this moment drawing us toward him. Hope helps us understand that mysteriously, yet really, eternal life in Christ forever is not entirely distinct from life in Christ now; that, in truth, eternal life somehow begins now. Finally, hope signifies that all the necessary means we need to achieve salvation will be ours: grace, mercy, pardon, and the ability to overcome obstacles to these.

Hope means all this, plus, once again, the lesson of today's Bible Readings: namely, God's willingness and readiness to forgive us.

TWENTY-FIFTH SUNDAY IN ORDINARY TIME (C)

Conscience Formation and the Magisterium

Amos 8:4-7; First Timothy 2:1-8; Luke 16:1-13.

Aim: to explain (1) where a Catholic goes to get official Catholic teaching in faith and morals; (2) the extraordinary and the ordinary magisterium, and (3) the development of a mature Catholic conscience.

Today's First Reading is from Amos, the earliest writing prophet, who appeared on the scene of salvation history during the eighth century B.C. Amos, a blunt, farm-worker, was called by God primarily to awaken the Israelites to the imperatives of social justice. The *consciences* of God's covenanted people had become dull. (In today's Second Reading, the Biblical foundation for the Prayer of the Faithful at Mass, we are reminded of our duty in conscience to pray for all men as brethren.)

Conscience, we hold, is the fundamental *subjective* norm of moral activity. St. Augustine called this power "synteresis" (sometimes misspelled "synderesis"). Synteresis means conscience as an inner disposition, as distinguished from conscience viewed as an act, or a concrete moral judgment made by an individual.

Thus, the "little voice inside us" theory about conscience has much to recommend it. In a real sense, conscience manifests itself in a sense of obligation that in a specific experience one ought to act, or else not act.

Some argue that conscience is merely a behavioral reflex rooted in environment. Others theorize that it may arise from the action of authority figures, such as parents. Such explanations fail since conscience often contradicts authority and society both.

No, the source of conscience lies somewhere in the innermost personality. Somehow conscience flows from man's mind and free will, precisely in their reflection of God acting within the soul. In other words, the "little voice" which is conscience is the voice of God mysteriously illuminating personal insight.

Since conscience represents God's Spirit drawing us, a true conscience cannot contravene God's known will. Conscience may be the supreme *subjective* norm for moral action, but it is always dependent on an *objective* norm, which is Truth personified: God himself. By its nature, conscience must look for enlightenment in the natural order of created things, in the supernatural order of divine Revelation, and in the Holy Spirit as he continuously teaches in Jesus' Body, the Church.

The means by which the Church helps form consciences is called the magisterium. The extraordinary magisterium refers to this means exercised in a solemn way, as when the Holy Father defines an article of faith, or when an Ecumenical Council witnesses to the faith. The ordinary magisterium means the Church's less solemn, everyday guidance and direction.

Today's Gospel provides an interesting observation regarding the role of conscience. Conscience is very much like a trust; it can be treasured and enlarged upon, or it can be treated nonchalantly and compromised. If compromised, it is destructive of true life.

TWENTY-SIXTH SUNDAY IN ORDINARY TIME (C)

Justice, and Church Support

Amos 6:1, 4-7; First Timothy 6:11-16; Luke 16:19-31.

Aim: (1) to explain that the imperative of justice is linked with our covenant duties as God's People; (2) to relate this imperative in the context of the local parish; (3) to comment on Church support.

As on last Sunday, today's First Reading is from Amos, the eighth-century B.C. blunt-worded prophet who warned that belonging to God's People means being united as one, and being united as one means that it is a sin against the Covenant—against religion—to ignore the hungry, or the aged, or the sick, or the poor. By the very fact that we are members of God's Covenant, we *are* our brothers' and sisters' keepers. We are obliged to see to it that we do not squander the resources of this world while others, like Lazarus in today's Gospel, go hungry and deprived.

Today's Gospel, in fact, underlies one of the Church's basic social justice doctrines, spelled out eloquently for contemporary man by papal encyclicals such as John XXIII's *Pacem in Terris* and Paul VI's *Populorum Progressio*; namely, that one's superfluous wealth may not be used merely according to one's whim.

What precisely, was the sin for which the rich man in the Gospel was rejected by God? *Rejected*; the Gospel makes this clear. Wasn't it that he in his wealth ignored Lazarus' needs? Thus, anyone who chooses to ignore the hungry or the oppressed or the needy in any way today, occasions divine repudiation. Fighting the good fight of faith—to borrow St. Paul's beloved phrase in today's Second Reading—means fighting material selfishness, a diabolical nonattention to others as if we had no obligation at all in this regard.

Keep in mind that Jesus said that even giving a thirsty person a cup of water in his name will never be forgotten by him. What if we do much more?

Like, for example, "adopting" a poor child in some ghetto, in the sense of making a contribution of a few dollars a year? Or, what if, in one's life, one becomes a nurse, or a social worker, or a teacher, and thereby helps poor children escape ignorance and poverty? What if, as a mother, one takes in a foster child who needs love?

Or, what if one joins one of the many Church or service organizations whose members visit the sick or elderly? Or what if one just does the shopping once a week for an incapacitated neighbor?

Justice can also be translated into terms of parish support. Simply by its existence, this parish is a reminder that we are one in Jesus, that by virtue of the Covenant we are responsible for each other. To this end, this church building must be maintained, for it is here that we are both constantly reminded of, and energized for, our communal tasks. The same holds true for our entire plant: this is the center of the whole educational, charitable, and spiritual apostolate for those to whom we are joined in Christ.

Thus we give to our parish, and, occasionally, to the needs of the Church universal as Catholics all united in faith. The little we have, we gladly share, in the belief that God's covenant with us unites us as one, and for this we are grateful.

TWENTY-SEVENTH SUNDAY IN ORDINARY TIME (C)

The Sacrament of Confirmation

Habakkuk 1:2-3, 2:2-4; Second Timothy 1:6-8, 13-14; Luke 17:5-10.

Aim: (1) to explain this sacrament as the confirming of one's baptism and the sacrament of Christian maturity; (2) to encourage all to be confirmed and to live up to confirmation commitments.

Faith, the Old Testament prophet Habakkuk tells us today, gives us life. Habakkuk lived about 600 years before Christ; his message was, in summary, that whatever the evils of this world, the person of faith will always emerge victorious. Faith, the Second Reading reveals, makes us strong, gives us the character never to be ashamed to witness for Christ. Christ, in today's Gospel, declares in a magnificent poetic statement, that faith can be strong enough to uproot a tree—to transfer it, even.

In one sense, all Bible readings today converge on confirmation in faith; or, more precisely, the Sacrament of Confirmation, which exists to extend to the Church of today and tomorrow the Gift of the Holy Spirit, sent to strengthen and stir up the disciples on the first Pentecost.

Confirmation is a sacrament of initiation whereby the baptized receive the special gift of the Holy Spirit, through the anointing with chrism on the forehead, which is done by the laying on of the hand,

and through the words, "Be sealed with the Gift of the Holy Spirit." The chrism is consecrated by the bishop in the Mass of the Chrism, celebrated annually on or just before Holy Thursday, in the cathedral church. Usually the minister of confirmation is a bishop, although priests may also confirm in necessity, or in other special circumstances, as when converts are baptized.

Confirmation, Cardinal Richard Cushing of Boston once remarked, is "the Cinderella of the Sacraments, neglected and little understood."

The other sacraments, commented Cardinal John Wright in the 1 June 1978 issue of *L'Osservatore Romano*, all but explain themselves. Confirmation, on the other hand, "cannot be easily identified with a clearly spelled out act or state, and yet it is the Sacrament, in a way, of everyday Christian vitality because it gives us the Holy Spirit in a special manner to fortify us in the day to day struggle with the powers of darkness, to enable us to answer the enemy, to come to maturity, prepared to show our faith in word and action, to live it and defend it, to persevere as witnesses to that faith..."

To quote Cardinal Wright again, *now* may be the right time "to take a second look at the 'Cinderella of the Sacraments' so that she can grow to full maturity in a Church which desperately needs that all members be aware of their responsibilities in and to the total community of the Holy Catholic Church as well as to the salvation of their individual souls."

"In a way," Cardinal Wright argued, "Confirmation might be thought of as a kind of ordination of the young layman or laywoman to a place in the total life of the Church, to a specific calling in the life of the Church."

At any rate, if we find ourselves "waffling" in our faith-witness; if we find ourselves sometimes ashamed to speak out on the Gospel, or too timorous to take a stand; if we find silence especially comfortable when faith affirmation must be made, we should examine our consciences as to whether we are allowing the Holy Spirit to help us be aware of his gifts, infallibly given us in confirmation, and which we can summon any time we need them, though only in faith: wisdom, understanding, counsel, fortitude, knowledge, piety, and fear of the Lord.

TWENTY-EIGHTH SUNDAY IN ORDINARY TIME (C)

The Kinds of Prayer, Especially Thanksgiving

Second Kings 5:14-17; Second Timothy 2:8-13; Luke 17:11-19

Aim: (1) to teach the four kinds of prayer; (2) to encourage prayer, especially thanksgiving.

One wonders how modern day pollsters—those people who ring your doorbell and ask you whether you think the Congress is fulfilling its role or not, or who call you on the telephone and ask you what television show you're watching—would react to the statistic cited in today's Gospel regarding appreciation. One out of the ten lepers cured by Jesus was decent enough to return and thank him for his having been cured. That's ten per cent of the total number. That means 90 per cent declined.

We all have reason to suspect—from our own neglect, at least—that this "low appreciation rate" approximates the real-life situation; *my* situation (to be blunt).

Thanking God for favors is, we sometimes forget, a form of prayer. From the Bible we can discern four kinds of prayer. The first we hardly ever forget, especially in moments of tension or crisis: petition, "asking God for favors," as we say. A third form is adoration: acknowledging our dependence upon God. Finally, there is contrition: expressing our sorrow for sin, detestation for sin, and resolution not to commit sin. All these forms can be found in the perfect prayer which Jesus gave us; namely, the Lord's Prayer, or the Our Father.

But back to today's Gospel and the prayer of thanksgiving. Mark how all ten lepers did not hesitate to voice their *petition* ("Jesus, Master, have pity on us!") in a spirit of adoration and contrition ("Keeping their *distance, they raised their* voices and said . . .") But only one came back to *thank* Jesus for being healed, and he was a Samaritan, an alien, like Naaman the Syrian in today's First Reading, who went out of his way to register his gratitude for God's good gift.

When was the last time *we* thanked God for his presence in our lives? Really thanked him, we mean?

Yet we have so much for which to be thankful. We know the true God. We know that God has revealed himself in Jesus of Nazareth, that Jesus lives in our midst and will never desert us—so long as we hold firm to our faith, as St. Paul reminds us in today's Second Reading.

Too, isn't our very identity as persons principally defined in what we as Christians possess? Leper like, we too have washed in the purifying waters of life, as Naaman was. How appreciative are we?

Test ourselves. For a Catholic, the subject of gratitude can hardly be discussed without reference to the Eucharist, a Greek derivative signifying "Thanksgiving." Is Communion a routine act of worship in our life? Can we even remember the last time we made a sincere effort to express heartfelt gratitude for so great a gift, by making what we learned so long ago in grade school religion class—to call our "Thanksgiving for Communion?" Even in the few moments of silence or hymn singing which the liturgy allows just for this, as the beginning of an attitude of thanksgiving in our everyday lives?

Cultivation of the virtue of gratitude properly begins with humble appreciation for the Eucharist. All one need do is speak gratitude in one's own heart, in one's own way. Be at least among the ten per cent that came back to Christ. Why must most of our prayers be petitions; and but a few, thanksgivings?

TWENTY-NINTH SUNDAY IN ORDINARY TIME (C)

Prayer Reflecting Faith

Exodus 17:8-13; Second Timothy 3:14, 4:2; Luke 18:1-8.

Aim: (1) to explain prayer as a reflection of firm faith in a secularist climate, and (2) to specify the need for morning and evening prayer, prayer before meals, and meditation.

Prayer reflects a firm, never-compromised faith, especially in adversity and is one theme sounded in today's liturgy.

The story of Moses' praying in today's First Reading, one of the best known stories of the Bible, signals this leitmotif. Victory depended on the faith of Moses in prayer; just when the forces of evil seemed to gain ascendancy, the prophet's firm prayer helped God's people to overcome.

We too "must remain faithful" to what we "have learned and believed:" today's Second Reading reminds us.

The widow in Today's Gospel had faith. She *kept* interceding; she maintained prayer despite the odds; she overcame.

The question put by today's liturgy—by Jesus himself—to us is: when he comes again to this world as judge, will he find faith?

Faith and prayer go together. True prayer always witnesses to belief. And belief overflows in prayer.

Today both prayer and faith, even in adversity, are challenged on several fronts. One is the spiritually enervating climate of secularism.

Secularism is a widely accepted attitude by means of which all reality is allegedly "explained" exclusively on the horizontal level, without any reference to God and revelation.

Wedded to this view of life is pragmatism or utilitarianism, a theory which defines that which is "true" in terms of its social usefulness or fruitfulness. Hence contemporary man has been conditioned to ask about Christianity, as he has been conditioned to ask about the world in general: "What is faith's utilitarian value?" And, consequently: "What is prayer's pragmatic worth?"

But are these fair questions? Is it appropriate to ask whether faith or prayer has practical value? Did not our divine Lord ask the same when he said: "What profit would a man show if he were to gain the whole world and destroy himself in the process?" (Mt 16:26).

Specifically, what more *useful* personal norm is there than that Christ, who is God, and hence our Beatitude, lives in our midst, intervenes in our historicity, and awaits us at the Omega Point of our life's pilgrimage?

Further, what more practical way of life can there be in praying to this God we know and experience in Jesus, his only incarnate Son, who now lives as risen Lord?

Isn't this why we as Catholics begin and close each day with our morning and night prayers? (The Our Father and Hail Mary we say, perhaps, upon rising. The Act of Contrition we may recite daily before retiring.) Too, isn't this why we pray before meals—with our traditional "grace;" why we take time to meditate on God and his word, at least a few minutes (ten or fifteen) every day—simple, loving thought on our faith? Isn't this also why we find ourselves praying almost spontaneously in times of adversity: in the hospital before surgery, at a deathbed, in a family crisis, in a moment of depression?

We pray so readily and daily, again, because in spite of the secularist, pragmatic climate all around us, we believe. Again, faith and prayer naturally go together.

Will Jesus find strong faith when he comes again? Check first to see whether he will find firm prayer. Check ourselves.

THIRTIETH SUNDAY IN ORDINARY TIME (C)

Prayer and Justice

Sirach 35:12-14, 16-18; Second Timothy 4:6-8, 16-18; Luke 18:9-14.

Aim: (1) to show that efficacy of prayer depends on an honest relationship with God; and that (2) God in his justice readily recognizes the person of true faith.

We have just listened to Jesus' parable of the Pharisee and the Publican, as recorded by St. Luke. It is Luke's own parable, incidentally; it doesn't appear in Matthew or Mark. And in John's Gospel there are no parables.

A parable, remember, is a somewhat mysterious form of preaching used by the Lord—*deliberately* used. Parables let in just enough light for the seeker who *wants* to believe. Christ never interferes with human freedom; he *never compels*, but as he once reminded, simply *draws* us.

Each parable is a challenge, therefore. It is not merely a riddle, though. On the contrary, it puts an existential question to us. Or more precisely, it puts *us* in question. Which is why, in Biblical language, parables are defined not only in terms of revealing the Kingdom of God. More, they have the power to reveal hearts—our hearts.

Take today's parable. The Pharisee was obviously self-confident. He had reason. A person of status, he did not hesitate to stand before God and recite a litany of his legal observances. He "told" God, as we say, of his righteousness. Is prayer "telling" God?

Note, too, that in his prayer, the Pharisee separates himself from others: "I am not like the rest of men. . ." Did not Jesus teach us to pray, "*Our* Father?" (Mt 6:7 ff.). Are our prayers prayed in isolation from others?

Consider the publican, now. A person of insignificant stature, an outcast in a sense, wasn't he like the humble man of today's First Reading? He did not tell God; he *asked* God. Nor did he recite his virtues; on the contrary, he made a general confession, and while standing afar off.

Do we approach God primarily to *tell* God? Or do we petition him, in full awareness of our nothingness before his presence? When was the last time we confessed our sins contritely while standing afar off—spiritually—in recognition of his holiness, contrasted with our sinfulness?

Jesus tells us that the publican went home justified. At the begining of the parable, he remarks that the Pharisee thought himself just.

Isn't one point to ponder here that whether or not *we* consider ourselves just, is of no real consequence. Of consequence is whether God holds us just, whether *God*—as Paul says in today's Second Reading, is on our side.

There are other rays of light in today's Gospel; like a diamond, a parable is multifaceted. The Pharisee takes his observance of the law seriously, we are told. In justifying the publican, then, was Jesus minimizing the need for good works? Of course not. But we do not rely on *our* good works, either. What we rely on is God's infinite mercy. The publican took God's mercy seriously.

One final insight. Whereas the publican knew he needed God— desperately—did not the Pharisee think that God needed him?

Do we go to Mass, do we approach the sacraments, do we dare presume that we are Christians because God needs us? Or do *we* need the Church?

THIRTY-FIRST SUNDAY IN ORDINARY TIME (C)

What God Looks Like

Wisdom 11:22, 12:1; Second Thessalonians 1:11, 2:2; Luke 19:1-10.

Aim: (1) to explain how Jesus reveals God to us.

Today's First Reading, from the Book of Wisdom, composed only a century before Christ's coming, opens up with a magnificent song of praise for God's awesome nature. But it quickly goes on to say, in effect, that God's love and mercy transcend his ineffable power and might.

Today's Gospel, the familiar story of the man who climbed up a tree just to see Jesus and Zacchaeus, the chief tax collector in Jericho—sounds the same theme of God's overwhelming love and mercy, as revealed in Jesus of Nazareth.

If we were to draw a portrait of God, surely it would accent his love and mercy, as revealed in Jesus.

There is a story about a little girl who, with crayons in hand, sat down to draw a picture of God. When her mother cautioned her that no one knows what God looks like, she replied, "When I finish my picture, everyone will know what God looks like."

The girl in a sense was right: we *can* know what God looks like. We *can* have an accurate picture of God—sufficiently accurate, at least, for our purposes as creatures striving for eternal life with him.

How? Need we—*Christians*—be reminded that God has revealed

himself in our midst in Jesus? We have but to contemplate Jesus of Nazareth to know what God looks like, how God acts. We have but to contemplate Jesus to know all that we need know about God. As Christ said to Philip: "To have seen me is to have seen the Father" (Jn 14:9).

What is God like, as we see him in Jesus? Simply contemplate Jesus. Jesus, who had compassion on the deaf, and brought to life a teenage girl, and returned a dead youth to his widowed mother. Jesus, who forgave a tax collector like Zacchaeus, in today's Gospel. Jesus, who excoriated hypocrisy, who exalted the downtrodden, the alienated, the impoverished. Jesus, who pardoned the penitent woman and made the vacillating Peter chief of his Apostles. Jesus, who not only calls us to his embrace forever—as today's Second Reading reveals—but makes us worthy of his call.

There is another story about a little girl who asked a question of her mother; theologian Yves Congar recalls it in his masterful book, *Jesus Christ* (Herder and Herder, 1966). The question put by the girl was: "Is the great God the same God as the loving God?" In other words, is the God who made the atom and the farthermost galaxies receding from us at fantastic speeds, the supreme intelligence who created and sustains all things; is this Almighty God the same God who comes to us in the Eucharist and in the Sacrament of Penance, and who seeks us out with his merciful love?

For us who believe, the answer is a clear and certain affirmative. We have a Revelation to go on. It is this God, who reveals himself in Jesus the Good Shepherd to whom we hope to gather—as Paul says today—for ages to come.

THIRTY-SECOND SUNDAY IN ORDINARY TIME (C)

Heaven

2 Maccabees 7:1-2, 9-14; 2 Thessalonians 2:16, 3:5; Luke 20:27-38.

Aim: (1) to give the Church's teaching on heaven; and (2) to encourage all to work for heaven as our true home and goal.

We read from Second Maccabees in today's First Reading. The name Maccabees means "hammer;" it was affixed in a special way to a great Jewish leader, Judas, who crusaded against the pagan Seleucid kings who persecuted the Jews beginning about two centuries before Christ.

(Incidentally, the Jewish feast of Hannukah, the Dedication of the Temple, was instituted in the time of the Maccabees, about 165 B.C.; it occurs around our Christmas time. The two books of Maccabees are not in the Jewish canon of inspired Scripture, but the Church has always held them as inspired.)

Today's First Reading relates the story of seven brothers tortured for their faith; they resisted because of their hope in life after death. Second Maccabees is one of the Old Testament witnesses to the reality of an afterlife, and to the efficacy of our interceding in behalf of the dead.

Sometimes we forget that it was not until Jesus rose from the grave of Good Friday that the doctrine of the resurrection of the flesh was revealed in all its fullness.

The Israelites of old knew that man can survive death; the Greek philosophers also knew this. The Pyramids of Egypt testify to the same. The Israelites also knew that the just person will somehow rise. Ezekiel's famous vision of the dry bones points toward a restoration to life of the Godfearing person.

There are similar segments of afterlife theology in the Old Testament: Daniel 12:1-3, for example, Psalm 49, and Wisdom 1-5. There is also a celebrated passage in the Book of Job which hints (at least) so strongly as to the prospect of resurrection that the musical genius Handel dwelt upon it in his immortal oratorio, *The Messiah*. Note, though: even as recently as Jesus' time there were some Jews who rejected the resurrection; such was the stance of the Sadducees in today's Gospel.

The New Testament completes and perfects the budding hope of resurrection found in the Old. It is only in the Resurrection of Jesus from the tomb that exciting texts like today's First Reading can fully be understood. Jesus is the model as well as the cause of our resurrection; like him, St. Paul reveals in Second Corinthians, we will rise again, though to a new life, to be with him forever. For his Resurrection was nor merely an historical event and the key sign of all salvation history, but also the power by means of which we too shall rise to eternal life.

Eternal life we describe as "heaven" (from an old Saxon root signifying the "skies"). For St. Paul, death meant simply to go home and be with Christ forever (Ph 2:23). Whether heaven is a place or a state doesn't change this basic truth: heaven is where Christ our goal is.

In heaven our reward will be the Beatific Vision: we shall *see* God. "See" is a verb used in the New Testament to describe the life of heaven; Mt 18:10 uses it with respect to the angels, and the First Epistle of John says that in heaven we shall "see him (God) as he is" (3:2). Since God is our goal, for whom we were created, heaven means perfect and endless personal fulfillment, peace, and joy.

It is Jesus' Resurrection—the power of his Resurrection and our faith in it—that gives us the courage to go on here below: the courage to say that the world is wrong when it denies God or his law, to maintain our course despite opposite currents everywhere: perjury, greed, contraception, abortion, divorce and remarriage, godless self-seeking and all the rest.

It is the risen Lord who delivers us from confused men, as today's Second Reading reminds us; the risen Lord toward whom we are being drawn this very hour, please God.

THIRTY-THIRD SUNDAY IN ORDINARY TIME (C)

Hell

Malachi 3:19-20; Second Thessalonians 3:7-12; Luke 21:5-19.

Aim: (1) to present the Church's teaching on the existence and nature of hell; (2) to inculcate a salutary fear of hell.

Today's Bible readings focus on God's judgment. Specifically, they can be read against the *real possibility*, in judgment, of our separating ourselves from God forever. The First Reading, from Malachi, the last of the twelve minor prophets (about 440 B.C.), accents this specific theme. And the Gospel's depiction of the "fearful omens and great signs" that will accompany the Lord's Second Coming in that last great trial, carries through this theme in the context of our need to persevere in our faith regardless of the evil forces aligned against us. Like the Thessalonians in today's Second Reading, we must not live lives of disorder, but patiently await a judgment that will come, though *when* no one knows.

Surely this is an opportune time to reflect on the doctrine of hell. Hell—our English word derives from a Germanic root signifying "realm of the dead"—*is* a doctrine.

To put this bluntly, we hold it on faith that life here is subject to total shipwreck, since it is possible for man, in his freedom, to reject God definitively.

Christ as Savior made this clear many times, in imagery that must be taken seriously as to its essential meaning. He told us that he himself would "send his angels to cast the workers of iniquity into the burning furnace" (Mt 13:41 ff.). Moreover, it is Jesus—the same Christ who went to the Cross of Calvary for us—who said in the parable: "Begone from me, ye cursed, into eternal fire!" (Mt 25:41).

The existence of hell has been defined by the Church; solemn statements on it are multiple. For example, there is the fourth-century creedal declaration, *Fides Damasci*; also, a declaration of the Council of Florence in 1439.

Theologian Karl Rahner has made the point that the doctrine of hell is not primarily for the purpose of giving man "advance coverage" of the end of time. On the contrary, hell should be preached in order to illuminate the present existence of man before God. The dogma is "not to provide abstract data or to satisfy our curiosity," but rather "to bring us to our senses and to conversion" (*Theological Dictionary*: Herder and Herder, 1965).

The doctrine of hell does not rule out the doctrine of the universality of salvation, obviously. But the latter does not rule out the former, either. How these two truths can be reconciled really doesn't matter, so long as they are both accepted.

One must of course distinguish the reality and eternity of hell, from the literary or artistic forms in which hell is described. Even in interpreting the Biblical data, care must be taken to observe the rules for determining the true sense intended. Thus, Scriptural images reflected by poets like Dante or painters like Michelangelo (e.g., fire, darkness, etc.), are borrowed from apocalyptic language. But their meaning is the crucial point; namely, the core meaning of hell: the real possibility of eternal alienation from God.

Hence a salutary fear of hell is characteristic of Jesus' disciple. That we can separate ourselves from our only true goal, God, is a most relevant truth to human existence.

We must live in the shadow of this truth.

SOLEMNITY OF
CHRIST THE KING (C)

Christ and Freedom

Second Samuel 5:1-3; Colossians 1:12-20; Luke 23:35-43.

Aim: (1) to explain that Christ the King draws us in our freedom, God's gift to us to permit us to love him.

Again, we celebrate, at the close of another Church year, the Solemnity of Christ the King.

What does it mean? In a word, that the claim of God's law upon the human heart takes priority over all other claims. "King of Kings and Lord of Lords . . . forever and ever," that awesome phrase put to music by Handel in the immortal oratorio, *The Messiah* means just this: Jusus is a king of hearts; the principal tributes due him are faith, hope and love.

When we speak of the heart, we also speak of freedom. The heart is meaningless outside of the mysterious concept of freedom, which as God's gift, permits love.

Recall today's Gospel. At Calvary, Jesus' executioners taunted him: "If you are the king of the Jews, save yourself." The Russian novelist Dostoevsky, in his *The Brothers Karamazov*, asked the question as to why Christ did not come down from the cross when he was so challenged. Our Lord did not come down, Dostoevsky argued, precisely because such a miracle would have compelled the jeering soldiers to believe in him; hence, he would be in effect forcing their faith. This is not Christ's way. Christ wants to *draw* us to him, not compel us. He wants us to accept him freely. Which is the reason why he never worked a miracle before he saw evidence of antecedent faith. It was never the other way around. First faith, then miracle; never, the miracle first.

In freedom, therefore, Christ the King calls us to his reign, so beautifully foretold in today's First Reading (David's anointing), and described by St. Paul in today's Second Reading.

As we grow and mature in life we become increasingly aware that we possess a faculty allowing for varied actions in any given situation. This is freedom, a mysterious power which still baffles philosophers and which separates human beings from all else in creation. As we come of age we realize that this freedom is all *ours*; that, too, we can use it to make of ourselves what we truly aspire to be for all eternity. And as we use it, we either enlist in, and deepen our commitment to, the reign of Christ; or we delay our enlistment and neglect God's graces drawing us to him. In any case, Christ will never force us; he is a king who will have no part of robots, automatons. He will only accept us as free persons, creatures able and willing to respond with their hearts to his invitations of love.

Christ is a king of hearts, then. Thus he invites us, *draws* us, to himself. He himself used this word of his action upon our souls (Jn 12:32).

We pray today that we will utilize our freedom to follow Christ our king, to allow ourselves to be drawn by his love. We ask him to enlighten our consciences, where he speaks to us in the innermost recesses of our personhood, and helps us to respond to his subtle summons. We do this by renewing our allegiance to him today as Lord of Lords and King of Kings forever.

And in our hearts we say, as Peter did that day when Christ promised the Eucharist (Jn 6:68-69): "Lord, to whom shall we go. You have the words of eternal life. And we believe . . ."

The early believers had an expression, *Marana tha!* (Come, Lord!). References to it can be found in the body of Scripture itself; in I Cor 16:22 and Rv 22:17, 20. It is a profound and intense plea that the Lord Jesus will be pleased to organize his kingdom without delay. Nor is it an empty poetic cry. The Spirit himself tells us that the prayer of the saints our prayer can actually quicken the advent of the Day of the Lord. Read and ponder Rv 6:9-10 and Lk 18:7.

Marana tha! The annual Solemnity of Christ the King gives us fresh opportunity to rehearse the truth that the coming of Jesus' Kingdom—when illness and ignorance and sin and death will all be finally vanquished—can be accelerated by our daily witness and prayer. Come, Lord Jesus!